Organizing the Movement
The Roots and Growth of ACORN

In the series
Labor and Social Change,
edited by Paula Rayman and Carmen Sirianni

activists who'd had recent success in the anti-war and civil rights movements and who were determined to build a mass movement for social change "from the ground up." Third, there were financial resources. Governmental grant programs, private foundations, and liberal churches were all "putting their money where their mouth was" to fund the development of local grassroots organizing. In addition, two forces greatly contributed to the development of community organization in the 1970s: (1) macro structural trends that made cities prime arenas for organizing, particularly among low-income and minority groups; and (2) the influence of the anti-war, Alinsky, civil rights, and welfare rights organizations that produced the organizers and set the political stage.

The Fight for the Cities

The development of community organizations during the last decade is related at least in part, to the attempt of local city governments to reallocate fiscal resources away from (particularly poor) individuals and redistribute them to business and corporate entities. This tendency has been compounded by the phenomenon of the shrinking pot. While business demanded a greater share of the fiscal resources, particularly in the industrial cities of the Northeast, business contributions through taxes were considerably lower, as evidenced by the decrease of the corporate tax share of the national budget from 23.3 percent in 1960 to less than 8 percent in 1984.

In the last fifteen years there have been escalating attempts within local, state, and federal bureaucracies, fueled by both the ideologically conservative Republicans and the fiscally conservative Democrats, to change the redistributive role of the state. This was to be accomplished by reversing the expansionist wave of welfare state policies, which functioned—at least on some levels—to distribute goods and services to the economically and politically disadvantaged, and replacing it with a "Robin Hood in reverse" policy, shifting resources to corporate entities. Faced with an eroding tax base, local governments initiated service cutbacks that detrimentally

1

Staying Put: CO's Bottom Line

Sometimes I could close my eyes and almost forget what city I was in because the feeling everywhere was the same. People were ready to organize!

—Bruce Thomas, Statewide Organizer,
National Welfare Rights Organization

When organizers arrived in Arkansas in 1970 to launch ACORN—the Arkansas Community Organizations for Reform Now—none had ever heard of mass-based, multi-issue, multitactical, community organization. In fact, as late as 1975 there were fewer than ten statewide community organizations (COs) in the United States. Yet in the mid 1980s there are over 8,000 community organizations in fifty states, and independent training operations to assist them in increasing and consolidating their fiscal resources, developing staff and leadership, and providing access to key decision-makers. What are the reasons for the explosion of community organizations since the early 1970s and how did these organizations intervene in the political life of urban communities?

Community organizations emerged and grew in the late 1960s to mid-1970s for a number of reasons. First, organizing was proved legitimate as a viable mechanism for empowerment by the success of the civil rights and anti-war movements on the one hand, and on the other, the Johnson-initiated mandate of "maximum feasible participation." Second, an experienced and talented group of people were interested in developing community organizations: the same

Acknowledgments

Many people in both the organizing and academic communities made important and insightful contributions to the process of focusing and developing this book. I am indebted to Russ Ellis, Bill Friedland, Michael Buroway, and Troy Duster for encouraging me in the conceptual stages to develop an organizational ethnography. David Matza, the chairman of my committee, consistently provided insightful comments, leads, and encouragement through the dissertation process.

I also received considerable support from Basil Browne and Tim Sampson, who read and reread all of my drafts; Hardy Frye, whose advice to "go on and write it up already" finally moved me to complete the study; and Carol Hatch, who always acted as if she knew I would finish this study, even when I was unsure.

In researching the dissertation I am indebted to Seth Borgos, John Beam, Larry Ginsberg, Mike Shea, and Madeleine Adamson, who loaned me their personal files and gave me access to the ACORN archives; and to Ginger Shiras, formerly of the *Arkansas Gazette*, for arranging access to the *Gazette* and *Democrat* archives in Little Rock. For providing access to unpublished, mimeographed essays on organizing, I thank Mike Miller and Spence Limbocker at the Organize Training Center in San Francisco.

All the research in the world would not have made this book presentable or acceptable without the long hours of editing and typing contributed by my wife, Marcia Henry. Not only did she type and edit; she also joined in on fourteen months of field work

ACKNOWLEDGMENTS

in New Orleans with our new baby. Margaret Shockley was also extremely helpful on short notice in the final editing of the dissertation.

For help in transforming an academic dissertation into a readable book, David Plotke's practical and politically oriented editorial comments were important, as was Frances Goldin's help in "agenting" and editing a draft.

Finally, my warmest thanks to Wade Rathke and the men and women of ACORN, whose struggles gave me something meaningful to write about.

Organizing the Movement
The Roots and Growth of ACORN

and (3) the connection of all electoral work to militant disruptive action and to a set of programmatic political demands.

This conclusion is based on three observations: First, the oligarchical structure of the organizations within the community organization movement, while useful in the formative stages of organization, is a barrier to real constituent development. Second, the economic context of CO development does not sufficiently address larger social justice concerns—disarmament, race, gender—and hinders the ability of community organizations to make strategic alliances with other groups and with the Democratic Party. Third, the level of political opposition to progressive organizing necessitates a cooperative division of labor as well as a pooling of political and fiscal resources.

My real question in beginning this study, after years of work as a community organizer, was this: what are community organizations really good for? Or, in less delicate terms, had my friends and I been wasting our time for the past ten years? While my own strong commitment made it unlikely that I'd discover CO to have been a wasted effort, the answer to this question is still complicated. On a general level, community organizations have the ability to demystify the economic system as well as create an alternative system of social practices that validates oppositional behavior. The value of community organizations lies in the process of organizing as well as in the "specific, immediate, realizable" victory. Community organizations help people get a sense of the way the world works, open a path for them to think about how it could be, and provide them with an opportunity to change at least a small part of it.

I was actually hoping to find that with their tremendous growth, community organizations could be the vehicles for the attainment of power. What I discovered was that the vehicle for power is the people themselves.

PREFACE

the major models of community organizing, and examines the relationship between the availability of resources—funds, personnel, and ideology—and the attainment of organizational goals. Finally, the study explores the extent to which community organizations in general and ACORN in particular might contribute to the development of a mass-based movement for social justice.

For over 14 years I worked as an organizer, trainer, and recruiter with ACORN, the single largest community organization in the United States, with over 50,000 members in 27 states. I was given access to all organizational files, including internal memos and organizational archives. In addition, I was able to conduct some forty interviews with ACORN leaders, organizers, and supporters. This book, therefore, is not the unbiased view of an "objective" outsider; indeed, in my years with ACORN I consistently attempted (with varying levels of success) to influence its political direction, social composition, tactics, and strategy—not only during my initial stint as a raw recruit in 1970 but also in 1979 when I ran the platform development portion of the 1980 political campaign.

While this study is informed by a number of theoretical frames—the work of Piven and Cloward on social movements;[3] Haggstrom on organization;[4] Castells, O'Conner, and Fainstein and Fainstein on urban political movements,[5] and McCarthy and Zald on resource mobilization[6]—the bottom-line analytical frame reflects the pragmatism of the organizer: *what will really work on the streets.*

My conclusion is, I believe, unusual. Given the drying up of resources for community empowerment, the difficulty of recruiting organizers from the traditional sources of liberal institutions, and increased repression in low-income communities (evidenced by funding cutbacks, massive dislocation of low-income residents, and direct attacks on progressive organizations by both the IRS and right-wing forces), I argue that the ability of ACORN or any other community organizing network to influence national politics will be determined by (1) the ability of the CO networks to make alliances and coalitions with one another as well as with organizations based on peace, gender, and racial issues; (2) the development of analytical and political skills among the primary constituency of the organizations;

Preface

Community organizations are not what they used to be. They are no longer the turf-oriented, confrontational instruments of citizen empowerment and municipal reform. Community organizations have evolved from the vague philosophy of simply "organizing ordinary people for power" to sophisticated networks replete with replicable organizational models, codified strategies and tactics, and complex staff-constituency relationships.

The activities of community organizations currently range from direct action confrontation to community-based economic development and, most recently, to electoral activity. One observer has called community organizing the "growth industry of the 1970's",[1] while the *New York Times* notes that activism at the local and state levels is so scattered and diverse that no one has been able to measure its precise nature or extent, though it has certainly grown.[2]

The question is, with all this smoke, is there really a fire? What have community organizations really accomplished? What are the strengths and weaknesses of community organizations? Under what conditions might COs play a key role in building a progressive coalition for social justice in the United States?

This book examines the general social and political context of community organization by analyzing the development of the Association of Community Organizations for Reform Now (ACORN). With ACORN as its focus, this study provides a narrative account of the development of community organization from the early 1970s through the mid 1980s, discusses the strengths and weaknesses of

FOREWORD

on ACORN's experience, but on any serious and successful organizing venture. Delgado draws on the ACORN history to probe a series of dilemmas that have plagued a good deal of organizing work. He considers, for example, the difficulties and advantages of building alliances among different political groups with different agendas. He uses ACORN's efforts to illuminate the process through which the felt grievances that are the organizer's touchstone in reaching out to people are transformed into a large political agenda that reflects those grievances but moves people beyond them to a larger consideration of the structure of American society. He worries with illuminating effect about the interplay and tensions between organization-building concerns, electoral work, and direct action. And finally he casts light on what is in some ways the great mystery in mass organizing, the role of those who put aside career and class status to take up the life of the activist-organizer.

Indeed, Delgado himself is one manifestation of that mystery, and that makes him uniquely qualified both to be the historian of ACORN and to reflect analytically on the ACORN experience. He is a trained social scientist. More to the point, he is an activist-organizer product of the NWRO and ACORN tradition. In the late 1960s and early 1970s, he worked first as a welfare rights organizer in Providence and then in New York City, and subsequently spent a number of years as a senior staff member with ACORN. He now directs the Center for Third World Organizing. Indeed, one puts this book down with an urgent sense that we need to know more about the young women and men who dedicated themselves to the vocation of organizing when others dropped out to return to schools and careers, or to make sandals. What we most need to know is what their lives have been like, and how they sustained their commitment over the course of nearly two decades when the national political climate gave so little encouragement to ideas of social justice. That faith is their achievement, and ACORN's.

FOREWORD

organizers, this term connotes an organizing strategy in which a broad range of issues is supposed to attract and sustain the participation of a broad constituency. In the ACORN lexicon, multi-issue organizing indicates not the search for a broad constituency, but rather a broad range of organizing campaigns directed against the diverse conditions that constrict the lives of their low-income constituents, from AFDC practices, to life-threatening power plant installations, to excessive utility rates, to unemployment, to lack of decent housing.

In all of these issue areas, the ACORN organizing style has been distinctive, irritating a good many people even while earning it the loyalty of its members. ACORN organizers never turned away from the direct actions of the sixties. To the contrary, they rely on bringing out crowds, and they rely on defiance. Even now, in the mid-1980s, a somber time if there ever was one, ACORN is in the middle of a squatter campaign in which it organizes local groups to help poor people occupy, claim ownership, and then repair abandoned houses. In part, this protest-oriented style is a reflection of the ACORN constituency. Poor people who enter politics are inclined toward direct action. They are skeptical of the usual sort of petitioning and lobbying because experience has taught them to be skeptical.

ACORN's senior staff have been out in the streets for half of their working lives; they are the most experienced and seasoned cadre of community organizers in the United States. Equally important, they have attracted a continuous stream of young recruits who share their commitment to organizing as a vocation. Perhaps most unusual, the ACORN organizers have cultivated an approach that is self-consciously experimental and self-consciously analytical. If, over fifteen years, ACORN has not shifted from its commitment to organizing the poor, it has nevertheless continuously invented new organizing campaigns, using new strategies to raise new issues. And each campaign begins as an experiment: the strategy is discussed, tactics invented, implemented, evaluated, redirected, or expanded.

ACORN thus merits the historical accounting that Gary Delgado here provides. It also deserves to be examined from the perspective of the large and searching questions Delgado asks that bear not only

FOREWORD

most of the movements of the sixties, particularly those that had mobilized the minority poor, fell into disarray. It seemed that the brief period of time in which the poor and minorities could exert influence had passed. NWRO, as an organization of the most demeaned people in America, was especially vulnerable to this discouragement, and the young organizers began to explore the possibility of organizing constituencies that would be stronger because more numerous and less easily isolated.

There were different solutions to this problem. A good many of the activists who had worked to organize the poor in the 1960s turned in the 1970s to organizing middle- and working-class constituencies, and turned also away from "direct action" to concentrate on lobbying and education strategies compatible with their new constituencies. The "citizen action" groups are the product of this turn. In some ways, the creation of a national network of citizen action groups is a noteworthy accomplishment. But it also has to be said that it was achieved by turning away from the impoverished constituencies whose plight had galvanized the organizers of the sixties, and by turning away from the protest tactics that had not only made the sixties memorable, but had yielded the movements what victories they had won.

The ACORN solution was different. Rathke went to Little Rock with the blessings of George Wiley and the NWRO to build an organization in which welfare recipients were the core group. In the fifteen years since the first Little Rock group was established, ACORN organizers have consistently and self-consciously targeted the poor and minority neighborhoods, carefully avoiding cutting too wide a geographic swath in their organizing work because experience has taught them that if they do, middle class residents will come to dominate their organization. ACORN has grown to a national organization with chapters in 26 states. It has developed an affiliated union organizing drives among the lowest-paid workers—such as CETA clients or fast-food workers—who were neglected by established unions. But neither organizational growth nor the passage of time has diluted the commitment to "organizing the poor."

ACORN calls itself a "multi-issue" organization. To many

FOREWORD

the fashion of scorning the turbulent movements of the 1960s, and of dubbing the period a failure.

The civil rights movement, the northern black movement, the antiwar movement—none of these were failures. They were part of one of those extraordinary periods in history when large numbers of people, most of them young, broke with their habitual acquiescence and rose in defiance to claim new rights from state and society. It was a period when for a moment those who were least became most, when those who were black, or poor, or young, asserted at least a measure of moral authority and political influence. True, the moment ended and the movements subsided. But they left remarkable accomplishments in their wake, including the dismantling of the southern caste system; the expansion of income-maintenance programs for the poor, the unemployed, the disabled, and the old; and at least a limit to the use of American firepower in Southeast Asia.

There was a less obvious accomplishment that also endured, and ACORN's emergence and growth is evidence of it. The movements of the sixties established a community organizing tradition in the United States. Although there had always been neighborhood organizing, which Saul Alinsky had developed into a kind of credo, in the context of the 1960s, organizing acquired a meaning that went beyond the essentially localistic, neighborhood-based focus of past efforts. It came to be thought of as a way of empowering the most subjugated people in the United States to transform society itself.

ACORN originated in just such a vision. It began as an offspring of an organization of Aid to Families with Dependent Children (AFDC) clients called the National Welfare Rights Organization. In the tumultuous climate of the late 1960s, NWRO chapters mushroomed across the country as welfare mothers began to recast their stigmatized status into a status founded on rights, and organized protests against restrictive local welfare practices. Wade Rathke (who started ACORN and has been its lead organizer ever since) was a student at Williams College who, like many others, was drawn to the NWRO by the visionary meanings of "organizing the poor."

As the national political climate turned conservative after 1968,

Foreword

Richard A. Cloward
Frances Fox Piven

This is a book about the pre-eminent poor people's organization of our time—an organization whose members and leaders are mostly poor, mostly women, and mostly minorities. It is also a book about the extraordinary young people who began building poor people's organizations in the 1960s, and who went on to dedicate their lives to the craft of organizing and to the vision of empowering the poor.

ACORN began mainly as an organization of welfare mothers in Little Rock, Arkansas, in 1970, but then broadened out to include the working poor and unemployed. It also spread to cities across the country, and became in time the largest poor people's organization since the unemployed movement in the 1930s. These features alone make ACORN remarkable, for there are no other contemporary community organizations of comparable scale, durability, and militancy that have kept faith with the injunction of the 1960s that justice and democracy depend on "organizing the poor."

ACORN is very much a creation of the halcyon days of the 1960s, and the *zeitgeist* of that period has continued to influence the young organizers who successively flocked to the ACORN banner. This may seem an odd assertion, considering that the movements of the 1960s have lately fallen into disrepute, as conservatives rewrite the history of the Vietnam War to discover some grounds for national glory on the one hand, and to heap disgrace on the antiwar movement on the other hand. Even people on the left have fallen in with

Contents

	Foreword	
	by Richard A. Cloward and Frances Fox Piven	ix
	Preface	xv
	Acknowledgments	xix
1	Staying Put: CO's Bottom Line	3
2	The Sixties Movements: Roots of Community Organization	13
3	The Roots of the ACORN Oak	39
4	The ACORN Model	63
5	Expanding the Turf	91
6	Jamming the Democrats	123
7	Cooperation in a New Political Climate	163
8	Internal Organization and Social Structure	179
9	The Prospects for Community Organizing	211
	Notes	233
	Bibliography	253
	Index	263

To my parents, Marjorie Elaine and Vernon Ivanhoe,
and their mothers, Marie and Ruth

Temple University Press, Philadelphia 19122
© 1986 by Gary Delgado. All rights reserved
Published 1986
Printed in the United States of America

Library of Congress Cataloging in Publication Data

Delgado, Gary, 1950–
Organizing the movement.

    Bibliography: p. 253
    Includes index.
    1. ACORN (Organization). 2. Community organization
—United States—Case studies. 3. Community develop-
ment, Urban—United States. 4. Urban renewal—United
States—Citizen participation. I. Title.
HN85.A3D45   1986   307'.14'06073   85-12608
ISBN 0-87722-393-9

Organizing the Movement
The Roots and Growth of ACORN

Gary Delgado

With a Foreword by
Richard A. Cloward and Frances Fox Piven

TEMPLE UNIVERSITY PRESS Philadelphia

affected disparate elements in the urban core and made them ripe for organizing. Urban housing deterioration, the attempted dislocation of low-income minority communities, and systematic cutbacks in social services gave fledging community organizations a definitive "terrain of contest" and a formidable protagonist. Community groups sprang up in response to the reallocation of fiscal resources, and their major target became local government itself. The emergent fights over the cost, conditions, and availability of housing, cutbacks in services, land use planning, the environmental movement, the control of police and schools, and efforts to end mortgage and insurance redlining effectively shifted part of the struggle of labor-capital relations from the shop floor to the state.

Habermas, in *Legitimation Crisis*, notes that class structure is maintained over the administratively (government) mediated distribution of increases in the social product. "It is in these struggles," he writes, "that the state acts as an arena in which a displacement of relations of production finds expression."[1] Summarizing this trend, Piven and Cloward observe in *The New Class War* that "while once working people looked to the marketplace for action on their economic grievances, they now more often look to the state . . . and not only in times of extraordinary disruption, or popular mobilization." "The state," they conclude, "has finally become the main arena for class conflict."[2]

What role did community organizations have in focusing pressure on local units of the state? How did local struggles unfold? Probably the organizing principle that initially forged the most militant and the largest number of groups was the most fundamental: the right to stay put.

The struggle over resources within the cities was characterized by increases in crime, the explosion of the welfare rolls, and the loss of direct political control by corporate interests in the inner cities. In central cities all over the country, local struggles emerged over minimum standards for rental housing (which in New York allowed tenants a warranty of habitability for rental units), the quality of education (which materialized in many cities as the community control movements), welfare rights, and the general growth of entitlement programs, including the federal attempt to subvert the power of the cities and set up a federal pork barrel through the "war on poverty."

A 1968 report by the President's Commission on Law Enforcement and the Administration of Justice noted that the poverty in the cities evidenced not only by the conditions of urban dwellers but also by the rise in street crimes left the city's social order "seriously threatened."[3]

Corporate leadership took this threat seriously. Already in the 1960s there were serious attempts on the part of capital to reappropriate urban space by manipulation of populations through urban renewal, a program known in low-income neighborhoods as "poor people removal." These programs, which successfully displaced a half million households nationwide, floundered when private investors shunned the cleared land encircled by deteriorating neighborhoods, or, worse yet, empty lots surrounded by more empty lots.[4]

A growing concern among urban corporate elites was the increasing domination of central space by blacks and Latinos who could not be exploited at the same rate by industry and landlords as earlier generations of immigrants. Fainstein and Fainstein write, "Because these populations were only a limited source of profitability for employers, merchants and property owners, cities began to experience serious problems of both accumulation and realization. Labor elsewhere provided a higher return; tax revenues declined relatively and absolutely; retailing died; and the tenement landlord began to experience severe difficulty in meeting his cost."[5]

The relative increase in the percentage of minorities in urban centers between 1960 and 1978 is indeed staggering. According to figures from the U.S. Department of Housing and Urban Development (HUD), central cities lost 9 percent of their white populations, while their black populations grew 40 percent. By 1980, 55 percent of blacks but only 24 percent of whites lived in center cities; almost one-third of center-city population nationally was black or Latino. In addition to the population shifts, there were, of course, economic ramifications: in 1976, 31 percent of blacks living in central cities of any size were poor.[6]

Corporate leadership, however, was not ready to simply abdicate in the urban centers. The expansion in the relative number of households, coupled with state restrictions on land use, made urban land increasingly valuable. As Roger Friedland points out:

> Given the importance of the big city vote for national elections, the continued concentration of corporate and financial headquarters in the major central cities, and the economic imperative of maintaining the value of public infrastructure and private construction in the central cities . . . the value of central city properties is the bedrock upon which the residential, commercial and municipal loans are based. Thus the viability of the financial institutions of this country and ultimately the nation's capital market itself are dependent *on maintaining the value of central city properties* [emphasis added].[7]

The urban renewal plans of the 1960s largely failed. However, the plan to retake the cities reemerged in the mid-1970s under the name "revitalization." In most urban centers, at least some sections are being "revitalized." This activity is characterized by increased tourism, the construction of convention and/or sports centers, and the physical refurbishing of buildings in the urban core. Consequently, the city is changed on two levels. First:

> Construction and rehabilitation is directed toward office buildings, upper income residences and specialized consumption activities. Isolated, "defensible" office towers are joined by luxury highrises and a network of shops and restaurants. Manufacturing space in core locations is converted to either offices or expensive housing. The existing architecture of the core is, in effect, rehabilitated

for service production or for consumption by the upper classes.[8]

Second, the character of core merchandising changes, as both a cause and an effect of the changing demographics:

> The core is no longer the purveyor of mass consumables, but rather of specialized goods and cultural activities. These commodities are aimed at the particular interests of fractions of the middle and upper class: travelers, tourists, and life-style groupings which require critical masses in order to permit individual consumption—e.g., homosexuals, singles seeking mates, and so forth. The manifestation of these new core consumption functions may be seen in rehabbed old markets, dockside restaurants, small and highly specialized shops, hotels, resurrected "historical" districts, singles bars, restaurants with tin ceilings, plants, fans, and—as the food reviewer comments—well-meaning if unprofessional waiters in blue jeans.[9]

However, even given these trends, one thing is clear: though many cities have managed to convert some sections into havens for the urban gentry, replete with fern bars and new "old towns," the reappropriation of urban space by corporate interests has not yet been accomplished.

Gentrifying the cities is dependent on two factors: the removal of the lower class—especially racial minorities—from the core; and the replacement of this displaced population with a more stable tax base—the new urban gentry. As early as 1969, social scientists at the Brookings Institute and the Rand Corporation[10] began to articulate a notion of "spatial deconcentration" and (white) middle-class dominance that argued for lowering the concentration of minorities in urban centers to lessen the probability of urban rebellion.

Almost as if the Rand study were being used as a battle plan, a pattern of spatial deconcentration began to emerge in the largest cities in the Northeast. First, the displacement of racial minorities from the core would be accomplished through a market function: rehabilitation and conversions would drive up the price of rental property; housing stock would be consumed by middle and upper classes; government housing policies would simultaneously cut back housing subsidies in the core and offer low-income people subsidized housing in suburban locations.

Second, a new urban gentry would be moved into the urban centers through a sophisticated series of public-private finance programs that would freeze home improvement loans to working-class neighborhoods (redlining), while offering rehabilitation loans to the new stable, more middle-class, gentry. Third, local and federal monies would be reallocated for "downtown development" (as evidenced in Detroit, New York, Chicago, St. Louis, and Baltimore). Fourth, after the removal/development process had begun, a program urban geographers have referred to as the Latin Americanization of American cities began. Monies previously allocated for services were systematically cut back.

This "planned shrinkage"—the closing of public schools, health care facilities, and public entitlement programs—was intended as a modern-day scorched-earth policy to ensure that, once removed, there would be no infrastructure to support the return of minorities to the urban centers. It was the resistance to this phenomenon, the reappropriation of urban space, that became the context for the formation of community organizations in the 1970s. As Table 1 illustrates, COs were set up to fight evictions, resist urban removal, control schools and police, and address neighborhood safety, zoning, and the threat of superhighways dividing the neighborhood.

On one level, community organizations were formed to address concerns specifically related to the delivery of services by government and to the impact of housing, transportation, and education on the spatial and social structure of the city. The conflicts that ensued were, at another level, direct responses to capital's attempt to reappropriate urban space and reallocate the social wage. As O'Connor notes, "The struggle for wages based on productivity has been transformed into a struggle for wages based on need.[11]

TABLE 1. ISSUES ADDRESSED BY COMMUNITY ORGANIZATIONS AND ACTION PROGRAMS

	No.*	%*		No.	%
Deteriorated housing	59	5.0	General disinvestment	31	2.6
Abandoned housing	53	4.5	Muggings	31	2.6
General city services	50	4.2	Mass transit	30	2.5
Burglaries	49	4.1	Loitering	28	2.4
HUD housing	47	4.0	Highway construction	26	2.2
Street safety	46	3.9	Drug abuse	24	2.0
Vandalism	44	3.7	Mental health	24	2.0
Recreation	41	3.4	Ethnic arts	23	1.9
Juvenile crime	41	3.4	Day care	22	1.8
Senior citizen needs	39	3.0	Vocational programs	20	1.7
Crimes against elderly	36	3.0	Crime against business	18	1.5
Education	36	3.0	Rape	18	1.5
Unemployment	36	3.0	Domestic violence	13	1.1
Health services	35	2.9	Unwanted programs	11	.9
Street traffic	35	2.9	Auto theft	10	.8
Street lighting	34	2.9	Child abuse	9	.8
Commercial revitalization	34	2.9	Planning & development	9	.8
Jobs for youth	33	2.8	Utility rates	5	.4
Mortgage disinvestment ("redlining")	32	2.7	Zoning	5	.4
			Tenant issues	4	.3
			Pollution	4	.3

*Number of citations and percent of total.

SOURCE: Gerson Greene, "A Self-Portrait of Some Community and Neighborhood Organizations" (National Center for Urban Ethnic Affairs, Washington, D.C., March 1978), 35.

The evolution of urban fiscal policy explains the structural strains that set the preconditions for organization: fights over the allocation of urban space, housing rights, and service cutbacks sprang up in cities all over the country. In this context, particular forms and tactics that mobilized poor minorities as a vanguard constituency can best be accounted for through an examination of the organizations and movements that immediately preceded community organization and provided CO's roots: the student antiwar movement, the Alinsky-initiated Industrial Areas Foundation; the welfare rights movement, and the civil rights movement.

2

The Sixties Movements: Roots of Community Organization

Almost every week we'd hear about a new organizing effort starting up. Welfare rights organizers, civil rights activists and an assorted array of lefties—we were making it happen in local communities all across the country. We had wounded the great beast of state in the 60's and we were convinced that in the 70's we were going to blow it away!

—Bert DeLeeuw,
Movement for Economic Justice

When asked to define the differences between ACORN and the Industrial Areas Foundation (IAF), an ACORN leader in Houston replied that "ACORN organizes communities, we don't organize industrial areas."[1]

Nevertheless, the IAF was the training ground for many community organizers. When a 1976 national survey of thirty-two COs asked organizers and leaders to identify their roots, the movements and organizations most often mentioned were the civil rights movement (twelve responses), and the National Welfare Rights Organization, the Industrial Areas Foundation, and the Students for a Democratic Society/antiwar movement (six each).[2] All four were training grounds for the organizers of the major community organization networks, and all had ideological and organizational inclinations that reemerged in the community organization movement.

THE SIXTIES MOVEMENTS

The Civil Rights Movement

The principal organizations within the 1954–69 wave of the civil rights movement included the Urban League, the National Association for the Advancement of Colored People (NAACP), the Congress of Racial Equality (CORE), the Southern Christian Leadership Conference (SCLC), and the Student Nonviolent Coordinating Committee (SNCC). Each of these represented a different analytical perspective and displayed its own tactical approaches to obtaining racial equality. While there is a tendency in social science to "think of the civil rights movement, organizations, and leaders, as if they were interchangeable or as if they were only parts of the same historical and social phenomenon,"[3] only by disaggregating its organizational components is it possible to ascertain the effects of the fight for civil rights on the social movements that emerged later.

The NAACP and the Urban League, founded in 1908 and 1910 respectively, had fundamentally different assumptions about the attainment of civil rights. While neither could be characterized as either mass-based or tactically (in the sense of direct action) militant, the NAACP did see its role as adversarial and viewed the legal manipulation of the state as an organizational mandate.[4] The Urban League, on the other hand, accepting an almost literal assimilationist view of social progress, "assumed that the problems of the Negro were primarily those of adjustment and that their need was for training and help."[5] In easing the path of southern rural blacks into the industrial working class, the League encouraged white business leaders to demonstrate their understanding of enlightened self-interest by hiring and training rural blacks.

The Southern Christian Leadership Conference (SCLC), formed in Atlanta in 1957, was encouraged by the success of the Montgomery bus boycott in 1955–56. It was not only the largest and most active civil rights group; it was also the first to start in the South. While the Gandhian philosophy Martin Luther King, Jr., brought to SCLC was not wholly embraced by many later organizers, the spirit of the movement SCLC engendered and the mass-protest tactics it employed have endured. While the whole social milieu of the country was profoundly influenced by the civil rights movement, the organizations with the most direct effect on community organization were the northern, urban-based Congress of Racial Equality (CORE) and the SCLC-affiliated, militant, student-based Student Nonviolent Coordinating Committee (SNCC).

CORE's influence was reflected in both the issues addressed and the tactics used. Founded in Chicago in 1942 and initially affiliated with the Quaker-sponsored Fellowship of Reconciliation, CORE had used the sit-in tactics that characterized the civil rights movement of the 1950s and '60s as early as 1943 when members desegregated a Chicago restaurant, and in 1947 when CORE cosponsored a freedom ride to address segregation on interstate bus routes. In the 1960s, CORE continued to be involved in issues affecting blacks in the northern urban centers, particularly housing and job discrimination. CORE groups based in New York, Newark, and Chicago became the northern counterpart to the explosion of activity that was taking place in the South. It was no accident that George Wiley, who in 1966 became the founder of the National Welfare Rights Organization, had his baptism by fire not in rural Mississippi but as chairman of a CORE group in Syracuse, New York.[6]

The other organization that fundamentally affected the scope and rationale of community organization, especially in the area of electoral politics, was the Student Nonviolent Coordinating Committee. Not only was SNCC instrumental in developing the organizational infrastructure for SCLC in a number of states in the South, including Alabama and Mississippi; it was part of the developmental group that advocated forming the Mississippi Freedom Democratic Party in 1963 and the Lowndes County Freedom Organization, the original Black Panther Party.[7]

It was also SNCC, within the civil rights community, that began to view the Vietnam War as imperialist, leading its members to adopt an appropriate organizational response to the war: "Hell no, we won't go!" This interpretive expansion in the scope of the civil rights movement caused the leadership, especially Dr. Martin Luther King, to begin connecting the war effort in Vietnam with domestic policy: "the war at home." Reflecting the expanded analysis of the

TABLE 2. A SUMMARY OF MAJOR TRENDS IN THE CIVIL RIGHTS MOVEMENT

	International	Mainstream	Other trends
1954–1966	Breakdown of European colonialism: 1957: Ghana—Nkrumah 1958: Guinea—Toure 1960: Cuba 1960–63: Independence of several Third World countries by Constitutional Convention 1963: Organization of African Unity formed	Integration: 1954: Brown vs. the Board of Education 1955: Montgomery bus boycott 1957: Little Rock school integration 1960: Sit-ins, freedom rides 1963: Birmingham; March on Washington 1964: Civil Rights Act; Mississippi Summer Project 1965: Selma to Montgomery March; Voting Rights Act; SNCC, SCLC, CORE, NAACP*	Nationalist movement: Elijah Mohammed Malcolm X Heirs of the Garvey movement 1964: Rochester, Harlem riots War on Poverty
1966–1972	1966: Vietnam; Armed struggle intensifies in Mozambique, Angola, Guinea-Bisseau, Zimbabwe, Namibia 1967: Martin Luther King anti-war speech, Riverside Church	Black consciousness: 1966: March in Miss.., "Black Power" 1967: Newark, Detroit "Burn Baby Burn" 1968: Black Manifesto; Black reparations; Ocean Hill-Brownsville, "community control" 1968: Congress of African People founded	Poor People's Movement: NWRO, NTO,* SCLC "end the slums" 1968: Poor People's Campaign; King assassination, riots in 100 cities Economic Development; rise of CDCs

Period			
		1968–72: Creation of Black caucuses in white institutions; Black Student Unions; Black elected officials: NCBL, ABSW, NBUF, NCBC*	
1972–1980	1972: March for African Liberation 1975: U.S. leaves Vietnam 1976: Formation of Patriot Front, Zimbabwe; Soweto demonstration, South Africa 1977: Andy Young named Ambassador to UN 1979: Support for PLO from black leaders	"Protest to Politics" Major wins 1972: Andy Young, first black Congressman from the South 1973: Maynard Jackson, Atlanta mayor; Coleman Young, Detroit mayor; Tom Bradley, Los Angeles mayor 1974: Mervin Dymally, California Lt. Gov. 1978: Dutch Morial, New Orleans mayor 1979: Richard Arrington, Birmingham mayor Major Losses 1975: John Bowser, Philadelphia 1977: Percy Sutton, New York; Otis Higgs, Memphis; Arthur Eye, Buffalo 1978: Yvonne Burke, Mervin Dymally, California	Community Development continued: Growth of CDCs Groups heavily dependent on government funding, OICs Crisis oriented groups: Anti-Klan Police Brutality Anti-Bakke, Weber Budget Cuts

*ABSW: Association of Black Social Workers, CORE: Congress for Racial Equality, NAACP: National Association for the Advancement of Colored People, NBUF: National Black United Fund, NCBC: National Committee of Black Churchmen, NCBL: National Conference of Black Lawyers, NTO: National Tenants Organization, NWRO: National Welfare Rights Organization, SCLC: Southern Christian Leadership Conference, SNCC: Student Nonviolent Coordinating Committee.

SOURCE: Hulbert James, "From Politics to Protest," *Just Economics* 8, no. 1 (January/February 1980).

movement, King's rhetoric also changed. Upping the ante of the civil rights movement to include economic rights, King was to note that it *"made no sense to be able to sit down and order a hamburger if you could not afford one."*[8]

This expansion of the scope of the civil rights movement led to two strategic shifts. First, an awareness of the role of the United States government in supporting imperialism in Southeast Asia and Africa lent support to the emergence of black consciousness—concretized by the first Black Power Conference in 1966—and resulted in the creation of black caucuses in white institutions, black student unions, and black community control organizations (see Table 2). Second, the notion that black political power could be realized in the electoral arena, and Bayard Rustin's 1965 argument[9] for the institutionalization of social gains through the attainment of political rights, met with wide approval from both black power advocates and urban social movement organizations.

A third tendency—characterized by the work of Black Muslims in the Northeast, the efforts of farmers' cooperatives in the South, and the development of black educational and cultural institutions—demonstrated a growing interest among black (and later Hispanic, Asian, and Native American) communities in building independent, alternative institutions that would promote both cultural pride and an alternative value system.

These three major questions—the relationship between domestic and international policy, the role of electoral politics in the activities of social-change groups, and the value of alternative institutions—would emerge as key topics for debate in the development of community organization.

The Antiwar Movement and Students for a Democratic Society

While there were clearly many organizations within the antiwar movement, the one that most influenced the direction of community organization was the group with the deepest roots in anti-communist social democracy: Students for a Democratic Society (SDS). Because SDS emerged in a turbulent period and was forced almost at once to cut the umbilical cord that attached it to the League for Industrial Democracy, it was no accident that SDS developed much of its identity in conjunction with SNCC. As Howard Zinn notes, SNCC students had a "tremendous respect for the potency of the demonstration coupled with an eagerness to confront policy makers with the power of people in the streets and on the picket line.[10] It was this power and energy, plus the view of the vanguard of the movement as both poor and black that prompted a young Tom Hayden to write to an SDS audience in 1963, "Working in poor communities is a position from which to expose the whole structure of pretense, status and glitter that makes the country's real human problems . . . . Students and poor people make each other seem real."[11]

While SDS continued to be the organizational backbone of the antiwar movement, Kirkpatrick Sale's history of the organization notes that "by the summer of 1963, the cause . . . seemed clear: organize the poor and unemployed. The means seemed to have been given: a SNCC-inspired movement."[12]

To evidence the growing ties between SDS, the emerging Northern Student Movement, and the black community-control organizations, Jesse Gray, black leader of the Harlem rent strike, was invited to speak at the December 1963 meeting of SDS. The organizational component formed in response to this new CO emphasis within SDS was the Economic Research and Action Project (ERAP). Influenced by the early black power position of SNCC, which insisted that white students organize in the white community, ERAP's first project was in Ann Arbor, Michigan—a project to organize white, unemployed, displaced southerners. By mid-1964, however, after much SDS infighting, ERAP emerged in ten cities and provided the organizational staff for Citizens United for Adequate Welfare in Cleveland, which won a free-lunch program for poor children in the city schools; and for the Newark Community Union Project (NCUP), which managed to improve local garbage collection and force housing improvements from landlords.

Although Rennie Davis was to confess that, by the end of the summer, "no project succeeded in giving life to our slogan: 'an interracial movement of the poor,' and certainly none 'organized a community,'"[13] the ERAP experience was important for a number of reasons. First, ERAP projects introduced the notion of systematic local organizing to a new left that had been involved only with "the movement." Second, it raised the question of serious white working-class mobilization outside the point of production. As Fructer and Kramer observed in their evaluation of NCUP in 1966, "students experience the secondary process of control rather than the primary process of exploitation."[14] In coming into contact with poor and working-class constituencies, organizers found that "this dual attempt to build the movement and to achieve specific concrete change generates a constant tension in all projects."[15] This tension reflected the organization's need for legitimacy, met by remedying individual grievances, coupled with a belief on the part of the organizers that the process of organizing was itself a means to radicalize the organization's members and orient them toward more fundamental structural change. This tension led organizers into a series of questions that laid the groundwork for new organizational forms all through the 1970s. The question of building a permanent local movement of opposition, for instance, was largely debated within SDS in 1966.

In addition, the ERAP projects came to be the basic units within SDS where women began to play key roles as organizers and eventually to question their own subservient roles in the movement. As Sara Evans notes:

> The ERAP projects created an environment far more conducive to female leadership than the highly intellectual campus movement. Community organizing in the North, like that in the South, allowed women to develop a strong sense of their own capabilities. ERAP represents the "SNCC-izing" of the northern movement. . . . women, utilizing the ideology that was embedded in SNCC and ERAP, led the critique of women's position in the new left, which was the beginning of the women's liberation movement.[16]

In the SDS view, the role of community organization was to develop consciousness (among the poor) and mobilize collective social action. As Kotler observes:

> The principal value of the SDS theory of community organization is its program for advancing popular revolutionary consciousness. As they organize, people in the community learn about the structures of national power and what they are up against. They see, by comparison among the communities of various cities that have SDS local projects, common conditions of inequality, and they formulate a view of the national elements of control common to all.[17]

It was therefore SDS that raised the question of how local communities could build both consciousness and organization to effect change on the national level.

The Industrial Areas Foundation

The Alinsky-founded IAF differed from the foregoing groups in several ways. Emphasizing the organizational imperative as the key to social reform, Saul Alinsky cited as his intellectual forerunners Jefferson, Paine, Lincoln, and Gandhi, as well as Hannibal and Machiavelli. Eschewing ideology, Alinsky's written work defines a context for making unacceptable social behavior justifiable. He writes in *The Professional Radical*, "The real question has never been: Does the end justify the means? The real question is and always has been: *Does this particular end justify these particular means?*"[18]

Many writers[19] focus on Alinsky's tactical abrasiveness while others are more critical of his lack of ideology,[20] but of one fact there can be no doubt: Alinsky was the first organizer to systematically project a purpose for community organizing (the obtaining of power) and to develop a replicable organizational model.

THE SIXTIES MOVEMENTS

The key to activating mass power in the Alinsky model is a territorial organization uniting existing organizations and action of issues of local grievance with achievable goals. Typically, organizers would develop a sponsoring committee that would be the basis for building a coalition of existing organizations, as well as bearing the responsibility for raising money. This model had the advantages of getting existing groups to "buy in" to the organization and of neutralizing political opposition.

The first significant variation on this model was independently developed in the early 1960s by Fred Ross of the Community Service Organization in California. Arguing that many poor people did not have organizations already representing their interests, Ross developed a new form of organizing technology: the house meeting. House meetings were evening sessions, held in poor communities where some six to twenty people would focus on the specific problems of the poor and develop a preorganizational infrastructure among the unorganized. This practice was translated into organizational formations in a number of ways. Cesar Chavez, picking up on the notion of community unions, used this type of infrastructural development *outside the immediate arena of conflict* to create farm workers' food- and gas-buying clubs, which would build up social cohesion in the farm worker community prior to confronting growers on the issues of wages, hours, and working conditions.[21] In urban centers, this method of directly organizing the poor around their self-interest and *then* linking the organization with existing, "legitimizing" institutions, was used differently: the new and often more militant groups provided the "pizazz" to the coalition; and their leaders were encouraged to manipulate the legitimacy of such existing institutions as churches and unions, to support rent strikes, marches, demonstrations, and other tactics that the legitimizing institutions might not initiate but would, in the context of the coalition, support. This procedure (known as "adding a live piece") though developed within the Alinsky model, had ramifications both in SDS and in the formation of the National Welfare Rights Organization.

In a move that linked students to Alinsky organizing, Margery Tabankin,[22] ex-president of the National Student Association, began working in Chicago for the IAF. The Citizens' Action Program (CAP)[23] was formed there in 1970, Tabankin remembers, when "Staughton Lynd sent me over to meet with Paul and Heather Booth and Bob Creamer and I got them involved."[24] Paul Booth became CAP's first chair and, together with his SDS colleague Bob Creamer, moved CAP into a campaign which pledged a number of community groups to withdraw money from local banks that had refused to lend money to residents in poor neighborhoods.[25]

Typical of Alinsky organizations, CAP was a coalition of community neighborhood groups with the strong participation of the Catholic Parish Councils. One of Alinsky's major contributions was the development of the use of the church.[26] Paul Booth, reflecting on his CAP experience, writes, "Saul Alinsky's major achievement was his Sherman's march through the Protestant churches, forcing one after another to re-orient their priorities to the need of grassroots organizations."[27]

CAP exemplified one form of movement merger: that of SDS and IAF. A special organizer training program conducted at the Syracuse University Community Action Training Center (CATC) in the summer of 1965 led to another form: the merging of CORE's northern-based civil rights organizing with the tactics developed by Saul Alinsky and Fred Ross to form the National Welfare Rights Organization.

The National Welfare Rights Organization

Unlike the other forerunners of community organization, which for the most part lacked theoretical clarity, the National Welfare Rights Organization (NWRO) had at its very beginning a theoretical framework and a tension between the development of a movement and organization strategy. Its theorists were Richard Cloward and Frances Fox Piven, both faculty members at Columbia University. In their controversial article "A Strategy to End Poverty," published in *The Nation* in 1965,[28] Cloward and Piven argued that the poor could be mobilized onto the welfare rolls, precipitating a political and fiscal crisis. The authors gave three reasons why their strategy would succeed. First, the mobilization would guarantee immediate economic benefits. Second, the strategy did not ask people to go outside their immediate experience or to be involved in formal organizational roles. Third, the prospects for mass influence were enhanced by the plan's practical basis for coalition between poor whites and poor blacks.

George Wiley, chairman of Syracuse CORE, was impressed by Cloward and Piven's argument. In a 1966 speech, Wiley stated, "This idea of releasing the potential for major economic pressure through trying to encourage people to gain their rights in the welfare system is one that has had immediate response and has been enormously attractive to activists working in urban areas."[29]

Although the major intellectual and material resources for NWRO were mobilized by Cloward, Piven and Wiley, the actual organizers included Bruce Thomas, President of Syracuse CORE; Rhoda Linton, an ex-missionary; and Bill Pastreich, an ex-Peace Corps worker who had been forced by the Peace Corps to leave Latin America because he had organized a series of mass rent strikes (despite the fact that he spoke Spanish very badly). All these, as well as a number of ex-SNCC workers, went through the CATC training and were influenced by Alinsky's notion of the organizational imperative, CORE's direct action tactics, and Fred Ross's house meeting infrastructure. Downplaying Cloward and Piven's plan for mass *mobilization*, these organizers called instead for a program of mass *organization*. What resulted was an organizational model, first tested in 1967, yet another step removed from Alinsky's coalition model. The welfare rights model ignored existing organizations and concentrated instead on developing a new local organization of welfare recipients. Through a six-week organizing campaign, it identified special needs (benefits) welfare recipients were entitled to but were not getting, and went on to mobilize organized recipients for protracted confrontation with the local welfare department. The "Boston model," developed by Rhoda Linton and first used extensively by Bill Pastreich in the summer of 1967, differed from Piven and

THE SIXTIES MOVEMENTS

Cloward's strategy on two important points. First, instead of organizing to add people to the welfare rolls, it mobilized a defined constituency: people already on welfare. Second, it developed semi-autonomous local units with indigenous leadership. Breaking initially with the Alinsky method of utilizing legitimizing institutions, as NWRO grew it began to build similar alliances on a national level.

When NWRO, as a single-issue organization with a single constituency, found itself unable to survive the state-initiated flat welfare grants (see Chapter 3), it sought to expand its constituency. As George Wiley wrote in 1973:

> It's time that a new majority be forged—one that is based on the real self-interests of its members. I believe that a political majority can be organized around a common set of fundamental economic issues such as tax reform, health care, and adequate income. This new majority could include all of the 79 percent of American families whose incomes are less than $15,000 a year (for a family of four). It could unite the majority that Nixon has wooed and the minorities he has ignored or oppressed. It could overcome hostilities that the Nixon administration sought to exacerbate between Blacks and whites, poor and working people, young and old.[30]

Three years earlier, Wiley had begun an experiment in Arkansas—then called the Arkansas Community Organizations for Reform Now—to test the viability of expanding NWRO's constituency.

ACORN, however, is only one of the "big four" national community organizing networks attempting to realize Wiley's dream of an organized new majority. Each of the networks (see Table 3) represents a different approach to building a majority movement. For example, even though the Citizen Action Program described earlier died in the early 1970s, the CAP experience gave Heather Tobias Booth the experience and connections to found the Midwest

25

TABLE 3. MAJOR COMMUNITY ORGANIZATIONAL NETWORKS IN THE UNITED STATES

Org'l Network	ACORN	Citizen Action	National People's Action	Industrial Areas Foundation
Organizational roots	NWRO, SDS	SDS, IAF, Women's Movement	IAF	Amer. populist/social work
Training center	Institute for Social Justice	Midwest Academy	National Training & Information Center	IAF
Publications	United States of ACORN/USA The Organizer	Citizen Action	Disclosure	(Local only)
Funding	45% Membership 40% Other internal 15% Foundation/ church	20% Internal 80% Foundation/ church	20% Internal 15% Government (through 1982) 65% Foundation/ church	20% Internal 80% Foundation/ church (older projects about 50% self-sufficient)
Organizational type	Membership	Coalition	Loose-knit network	Federation
Tactics	Confrontation Direct action Electoral Alternative institutions Negotiation	Confrontation Coalition-building w/ progressive candidates	Confrontation Direct action Negotiation	Confrontation Direct action Negotiation

Scope	27 States	18 States	9 Cities	10 Cities
Issues	Utility rates, jobs, redlining, housing, taxes, block grants, schools, welfare	Energy, plant closings, taxes, toxics, health, solidarity with Central America	Jobs, housing policy, utility rates	Crime, housing, health, education, insurance rates
Organizational connections	American Agriculture Movement, local AFL-CIOs in 30 cities	C/LEC, Conf. on Alt. State & Local Government, Working Women, Citizens for Tax Justice, UAW, AFSCME, Nat'l Council of Senior Citizens	National Center for Urban Ethnic Affairs, National Congress of Neighborhood Women, local labor & church connections	Catholic, Methodist, & Episcopal churches (Organize, Inc. has same strengths, fewer projects)
Media support*	ITT, *Social Policy*, establishment press, internal statewide newsletters	ITT, *Mother Jones*, *Democratic Left*, *Socialist Review*, established press, internal statewide newsletters	ITT, *Social Policy*, establishment press, internal individual organizational newsletters	Establishment press, internal individual organizational letters

*Media support is a question of quantity. In the establishment press, ACORN and NPA get more local coverage, while nationally, because of the infrastructural connections, Citizen Action gets more coverage, both in the establishment and the alternative press.

SOURCES: J. Perlman, "Grassrooting the System," *Social Policy*, September/October 1976, pp. 14–17; T. Sampson, "Roots and Branches of Mass-Based Citizen-Action Organizing" (mimeographed, 1977).

Academy, an organizer training institute that developed the organizers and leaders for the multi-state Citizen Action organization. Citizen Action's major strength has been its ability to use the sociopolitical relations of many former SDS activists and to mobilize their skills and talents into the building of powerful statewide coalitions of existing community groups (particularly senior citizen and labor groups). In contrast, the Industrial Areas Foundation has opted for a strategy of institutionally based organizing, rooted in the notion that such institutions as the church in particular can be transformed into social change instruments by developing the political acumen of key actors. National People's Action, a coalition that developed national prominence around its work with insurance and mortgage redlining, has attempted to consolidate local groups through both a yearly national confrontational event (usually with HUD) and local group training and development provided by NPA's training arm, the National Training and Information Center.

Whatever their differences, however, all four networks were instrumental responses to issues and debates about community organizing that were raised in the movements of the 1960s.

Debates within the 1960s Movements

As the movements of the 1960s developed, the hows and whys of social-change activity were argued in every setting from red-eyed all-night strategy sessions to church basement banquets and college journals, as well as in jail cell "reevaluations." The discussions were not especially calm or rational; specific "sides" seldom won, and many important tactical assumptions were never debated at all. But the pivotal issues raised —including tactics, constituency and infrastructure, the utility of movements versus organizations, the role of ideology, and the appropriate scope and size of the movement—set the tone for the strategic and tactical development of community organization.

Tactics

Within each movement, disruptions and demonstrations were the two tactics developed to a science. But as Michael Lipsky noted:

> Protest as a political tactic is limited because protest leaders must appeal to four constituencies at the same time. A protest leader must:
> (1) nurture and sustain an organization composed of people who may not always agree with his program or style;
> (2) adapt to the mass media—choose strategies and voice goals that will give him as much favorable exposure as possible;
> (3) try to develop and sustain the protest's impact on third parties—the general public, sympathetic liberals or anyone who can put pressure on those with power; and
> (4) try to influence directly the targets of the protest— those who have the power to give him what he wants.[31]

One criticism of the limitations of these tactics was, of course, ideological. As activist Ron Aronson wrote:

> The movement's main weapon of opposition is its power of disruption: picketing, sitting-in, destroying the business image of a city or state. Although useful for winning concessions, these tactics carry no implication of direct control over the levers that run the system. They *ask* for concessions rather than assert the power to seize them.[32]

Another question was posed initially in the civil rights movement and later echoed by the student movement: how could the movement consolidate the tactical gains made by demonstration and disruption? One answer is evidenced by the tactical shift within the civil rights movement toward electoral politics. The civil rights and the student movements also advocated setting up alternative economic and social institutions, both to develop models and to provide people with a concrete alternative to capitalist consumerism. The Alinsky organizations, on the other hand, opposed alternative institutions on the grounds that it is problematic to define "our clients as potential members or, worse, our members as potential clients."[33]

In choosing tactics, there is also the question of "keeping inside the experience of the people," a tenet of community organizing. Many critics have argued that disruptive actions are outside the experience of most working-class people; others have countered that voting is the experience of the middle and upper classes. This debate is clearly related to the second area of discussion: constituency and infrastructure.

Constituency and Infrastructure

The question of what strata to organize in order to effect social change is, of course, related to the kind of social change desired; it is ultimately a political/ideological question. Implicit within the splits in the civil rights movement is the question of coalitions: should they be based on class (the unification of poor blacks and poor whites) or race (the unification of all blacks)? In community organizing circles, both the IAF and NWRO viewed the question of constituent legitimacy as central. Should the concentration be on existing legitimate organizations; should new grassroots organizations of the poor be formed; or should both happen? The question of infrastructure is also key to community organization, on two levels. The first has to do with mobilizing the resources of semi-autonomous social institutions.

> According to Myles Horton, founder of the Highlander Folk School, which trained hundreds of civil rights activists, places like black beauty parlors provided enclaves for discussing strategy and centers for distributing literature precisely because they were relatively insulated from

white community sanctions. "We dealt with people who couldn't get in trouble with the whites—labor union people and professionals in the black community and the beauticians," Horton recounted. "We ran special workshops for black beauticians. We used the shops all over the South as a center for literature and discussions because the beauticians didn't care what white people thought about them."[34]

The role of semi-autonomous social or economic institutions was important not only in the civil rights movement. The women's movement has also underscored the importance of social networks in developing consciousness and organization. One of the values that fueled the student movement was the emergence of radical debate on issues of tactics and strategy. In an article assessing the movements of the 1960s, Paul Booth has pointed to the development of an intellectual infrastructure of journals including *Studies on the Left, Liberation, Ramparts, New Left Notes,* and *New University Thought.*[35] It was in these journals that the hot items of the day and the new ideas were fed to an eager group of activists. Very often these debates were important in shaping movement strategy. As Wini Breines reflects:

> *Studies on the Left* published a series of articles, the main contributor to which was James O'Connor, around the theme that contemporary working class agitation was increasingly generated by poverty, slums, inadequate educational facilities, and insufficient public services—*not job issues. This amounted to a shift in the traditional leftist notion of agency from the working class to the poor and the marginal* [emphasis added].[36]

This infrastructure, in many ways, provided the student movement with its intellectual underpinnings as well as access to university and monetary resources.

THE SIXTIES MOVEMENTS

Movements versus Organizations

As suggested earlier, the welfare rights movement was built within a context of tension between strategists who argued for mass mobilization leading to systemic breakdown (Piven and Cloward) and those who favored organized development (Wiley). These opposing views were represented in the civil rights movement through what was almost an organizational division of labor: SNCC in particular was interested in building local organization, while SCLC advocated broad strokes—large-scale marches and mobilizations. The tension was mirrored also in SDS. As one observer wrote:

> SDS just simply was not interested in talking about organizational problems or about political analysis. . . . SDS cannot be understood in terms of traditional political organization. *Neither ideological clarity nor organizational stability are fundamentally important to SDSers* [emphasis added].[37]

The Alinsky position on the movement/organization question was hard-line:

> In the IAF lexicon, "organization" is everything, while "movement" is almost a bad word. As Ed Chambers explains it, a movement relies on charismatic leaders, other people's money, indiscriminate recruitment, amateur devotion, and "flash, image, consciousness raising." An organization is built on dues, collective leadership, army-like regularity, systematic daily work, professionalism, and playing to win. Movements are ideological. In the Alinsky model of an organization, people act democratically in their own self-interest, and ideology is irrelevant.[38]

Even when organizations were chosen as the appropriate means for creating change, however, there was still the question of organizational form. As Jo Freeman observed in "The Tyranny of

Structurelessness," the women's movement in particular was antihierarchical. She noted that in its early years there was an emphasis on "leaderless, structureless groups as the main, if not sole, organizational form of the movement."[39] Characterizing this view, Aronson wrote:

> The system makes all important decisions for you, structures your life. We seek here a democratic movement, in which people make their own decisions and are treated as ends and not means. To move people to act by our own subtle means of persuasion, to be dishonest in any way, is to perpetuate what we are fighting against. Therefore we shall not coax, suggest, "lead" discussions, artificially maneuver people into situations, or seek to influence their thought and decisions. The power structure operates from the top down; if we accept that way of operating, we have no reason for being here.[40]

Paul Booth saw this tendency as opposing institutionalized leadership and discipline and favoring spontaneity, all under the false name of participatory democracy.[41] It is ironic to note that the very organization of which Booth was the initial chair, the Chicago-based Citizen Action Program, died—according to Moberg—precisely because of hierarchical control: "The trouble lay in CAP's very structure. The quick unravelling of the organization essentially came down to a matter of who would control things, and Alinsky's ideas, as practiced by the IAF, were central to the controversy."[42]

This IAF/SDS split over organizational structure continued with IAF-trained Mike Miller summarizing the basic function of organizations as "the education of community people; the legitimation of the organization; the strengthening of the organization; the escalation of demands followed by organizational victories; and the realization by people that a better life is possible."[43] It was precisely this focus, however, that led Danny Schecter, writing a critique of the Syracuse University Community Action Training Center (CATC) headed by Warren Haggstrom, to argue:

> Emphasis on structure leads him [Haggstrom] to a condemnation of social movements because of their unstable and anarchic nature. Unfortunately, his concern with form becomes a concern with content. A formal neighborhood organization is properly concerned with only neighborhood problems. This imposes an often parochial and unideological tone to an organization's activities.[44]

Underlying these charges and countercharges are some fundamental differences. The movement experience of the SDS antiwar efforts anticipates change through the mobilization of broad sectors of the population, the successful use of sympathetic media, and massive waves of local and national action. The experiential base of the traditional Alinsky approach is explicitly local, the demands immediate, specific, and realizable. The beneficiaries of the action are indirectly the community at large but *directly* the organization and its members. In one view, the organization is a means to power; in the other, the organization *is* power. Clearly, the relationship of organizational structure to purpose is related to the fourth area of debate: the role of ideology.

Ideology

At the base of all debates about organizing is a fundamental question: for what and for whom is the organizing taking place? It was only when the civil rights movement began to develop ideologically, connecting the exploitation of blacks in this country to a system of exploitation, that the first major splits developed. Similarly, the transition in the antiwar movement from an antimilitarist stance to a pro–North Vietnamese stance was to cause waves within both the "peace establishment" and the student movement. The welfare rights movement reached the height of its political power by linking the effects of the war in Vietnam to the "war at home."

These, however, were not the dominant tendencies. In the civil rights movement, transformed in the late 1960s to the black power movement, the major ideological stances were characterized either by Bayard Rustin's consolidation of political power through electoral politics or by a younger, more militant cluster of groups that were heavily influenced by Franz Fanon's *Wretched of the Earth*, Carl Bogg's *Racism and Class Struggle*, and Stokeley Carmichael and Charles Hamilton's *Black Power*. Young blacks became the backbone of such eclectic formations as the more working-class-based Black Panther Party on the one hand, and the party-building efforts of the October League, African People's Socialist Party, and the Bolshevik League on the other. While both the electoralists and the revolutionary nationalists could claim constituencies in the black community, neither group was successful or, in the case of the vanguard parties, interested in developing mass-based organization.

Although the student movement also split along ideological lines (one burning question being the role of women) and gave rise to a number of ultraleft organizations (including Weatherman), a major portion of the student movement argued for a "pragmatic approach" to politics, which focused on working for the Alinsky-esque "specific, immediate, and realizable" achievements. In part, this emphasis on the pragmatic reflects the relatively narrow scope of strategic debates. For instance, in his pithily titled ("Words Butter No Parsnips") 1964 address to the SDS Conference on Economic Issues and Community Movements, Field Secretary Steve Max called for "wresting from the hands of the exploiters the power through which they could exploit—that is, the political power of the city, state, and federal governments."[45] Tom Hayden mused that this was SDS's attempt to "create a new world with the tools of the old."[46] However, as theorist Ron Aronson notes, an antitheoretical and anti-ideological bias characterized the student movement:

> Ironically, organizers are applauded by nonradicals for their rejection of "foreign" ideology and their solid American pragmatism. What is meant, of course, is that they are not Marxists, are not opposed to basic "American" institutions like capitalism. Thus at one and the same time, the organizers violently reject American society—on

a personal and moral level—and accept many of its theoretical underpinnings. As their society rejects Marx as irrelevant, so they reject Marx as irrelevant; as their society is anti-intellectual, anti-theoretical and pragmatic, so are they anti-intellectual, anti-theoretical and pragmatic; as their society considers the term *capitalism* more pejorative than meaningful, so they consider the term no longer meaningful; as their society refuses to confront the roots of its problems, so do they refuse to examine structural causes; as their society proclaims the "end of ideology," so do they reject the term itself. Because the organizers have not reached a long-range theoretical and analytical level, their underlying attitudes and preconceptions thus acquiesce in the society they seek to reject. Were this not so, the organizers would seek to demonstrate the illegitimacy of the given system on all levels.[47]

The problem was reflected in Moberg's assessment of the earliest (1970) merger of Alinsky and SDS politics in the Citizen Action Program in Chicago:

It failed to develop even a modest ideological commitment that could keep people together for reasons beyond the necessary but often fickle motivations of self-interest narrowly conceived. Organizers' caution against placing any ideological stamp on CAP activities meant that ideas were not discussed openly, leaving people more subject to manipulation.[48]

It is evident that discussions of the role of ideology in developing organization took place on a number of levels. Both SDS and the civil rights movement raised questions about the U.S. government as an imperialist power and also began to question the basic economic order. On another level, ideology was linked to tactics, pitting the electoralists who argued for consolidation of power by increasing political clout against the Weather underground and some formations of racial minorities who argued for more militant attacks directly on state institutions and corporate targets.

In addition to such "purer" ideological concerns as whether and how an organization would take an anticorporate or anticapitalist stance, or how to express the ideological position tactically, other concerns surfaced in relation to the question of internal democracy. How could the organizers build an organization for social change that did not itself replicate the oppression of the larger society? It is these same concerns that community organizations face today.

Scope and Size

Related to discussions concerning tactics, constituency, structure, and ideology was the debate as to the best size for an organization and the scope of political issues it was attempting to address. Opposition to large-scale organization certainly characterized the IAF in particular—though as early as 1941, Alinsky himself wrote that the two major defects in the traditional community organization movement were (1) that it viewed each community problem as it if were independent of all other problems, and (2) that it viewed the community as a social, political, and economic entity more or less insulated from the general scene.[49]

Clearly, local organizing was the direction in which many former SDS organizers planned to move. Along with welfare rights activists, the former student radicals adopted what Harry Boyte refers to as the "localist tendency," the assumption that thousands of local organizations formed around local grievances would in the future merge and become the base of a new progressive movement.[50] The rejection of a national coordinating infrastructure in favor of local autonomous organizations was the initial political stance taken by organizers in virtually every newly formed community organization of the 1970s.

Associated with the question of size is the question of scope. Steve Max, describing parallels between community organizations and trade unions, writes that the former are "guided by many of the same principles of self-interest, pragmatism, and emphasis on constant small victories, with only slight attention paid to the long-term self-interest of the members."[51] In this same vein, Boyte argues that for all its militancy, the Alinsky approach could easily fit into the traditional interest-group form of American politics.[52] Summing up this line of argument, Friedland stresses that power in the United States is organized nationally and internationally; Thus, he asserts, community organizations that initially focus on and, all too frequently, remain centered on local, manageable problems are addressing only illusions of power and not its realities.[53]

In the last few years, all these questions concerning the role of community organizing within a larger movement have been raised anew. While the "localist school" has all but disappeared as three of the four major organizing networks move to consolidate in a national arena, debates still rage about the progressive impulses of working-class, welfare, and middle-class constituencies; ideological questions abound as community organizations win electoral office and participatory democracy becomes state planning. The political character of alliances becomes more important as three of the national networks develop formal relations with labor and church progressives.

One of these three, the Association of Community Organizations for Reform Now (ACORN), expanded in six years from one state to twenty, and attempted to wring ideological and pragmatic concessions from the Democratic Party.

3

The Roots of the ACORN Oak

> *"If we had known all about it [ACORN when it first emerged], well, I'm not saying history would have been changed, but it might well have been."*
>
> —A. M. Sandy Keith, former Mayor, Little Rock, Arkansas

ACORN's fifteen-year history has been guided by three basic principles: expansion, penetration, and consolidation (immediately followed, of course, by more expansion). The organization would expand geographically and in its constituent base; utilize the entree of traditional community organization to penetrate other spheres of community life; and then consolidate fiscal, personnel, and ultimately political resources for the next expansion. While this pattern did not always develop rationally and cyclically, it does characterize the development of the organization over its first ten years.

Of course, such a developmental pattern is not unique to ACORN; it is a growth model describing organization in general and, in particular, ACORN's direct predecessor, the National Welfare Rights Organization. ACORN's formation was authorized in 1970 by George Wiley, executive director of NWRO, in the hope of providing a model for expanding NWRO's constituency from welfare recipients only to a broad-based coalition that would include low- and moderate-income people—a new majority.

To understand the progress and development of ACORN, then, it is first necessary to examine the history of NWRO, which provided the impetus and initial funding for the "Arkansas experiment."

Founded in 1966, NWRO had grown out of a merger between the Industrial Areas Foundation (IAF) and the civil rights movement, sparked by a 1965 organizer training program that brought together veteran organizers Saul Alinsky, Warren Haggstrom, and Fred Ross to build an "on the streets" community organization model through the Syracuse University School of Social Work.

Most influential were theorist Warren Haggstrom and Fred Ross. Haggstrom's work had far-reaching implications for organizational growth in general (see Chapter 4). In California, Ross had developed a new twist to the Alinsky-IAF coalition model, which used existing community infrastructure (churches and unions, for example) to coalesce a neighborhood "federation," which would then confront local officials. Ross started instead with neighborhood-based house meetings to build a sense of community among potential members, then consolidated this sense of community by initiating nonconfrontational cooperative ventures (gas stations, food-buying clubs) that would strengthen interpersonal and organizational ties for the thrust into other organizational spheres. In the Ross model, constituents would first develop a cooperative working relationship based on group consensus before initiating a confrontation. This contrasted with the predominant civil rights model, which called for the use of confrontation to increase militance and consensus.

The emergent welfare rights model was based on an analysis of the degree to which the group targeted for organizing—mothers receiving Aid to Families with Dependent Children (AFDC)—had (1) developed infrastructural relations and (2) successful experience with confrontational tactics. NWRO built a grassroots organization through house meetings, which increased in-group solidarity, and direct confrontation with local welfare officials, which in turn increased militancy in the constituency. Though local welfare rights groups frequently did work with local churches and unions, the relationships were welfare rights–related; progressives from both those communities were mobilized around specific welfare reform issues. Coalition development, then, was not a major strength of NWRO.

The primary reason for NWRO's phenomenal growth was that its local organizing model could, with slight modification, be duplicated in every major urban center in the country. The "Boston model," developed by Rhoda Linton in Brooklyn in 1967 and further polished and used in Boston by Bill Pastreich in the fall of 1967, was the basis for NWRO's ability to send raw young white organizers like Bert DeLeeuw, Pam Blair, Marcia Henry, Mark Splain, Kathy Landry, Barbara Bowen, Gerry Shea, and Wade Rathke into Minnesota, Ohio, Illinois, Rhode Island, and New York, where, in a matter of months, they produced organization. The model emphasized the unearthing of a "minimum standard of need" welfare regulation specifying a material benefit to which welfare recipients were entitled but which they were not currently receiving. After scouring the state welfare regulations, organizers would create a form to be filled out by recipients who attended a group meeting and joined the organization. They would then march en masse to the local welfare department to demand cash for the benefit—usually specifying a check be issued within ten days. These "furniture campaigns" or "clothing campaigns" (so called because the minimum standard grants most commonly won in New York and Massachusetts were for furniture and clothing) would last approximately six weeks. At the completion of the campaign, previously unorganized recipients would have been through an organizational development process that included a minimum of one house meeting, two organization-building meetings (including an election of temporary officers), two demonstrations, and sometimes even a "grievance day," where members would negotiate individual problems with the local welfare office.

NWRO was extremely successful at building strong local groups in almost every major city in the country, and in getting material benefits for members, whose numbers peaked at over 100,000. The organization had the strengths of a truly grassroots, low-income membership of predominantly black women who could claim local, statewide, and even national effectiveness on the welfare issue.

On the other hand, the weakness of the organization was reflected in the too rapid development of leadership among welfare recipients. Often the officers "temporarily" elected at the first meeting would stay on for years, a tendency that eventually resulted in the entrenchment of national leaders who had little acccountability to the membership. This problem was accentuated by the group's inability to build meaningful coalitions and the its organization around a single issue—welfare—that was an anathema to many church and labor progressives, despite general acknowledgment that many job training programs did not work and that unemployment was an increasing problem, especially for minorities. Even when doing so appeared in the direct economic and political self-interest of labor unions, many did not support progressive welfare policies, while conservative forces in the church community took the position that everyone should engage in income-producing work.

The NWRO "break the bank" strategy produced yet another problem. The state welfare bureaucracies, grasping the significance of the open-ended organizing opportunities afforded by "special need" or "minimum standards" demands, responded by changing the grant structure so that all recipients received a "flat" grant that supposedly covered all their needs. By the end of the turbulent 1960s, the handwriting was on the wall: the welfare rights movement, by itself, was not going to move much further.

Cognizance of these weaknesses led organizers within NWRO to discuss ways in which the welfare constituency could forge meaningful ties with labor, church, civil rights, and other progressive groups, especially with other poor people's organizations. The established Southern Christian Leadership Conference and the fledgling National Tenants' Organization (NTO) were approached about the possibilities of coalition work and eventual merger. Both SCLC and NTO expressed interest, but the discussions never moved beyond vague promises to develop proposals of how the groups might work together. When these external merger plans bore little fruit, organizers within NWRO proposed two experimental plans: (1) the expansion of NWRO's organizational ties through the development of a "Southern Caravan," a traveling road show of NWRO leaders who would visit eight southern states to demystify welfare, develop leadership, and build the organization; and (2) the initiation of new organizing projects in New Orleans and Little Rock.

Why Arkansas?

When Wade and Lee Rathke drove their Datsun station wagon some 1,500 miles from Boston to Little Rock in June 1970, much of the debate about exactly where to locate a southern organizing project for NWRO was old hat. Unwilling to put all his eggs in one basket, George Wiley had balanced NWRO's self-perceived need to "start something in the South" with an assessment of the resources and organizing potential in a number of southern states before authorizing projects in New Orleans and Little Rock. New Orleans was chosen because Louisiana had one of the lowest AFDC grant levels in the country and because NWRO's southern regional representative, Annie Smart, lived in Baton Rouge and was willing to help Virginia-based organizer Andy Bowler get started. In addition, one of NWRO's arch enemies, Senator Russell Long, hailed from Louisiana, and the project would give NWRO a local base from which to raise the issues and concerns of welfare recipients.

Arkansas was chosen for a number of reasons. Census data indicated that the state had a median income of under $6,000; there was a large welfare-eligible population (though the average grant was under $200 per month); and black residents constituted 35 percent of the population. Given NWRO's strong history, a large low-income population of which a significant percentage was black was an important factor. Of the state's 1.9 million residents, over 200,000 resided in the area of Little Rock, the state capital, the only other significant population centers being Pine Bluff (60,000), forty miles south; Fort Smith (63,000), 180 miles west; and Hot Springs (35,000), fifty-five miles south. Little Rock, the center of money and power in the state, had the additional advantage of being located almost in its geographical center. In sum, Arkansas was a southern state with a relatively small population, and without a well-entrenched political elite—a state where a new organization could really make a dent with a well-executed organizing strategy.

Demographics and geography, however, were not the only considerations. A small welfare rights group in Little Rock had issued a *pro forma* invitation to organize a statewide welfare rights organization, and there was the not unimportant endorsement of the project from Johnnie Tillmon, a former Arkansas resident and national chairwoman of NWRO. Tillmon's interest was based not only on her concern for the development of organization in her home state; but, in addition, the Arkansas experiment would give NWRO an opportunity to deal on his home turf with one of the organization's principal legislative opponents: the formidable Wilbur Mills. As Andrew Kopkind has noted:

> Arkansas appeared as an intriguing locale for the experiment in majority organizing. For one thing, it was the lair of Wilbur Mills, then the most powerful manipulator of social and economic legislation in the country; before Mills self-destructed with his own folly, no political opposition to his power was operating in Little Rock.[1]

Arkansas clearly did not have a history of liberal politics. Little Rock is historically a city synonymous with resistance to social change, exemplified by Faubus's 1957 busing desegregation stand. While the Little Rock school desegregation problems were an impetus for civil rights organizing all over the country, the civil rights movement had never established a viable organization in Arkansas. Unions had also been relatively unsuccessful in establishing an organizational base in this right-to-work state.

Nevertheless, the state had been the site of a number of successful populist efforts: H. L. Mitchell's Southern Tenant Farmers' Union in the 1930s, an interracial organization that advocated fair cotton prices for tenant farmers, as well as Huey Long's "Share the Wealth" clubs, which had found strong support in rural Arkansas.

Moreover, electoral politics had begun to have an effect on the infrastructural development for blacks. In 1966, the people of Arkansas had elected as governor Winthrop Rockefeller, a liberal Republican who, in his first three years in office, had initiated a series of OEO (Office of Economic Opportunity) programs that resulted for the first time in the appointment of blacks to political positions. By

1969, then, Arkansas was beginning to form a new political infrastructure that made Arkansas ripe for organizing.

The Organizer

When he emerged as the leading contender to initiate the Arkansas piece of NWRO's southern expansion strategy, twenty-two-year-old Wade Rathke had had only two years of organizing experience. Hired in June 1969 by veteran Bill Pastreich at a rally for welfare recipients on the Boston Common, Rathke had been sent to Springfield, Massachusetts, where four months later he led a newly organized group of welfare mothers in a demonstration for guaranteed welfare benefits that, according to the press, turned into a rock- and bottle-throwing riot. Rathke and Pastreich were both arrested for inciting to riot. By January 1970, Pastreich left Boston to build welfare rights organizations in Ohio and Washington, D.C., leaving Rathke, whom he called "the most talented organizer ever to work for me,"[2] in charge of the Massachusetts organization (MWRO). In early 1970, then, the largest statewide welfare rights group in the country was headed by the youngest organizer on a national staff of almost fifty.

From his position with MWRO, Rathke noted that the organization was severely limited in potential by sticking to the welfare issue, as well as unable to take full advantage of relationships with other groups. Summing up this position in the *ACORN Organizing Handbook*, Steve Kest observes:

> WRO, especially in Massachusetts, welded its constituency of welfare mothers into a highly effective pressure group which brought about countless positive changes in the welfare bureaucracy and in this country's welfare laws, as well as giving the welfare mothers themselves a sense of pride and accomplishment that had been systematically shipped out of them by the institutions they dealt with day to day. But MWRO—and other poor people's

and minority-based organizations of the late 60's—never had the potential for achieving any real power. For one thing, they were, by definition, minority-based. Given America's political system, that meant they would never achieve any wide-ranging political power. But even more important, center and right-wing politicians, the welfare bureaucracies, and the media succeeded in convincing the broad working class majority of the country that what the minority groups wanted was a piece of *their* pie. And given the tax structure that was going to have to support increased welfare and poor people's benefits, it wasn't too hard to do the convincing. The necessary allies of the welfare and minority groups, then, became their enemies, and the majority coalition needed for progressive social change in this country found itself thoroughly divided, and ultimately defeated even before it had a chance to be born.[3]

Wade Rathke's ambitions for organizing in Arkansas, where he characterized the level of political activity as an "organizational vacuum,"[4] reflected his awareness of this analysis. He further noted that grassroots organizing had reached a state of uncertainty throughout the country as Alinsky's efforts in Chicago, Buffalo and Providence produced short-term victories but lacked long-term structures for social change. The welfare rights movement was stymied as the flat grant system eradicated the organization's primary leverage and Chavez's efforts, though effective in secondary boycotts, did not provide an effective model for neighborhood organization.[5]

In building ACORN, Rathke hoped to keep what he perceived to be good in his welfare rights experience (the membership base, the use of a replicable model, and the strategic manipulation of the press), while incorporating some parts of the old Alinsky model (strong ties with such existing organizations as unions and churches) and experimenting with electoral politics as a way to consolidate organizational victories.

ROOTS OF THE ACORN OAK

The Organization: For What and For Whom?

Like every other attempt to build a progressive organization that would empower a particular constituency, the Arkansas Community Organizations for Reform Now had to grapple with the same issues that plagued the movements and organizations of the 1960s. Addressing the fundamental question of for what and for whom should the organizing take place, Rathke's early writing asserts:

> ACORN deals with power, and not simply with winning issues, be they consumer issues or environmental issues or economic issues, or whatever; winning those issues is what ACORN does on a day to day basis.
>
> Behind the organization's concern with these issues is a basic understanding which says that all these issues are mere manifestations of a much more fundamental issue: the distribution of power in this country.... You can win stop lights from here to eternity, which is what many community organizations around the country have excelled at, but unless your organization addresses the question of who has the power to control what happens in a neighborhood, a city, a county, or a state—and who *should* have the power to control what happens in these areas—then all your organization will achieve is a proliferation of stop lights in low-to-moderate-income neighborhoods. Obviously, ACORN's goal is much more.[6]

Rathke postulated that what was needed for the distribution of power was a constituency attuned to building a broad-based, stable membership organization. Therefore, the answer to "for whom?" was what ACORN terms the "majority constituency"—"all of the people in this country who are shut out of that power." Noting that 70 percent of the population in Arkansas earned less than $7,000 per year, Rathke argued, "If you can fashion a program that will attract people who earn, say, $8,000 or less, then you're appealing (in Arkansas) to a very large majority. You can develop an organization with real power."[7] While this notion may be inexact in terms of what all these people will actually *do* with a powerful organization, it sets up class-based criteria for membership and advocates, at a minimum, *control* of local institutions by low- and moderate-income people.

A second set of questions concerned the means and process of building an organizational vehicle that could develop power for low-income people in Arkansas. Asserting that the major societal problem was the inability of low- and moderate-income people to control the institutions that affected their lives, ACORN adopted the state of Arkansas's 1836 motto, "The People Shall Rule," as its basis for a general plan of action. First, the organization would concern itself with multiple issues: any issue that concerned its potential membership was an issue on which ACORN would take a stand. "ACORN has the ability, and according to its members, the obligation, to deal with the manifestations of the maldistribution of power in whatever form they take. To ignore certain of the manifestations is to ignore segments of the majority—and that's no way to build a majority constituency."[8]

Linked to the concepts of mass constituency, a multi-issue focus, and the redistribution of power was ACORN's first real philosophical deviation from standard community organization practice: involvement in electoral politics. Before ACORN's conscious move into that arena, most electoral activity—with the exception of the community school control movement and the black electoral efforts—was shunned by traditional community organization: it was all right to demonstrate against politicians but dangerous to join their ranks. ACORN, on the other hand, has from its inception registered lobbyists, endorsed candidates, and worked on initiative measures.

In another break with traditional CO, which was and is largely supported by outside monies, ACORN elected to raise its operating funds through membership dues. Early on, Rathke wrote that "ACORN lives or dies based on its membership's willingness to organize and pay their dues. . . . It doesn't matter if I or the governor or anyone else thinks we're doing great. If the membership stops paying dues we're out of business."[9] Initially, this line was mostly rhetorical, but ACORN has in fact developed an internal financing system that has made the organization relatively independent of outside funding (see chapter 4).

Closely related to these principles was the complex notion and driving force that came to influence many decisions in ACORN's history: Rathke's disaggregation of the concept of organizing.

> I noticed that even in "organized" neighborhoods or constituencies, usually we only had 10–15% of the people active in our group. It seemed . . . important to expand, both in terms of neighborhoods and constituencies, into as many areas as we competently could, as well as using our point of entry—community—to penetrate into other spheres of people's lives—their jobs, schools, politics, culture, etc.[10]

In attempting to operationalize these ideas, ACORN complicated the tensions existing in most fledgling organizations; the trend toward maintenance and consolidation was constantly at odds with the organizational need to expand the membership base. Many major decisions in ACORN's first ten years were informed by discussions and debates framed in terms of the costs and benefits of "expansion versus maintenance."

Though ACORN's development took place on a number of levels simultaneously, its growth occurred in roughly five stages, each characterized by different emphases.

Phase I, 1970–72: The establishment period emphasized local infrastructural development, the definition of ACORN as a separate entity from the National Welfare Rights Organization, and the formation of the ACORN model.

Phase II, 1973–75: These years were characterized by ACORN's first major expansion of both issues and constituencies, as well as its development into a statewide entity. Phase II was also the most intense for the recruitment and training of staff.

Phase III, 1976–79: This was the greatest period of multistate expansion. In these three years, ACORN became a nineteen-state association, both by initiating organizing projects and negotiating affiliations and mergers. The organization also established several community radio stations and a sister organization, the United Labor Unions (ULU).

Phase IV, 1979–81: From mid-1979 through the end of 1981, ACORN consolidated its membership groups by waging a protracted struggle with the Democratic Party.

Phase V, 1981–1985: During these five years, ACORN has attempted to build major coalitions around electoral campaigns, merged its unionization efforts with the Service Employees Union of the AFL-CIO, and reclaimed its disruptive character and low income constituency through militant squatting and "Jobs-for-Residents" campaigns in 12 cities.

Phase I: The First Two Years

Armed with a kitty of $3,000 from NWRO and a guarantee of six months of his NWRO annual salary, Rathke had, by July 1970, located and secured a free office (a habit that later became part of the ACORN model) at the Arkansas Council for Human Relations. By August he had completed the research for his first campaign under the name of Arkansas Welfare Rights, choosing the familiar welfare rights standard campaign: furniture. There were several reasons for this selection. First, the issue appealed directly to the welfare constituency. Second, both Rathke and I, as the second NWRO-trained organizer sent to Arkansas, had conducted furniture campaigns in other states. Third, the state's "minimum standards" regulation was written in such a way as to include low-income, *non*welfare recipients—an immediate opportunity to expand the organizing base.

I arrived in Little Rock by bus in late June 1970 and on the ride from Washington, D.C., I had plenty of time to think about my big move south. As one of eight black organizers NWRO had just put through a summer "hands on" training session involving a D.C. furniture campaign that had resulted in hundreds of arrests (two of them mine) and *no furniture*, I had mixed feelings about my Arkansas assignment. Although both of the lead trainers, Bill Pastreich and Bruce Thomas, kept trying to convince me that the post was a "plum," a chance to work with "one of the best," my first meeting with Wade Rathke in NWRO's Washington office had been fairly inconsequential. He told me about the ACORN idea, the expansion of welfare constituency to include all low-income people. I agreed to go down and work on a six-week drive.

Growing up in New York (Brooklyn), I'd always had a fascination for the South, moderated by what I'd still characterize as a healthy fear. Rathke's protestations that Arkansas was "really sorta the Southwest" did not reassure me. Shortly after my arrival in Little Rock, Wade and I had a series of small arguments about the appropriate appearance for an organizer. Wade attempted to get me to cut my hair (which I did), shave my beard (which I didn't), and buy an American car (which I couldn't afford—and besides, *he* had a Datsun.)

After driving around the neighborhoods (I was glad to get a comfortable berth—far away from Central High School—with a VISTA attorney who would later become ACORN's first lawyer), Wade, his wife Lee, and I went to lunch at the local "Minuteman" restaurant to plan the campaign. In an expansive three-hour discussion, Wade laid out all the political factors, campaign possibilities, and contingencies, emphasizing *what would build the organization*. When we left the restaurant (which I was initially unwilling to enter because of its name—it was only after Lee showed me the slogan "It only takes a minute, man" that I agreed to go in), I was ready to organize the neighborhoods, convinced that we would win the campaign. Only one small incident dampened my enthusiasm: after we got into the Rathke's Datsun, Lee said to Wade, "Didn't you guys see everyone in that place staring at you and listening to your conversation? Am I ever glad to get out of there!" Thus began my organizing career in Arkansas.

Early Campaigns

In evaluating the campaign's chances for success, Rathke saw three potential obstacles. There was, first of all, no precedent that could be uncovered in the state for actually getting a $40 furniture allotment, despite provision for such grants in the state regulations. We talked to hundreds of welfare recipients, but neither we nor the recipients themselves could find anyone who had ever gotten a special-need grant. Second, although there was approximately $750,000 in the state budget allocated for special needs, it was not possible to discover how much, if any, of the money had been spent. Third was the question of allies. A sizable portion of the new black middle class in Little Rock was directly linked, through appointments, to the state Office of Economic Opportunity. Many had strong ties to liberal Republican Winthrop Rockefeller and were therefore likely to be pressured into supporting Rockefeller against a welfare rights campaign.

In order to tip the odds in our favor, Rathke's first organizational move was to dip into his $3,000 kitty and hire Peter Hobby, son of the most powerful and widely respected Methodist minister in Little Rock, to organize a support group for welfare rights called Citizens for the Abolition of Poverty. In what became a model for "neutralizing the opposition," Rathke, through Hobby, set up an interracial, middle-class pressure group that played a key role in the first organizing campaign.

After six weeks of doorknocking in six neighborhoods, the first seventeen (mostly white) women from the Silver City community—an area that George Wallace had carried easily two years earlier[11]—descended on the Pulaski County Welfare Department to demand "minimum standards." For the next four days, groups of black recipients totaling about four hundred followed suit. These actions were enhanced by extensive television and newspaper coverage, and much speculation about who or what this new organization was. Much was made of its interracial nature and the militancy of its leadership. The following week, members of the Citizens for the Abolition of Poverty, accompanied by the Reverend Mr. Hobby and his son

Peter, inspected the homes of several recipients and issued a press statement addressing the "inhumanity of a state where children are forced to sleep on the floor."[12]

This skillful manipulation of a potential adversary, coupled with a fortuitous blunder made by the state welfare commmissioner—who publicly tried in the middle of the campaign to change the regulations on eligibility for special needs and to make the change effective retroactively—allowed ACORN to win its first victory. (Although the action started as a welfare rights campaign, after a few weeks the leaflets said "Arkansas Welfare Rights, an affiliate of the Arkansas Community Organizations for Reform Now [ACORN]," and by the end of the campaign all the literature said "ACORN.") The ACORN campaign resulted in the creation of a new state agency: Furniture for Families, charged with collecting and distributing used furniture. Governor Rockefeller appointed a Republican Party worker to head the agency and paid his salary with personal funds. Thus, though recipients did not get the cash grants that NWRO had won in New York and Massachusetts, they did get furniture, and ACORN had succeeded in winning the first minimum standards campaign in the state of Arkansas. In recounting the incident, the Houston Post wrote, "A 22-year-old ex-SDS member organized a group of welfare mothers in a successful effort to resurrect the rusted remnants of southern populism."[13]

My own recollections of the campaign are somewhat more personal than analytical. One one level I was amazed at the sheer vitality and vibrance of the campaign. The demonstrations all made the front pages of the two major dailies, and the state secret service was on hand for the big action at the governor's mansion. In addition, Rathke always acted as if he knew we would win. Every day during the first series of demonstrations, he would go back to our commandeered office (considerable pressure was brought to bear on the Arkansas Council of Human Relations during the campaign), put his feet up on the desk, and "wait for the governor to call." To this day I'm surprised that we really did get the call. As to my own work on the campaign, of the initial seven groups organized, I was responsible for five, my biggest success being on the east end of

Little Rock where 125 people showed up for the first organizational meeting on a hot, muggy morning. My preparations for the meeting had included weeks of knocking on doors in the neighborhoods, speaking at local churches (a new experience for a nonpracticing black Catholic from Brooklyn), and numerous house meetings, at which I learned to arrive early to ensure getting dinner.

Other reflections on that first campaign refined my notions of life in the South. After three months of scrounging meals fairly regularly at the homes of members of my groups, I invited six or seven local leaders to have dinner on me at the place of their choice. After much sprucing up on my part, I picked up my guests—Where did they want to eat? *At the bus station*! When I asked why, the women answered, "Because the food is served cafeteria style so we can get anything we want, because it's not too expensive, and because it used to be we couldn't eat there and now we can." So ended the first campaign.

ACORN's second campaign exemplified the organization's ability to expand its membership base in terms of both constituency and geography, and to penetrate an area of social life in which people had an interest and where they were legally entitled to specific benefits. The campaign itself was simple. Under the National School Lunch Act, students from low-income backgrounds were entitled to free or reduced-price lunches in the public schools. Black children in North Little Rock schools were denied these lunches, even though the program was 100 percent federally subsidized. ACORN's role was to inform local residents of their children's rights, organize parents to win those rights, and expose the school boards' selective enforcement of federal regulations.

This second campaign, which ACORN also won, allowed the organization to expand from Little Rock into North Little Rock and to penetrate another income constituency, since the school lunches were potentially available to the vast majority of the children of low-income working people in Arkansas. Moreover, it changed the terrain of struggle: ACORN was able to leverage the United States Department of Agriculture to pressure the local school board into compliance with the school lunch regulations.

This strategy of using federal regulations to influence recalcitrant local governments had frequently been applied by civil rights organizations in southern states, but it was ACORN that filed the first lawsuit against a school board for noncompliance with the school lunch regulations. The legal action, coupled with the testimony that a local member and I presented at hearings of the Senate Select Committee on Human Needs, chaired by George McGovern, catapulted the issue into the national news. The assertion in ACORN's testimony that "for all intents and purposes the law on school lunches is not in effect in Arkansas"[14] caused a furor in the local press. The response from the North Little Rock superintendent was to hold up his fists (for a press photo) and decry the role of "outside agitators." The lawsuit, local action, press attention, and federal pressure all contributed to a winning campaign. The North Little Rock schools were forced to comply with federal regulations. Poor children received free lunches and ACORN's reputation grew.

The Attempted Buy-off

With the successful mobilization of hundreds of North Little Rock residents in the school lunch campaign, Governer Rockefeller began to take a second look at the new organization. In their first negotiations over furniture, Wade Rathke had, in the middle of the discussion, looked at Winthrop Rockefeller's monogrammed cowboy boots and facetiously observed that "since we have the same initials maybe we should trade boots." By the time the national press was zeroing in on school lunch regulation noncompliance (October 1970), Governor Rockefeller had, through one of his operatives, scheduled a meeting with ACORN organizers to discuss the possibility of our conducting a voter registration and get-out-the-vote campaign in the upcoming election. While the plan was never clearly articulated, it was the governor's assessment that ACORN could be useful in registering and mobilizing black voters, for which it would be paid $5,000 cash. ACORN never agreed to take on (and never carried out) the project, but shortly thereafter received a cash advance—$3,000 in the proverbial brown paper bag—which extended the organization's ability to hire staff and mount other campaigns. Because he lost the 1970 election to Democratic candidate Dale Bumpers and because the money was in cash, Winthrop Rockefeller was in no position to ask for an accounting.

ACORN "sat out" the gubernatorial race, making neither statements nor endorsements, but on the night of the election when the returns were in and it was clear who the winner would be, Rathke took a small group of ACORN leaders to the new governor's hotel victory celebration. His rationale: "It's free food, plenty of contacts, and it looks like we backed a winner all along."

By January 1971, ACORN claimed a membership base of about 1,000 in Pulaski county, and it was during that month that the organization took its first steps into the electoral arena. Fully seven years before electioneering became generally acceptable in community organization circles, seven ACORN group leaders registered with the Arkansas legislature as special interest lobbyists to represent poor people in the state.

As its first political platform, ACORN put forth a legislative package calling for

> an amendment in the state pharmacy laws to enable free health clinics to dispense drugs; free medical care for low-income persons not eligible for it under existing programs; increasing the size of Housing Authority Boards so tenants can be appointed to the Boards; the establishment of a public defender system in the Circuit Courts; elimination of the state income tax for persons with incomes of less than $3,000; higher welfare benefits for the elderly, blind, disabled and families with dependent children; a prescription drug program for welfare recipients; an expanded collective bargaining law, especially for public service employees, and measures to lower the voting age to 18.[15]

ROOTS OF THE ACORN OAK

Following up on the organization's demands for expanded health care services for poor people, ACORN began a spring offensive against the University of Arkansas Medical Center, demanding better treatment in that facility. Initiating the organization's first campaign in predominantly white neighborhoods, ACORN was able to use federal laws such as the Hill-Burton Act (which required all hospitals receiving federal funds under this act to provide some indigent patients with free or reduced-price health care) plus guerilla tactics to negotiate a series of concessions. These included the creation of a consumer board that gave low-income people a voice in the operations of the Medical Center. According to an account published in the *Arkansas Gazette*:

> With full media attention, 50 protesters marched on the office of James E. Crank, director of the University of Arkansas Medical Center, demanding better scheduling and medical care for patients at the Center.
>
> The demonstration surprised Crank, won Acorn headlines and put pressure on the Medical Center. Acorn kept up the pressure. One Friday morning, 12 Acorn members marched into the hospital emergency room, carrying a doll on a makeshift stretcher and a sign saying "I'm here to wait forever for prompt emergency room care."[16]

In the fall of 1971, ACORN organized its first worker constituencies: the Unemployed Workers' Organizing Committee (UWOC) and the Vietnam Veterans' Organizing Committee (VVOC). These efforts were important because they not only mobilized male workers (a consistently underrepresented constituency within the organization) but also enabled ACORN to win support from organized labor in a campaign against unscrupulous employment agencies (one of which was forced out of business)[17] and from the new Democratic governor Dale Bumpers, who supported more benefits for veterans, including free tuition at the state university. These organizing committees, which were later merged with local ACORN neighborhood

57

groups, were fertile ground for the development of grassroots leadership. Steve McDonald, for instance, ACORN's first chairman, entered the organization through the VVOC in 1971.

By the end of 1971, the organization had achieved a number of significant victories, including stricter enforcement of federal food stamp regulations and local movement on health care and employment practices. But ACORN was not without enemies—especially during the next five years, as it increased its tactical militance in an effort to uncover links between local government policy and business interests. In an October 1971 in-depth article on ACORN by Martin Kirby of the *Arkansas Democrat*, the North Little Rock school superintendent snorted, "I don't like the tactics they use—I have nothing against people getting what they supposedly justly deserve, but their tactics are not necessary or desirable."[18] This criticism from public officials never diminished; in fact, between 1971 and 1976, its language changed from "not necessary or desirable" to "a threat to capitalism and democracy."

The Break with NWRO

The year 1972 was characterized by the tension between two major objectives that exists within all organizations: the need to expend resources for organizational expansion, and the need to maintain and develop the fragile organizational entities already established. During the struggle to "organize as many people as we can" as well as maintain the existing organizational infrastructure, two things happened. First, Arkansas Welfare Rights, the NWRO affiliate, broke with ACORN.

Nationally, NWRO was having its own problems. The organization was clearly on the wane, given the trend toward "flat grants." Moreover, with George Wiley's interests being more directed toward a majoritarian model, there were disagreements about the ACORN experiment. The leadership among welfare recipients saw the project as a diversion which had attracted one of the organization's key organizers, absorbed scarce resources, and "organized around" the existing leadership structure by developing nonrecipient leaders. The NWRO staff, on the other hand, was wholeheartedly in support of the project, viewing ACORN as the "wave of the future." These structural tensions at all levels of the organization, coupled with the class and racial tensions in the Arkansas situation, led Barbara Hampton (one of the welfare mothers who originally invited Rathke to Arkansas) to call a press conference in early February 1972, during which she leveled a series of criticisms at both Rathke and ACORN, and disaffiliated Arkansas Welfare Rights from ACORN. "Wade Rathke is a middle-class white," said Hampton, who is black. "He had never had stomach cramps from hunger. How is he going to get the message over of the needs of poor people?" She went on:

> ACORN has taken credit for the achievements of the NWRO in Arkansas. ACORN has become a middle-class type lobbying group. . . . It only uses poor people or welfare mothers to do the demonstrations. . . . Paid organizers do all the work in the name of poor people, but not with poor people. . . .
> ACORN's desire for power is greater than its concern for poor people.[19]

While welfare mothers were indeed the troops for the first ACORN campaigns, there is litle doubt that subsequent campaigns mobilized other poor but nonwelfare people as well. Hampton's last charge, however, that ACORN's desire for power was greater than its concern for poor (welfare) people, may in fact have been true, especially given ACORN's willingness to expand its base to include "moderate-income" people. By 1974, a Little Rock reporter was writing in *Southern Voices*:

> The few WRO groups still surviving are powerless to do anything except make occasional public utterances, as they lack both numbers and effective advisers. Many welfare recipients now belong to neighborhood ACORN groups, and there are some groups, notably those made

up of residents of public housing complexes, that consist almost entirely of welfare recipients. ACORN probably has more people receiving public assistance on its membership rolls than the WRO ever did, and when they participate in an ACORN campaign they do so as members of an increasingly influential organization that is relatively immune to the usual anti-welfare insults. But a directness of approach has been lost. It isn't remarkable that the black president of one of the last struggling WRO groups referred to Rathke in a newspaper interview as "an ego-trippin' white dude from Louisiana." I don't agree with her implication but I can see her point.[20]

It was through a conscious attempt to redefine its constituency as broader than the initial welfare rights group that ACORN initiated a geographic expansion aimed at recruiting working-class homeowners. The effort was made through an anti-blockbusting, "Save the City" campaign in Little Rock's central residential community, characterized by yard signs reading "We like it here—this house is *not* for sale."

Other expansion efforts included the opening of the first Arkansas regional office in Fort Smith, and the introduction of a statewide campaign against tax loopholes, which won the support of the state AFL-CIO. In its first foray into local electoral politics, the group endorsed and elected a Little Rock School Board member committed to the ACORN school position: "Free textbooks, abolition of school fees, progressive special education and more funding allocated in eastern and central Little Rock . . . the low- to moderate-income areas."

By the end of 1972 ACORN was beginning to develop a reputation for accomplishments outside the state. In two years the organization had been successful in all its local campaign efforts. Its rolls included members not only in the Little Rock/North Little Rock area but also in Pine Bluff to the south and Fort Smith in the northwest corner of the state. It had begun to develop a staff of ex-VISTA volunteers, as well as local recruits. It had managed to build a support base within the churches, unions, and the liberal strata through the work of the Citizens for the Abolition of Poverty and by generating support for specific campaigns. Finally, the break with NWRO, coupled with Rathke's willingness to experiment with different organizational forms, marked ACORN as the first of a new breed of community organizations.

It is important to note, however, that while many community organizations begin with the same kind of success, few local efforts have lasted longer than a few years. The factor that allowed ACORN to send raw recruits into new towns and build grassroots organizations replicated in every other ACORN city was a new model in community organization: the ACORN Model.

4

The ACORN Model

> *This model is designed for ACORN organizers. . . . It is not to be used for mass distribution, rather it is designed as a brief training manual in the community organizing model developed by ACORN in Arkansas. Only vendors put their business on the street, never organizers.*
> —"ACORN Community Organizing Model"

The two major reasons for the successful expansion of ACORN into twenty-seven states in fifteen years are, first, the ability of the organization to train competent staff and leadership, and second, the use of a model that enabled ACORN organizers to replicate the basic organizational structure in more than thirty-five cities. The ACORN model was put in writing in early 1972, reflecting the experience and basic assumptions of its predecessor, the welfare rights–generated Boston model, as well as taking into account two years of organizing a working-class and less urban constituency in Arkansas. The model has as its goal the building of a "mass community organization" able to develop "sufficient organizational power to achieve its individual members' interest, its local objectives, and in connection with other groups, its state interests. The organization must be permanent with multi-issued concerns achieved through multi-tacticed [sic] direct action, with membership participating in policy, financing and achievement of group goals and community improvement."[1]

THE ACORN MODEL

Like the Boston model, the ACORN model relies on the need to offer tangible benefits, the need to build a cohesive community based on a consensually agreed upon benefit, and the need for professional organizers to identify issues to which the organization can rally. From the start, the model has been significant for a number of reasons: (1) it clearly delineated a modus operandi for organizers, especially when they entered a new town; (2) it elaborated a replicable organizational structure, which included membership base, local indigenous leadership, and a citywide alliance of ACORN groups; (3) it trained organizers; and (4) it defined a method by which organizers could use almost any neighborhood issue to build an ACORN group.

The core of the ACORN model is the organizing drive. It is the drive that mobilizes people to participate in the local group and defines the initial parameters of conflict between the organization and the social structure.

The Organizing Drive

> The trainee is twenty-three, white, well-educated and nervous. She was recruited to ACORN through an ad in the college paper which promised hard work, long hours and low pay—for exciting, meaningful work. Her twenty-seven-year-old trainer is a veteran, also white and well-educated. They have just gotten back from surveying the required three neighborhoods and they are ready to discuss which one the trainee will choose for her baptism of fire—her first organizing drive. It is her second week on the job.[2]

Since ACORN's early days, all new organizers have been required to build at least one local group when they become part of the staff. The six- to eight-week organizing drive is divided into seven stages: (1) research and analysis; (2) initial contact work; (3) establishment of an organizing committee and specifying the issue for the campaign; (4) preparation for the neighborhood meeting; (5) holding the neighborhood meeting; (6) initiating collective social action; (7) evaluation.

The purposes of the organizing drive are to delineate a geographic area (neighborhood) and a set of issues; to cast a wide social net so that a screened potential local leadership can be identified, followed by development of a secondary membership base; and the generation of a confrontational issue. An implicit part of the drive is to teach new organizers and indigenous leaders to think in terms of the model by systematically processing them through the seven-stage drive.

Research and Analysis

Part of the organizer's earliest research is information-gathering. Because an organizer should be knowledgeable about the working areas, s/he identifies the low-income sections of the city through census data; notes the areas of substandard housing; surveys the location of potential places of confrontation (e.g., the city hall and the chamber of commerce); identifies the issues that the local press has been interested in; observes the racial composition of the community.

The organizer is further encouraged to talk to known leaders, the staff of neighborhood centers, school personnel, and others. These early contacts offer two major benefits. First, they identify and give the organizer an opportunity to neutralize potential *opposition*, both from within the state and from other groups. The model argues that the organizer needs to know the history of an issue and who the competitors are—"to avoid them, freeze them out and not tread on 'their' issue until after you have built your base."[3] Second, the contacts identify potential resource people in the progressive community who could become *allies* in an organizing campaign; as the model points out, these give the organizer "your invitation and legitimacy in the area, since you are initially talking to them about the possibility of organizing rather than the fact of it. *The suggestions they have for ACORN give us the mandate to be there* [emphasis added]."[4] The model also cautions the new organizer that "many contacts will attempt to influence your eventual organizing plan to serve their self-interest and not ACORN's"; therefore, the organizer should "give on your agenda only when it doesn't matter, never give easily, and never give when it matters."[5]

This approach is markedly different from the traditional methods of the Alinsky-based organizations. In the Alinsky model, the organizer would attempt to figure out which organizations in the community were the most legitimate or had the broadest base, and bring these together to form a sponsoring committee. "The sponsoring committee," writes Shel Trapp, lead trainer for the National Training and Information Center and organizer of National People's Action (NPA), "is a group which recognizes the need for a people's organization and begins the process of gathering funds.... After the organizer is hired, the sponsoring committee monitors the funds, becomes the flack catcher for the organizer."[6] This method neutralizes existing organizations through their participation in the sponsoring committee. In the ACORN model, however, while legitimate organizations (churches, unions, other community groups) are asked for letters of endorsement, they are not given a role in hiring or organizational direction.

ACORN's procedure is inherited from welfare rights. NWRO built independent, semi-autonomous groups of welfare recipients, arguing that the interests of these recipients could be represented only in their own organization. ACORN similarly argues that the interests of low-income people would be diluted in a coalition of already existing groups; therefore, independent local units are necessary.

The multi-issue approach advocated in the ACORN model also protects the organization from the single-issue tendency of many ad hoc coalitions in which, ACORN organizers argue, "There is no guarantee that all those members [in a coalition of existing organizations] are going to have any understanding of the fact that organizations are not built, 'for better schools' or for 'safer streets,' but to address that basic maldistribution of power."[7] In starting a

THE ACORN MODEL

local group, all of the aforementioned data will be analyzed in a discussion between the trainer and organizer-trainee; the neighborhood will be selected; and the organizer will begin making contacts.

Contact Work

In this phase an organizer puts together a list of contacts from either a voter registration list, a criss-cross directory or even a "safe petition."[8] Contact work is very often the task that will drive a trainee out of organizing, because it may require going into a neighborhood and knocking on doors to develop a list. A list of "hot contacts" is not simply material for a mass mailing; it is an invaluable resource that may be transformed into the lifeblood of the organization—its members. Functionally, contact development trains the organizer in a number of skills: it develops a set of work standards (the model demands between twenty and forty contacts per day during the drive); it tests the organizer's ability to be systematic (each contact is spoken with twice and receives two letters and a phone call, all in the space of six weeks); and finally, contact work supports the organization through dues (45 percent of ACORN's budget is supplied by membership dues, and almost 70 percent of that is collected not through the mail, but by direct contact with members in meetings and during doorknocking).[9]

Early in the course of the contact phase, the organizer must chose between ten and fifteen people in the area who have leadership potential and/or legitimacy. These people will act as part of the neighborhood's organizing committee.

The Organizing Committee and the Issue

The model notes that "the organizing committee is your manpower on the drive, your legitimacy, your potential leadership, and the focus on the issues."[10] The committee is coalesced during the

67

first two weeks of the organizing drive in a meeting whose purposes are (1) to specify the initial issue the organization will address and map out the steps of an organizing campaign; (2) to legitimate the organizing drive by developing an organizing letter, signed by all of the participants in the meeting, which is then mailed to all neighborhood residents; (3) to collect dues, thus establishing the practice within the organization; (4) to involve members of the committee in contact work (petitions, doorknocking, phone calls); and (5) to prepare for the upcoming neighborhood meeting.

The organizing committee (OC) is the first opportunity for the organizer to begin developing leadership.

> Invariably the organizer will end up guiding the OC meetings, especially the first one. Draw people out to take roles in moving and running them. You will always have to maintain a complex dynamic in the OC, which allows for "testing," digressions, humor, enthusiasm on the issues and events, and consensus on the techniques, responsibilities, and committments [sic] which members of the OC will be forced to make.[11]

Of major import in engaging the members of the organization is choosing the issue and laying out the campaign. As Meg Campbell, former training director of the Institute for Social Justice (ACORN's training arm) has written:

> The wider and deeper the appeal of the issue, the better. Listen for issues people feel strongly about, things which make them angry. But also be sure it's an issue which has realizable, winnable, concrete goals. While maximum membership participation is a barometer for gauging a potential issue, it must be coupled with a longer-range concern for delivering the wins necessary to keep that membership participating over time. The organizer's job

THE ACORN MODEL

is to insure that the issue has pragmatism as well as common self-interest.[12]

The organizing campaign structures this common self-interest by defining and focusing on a specific issue, and making plans to exploit it through a series of confrontational actions designed to benefit both individuals and their organization. The organizer works with the organizing committee to identify targets for these actions by asking OC members: "Who has the power to redress our grievance?" Also involved in developing the campaign plan are strategies for cultivating allies and using the media, as well as the delineation of specific tactics and a timetable for achieving the goals of the campaign.

Once the plan is outlined, the organizing committee meetings become the place to test the commitment of the members to move the campaign and the organization forward. This commitment is demonstrated in a number of ways: paying dues, recruiting additional neighbors, and accepting responsibility for a part of the agenda at the first community meeting.

The emphasis on dues is derived not from welfare rights but from the work of Cesar Chavez and the United Farm Workers; early on, Chavez insisted on payment of dues.

> A union must have members who pay dues regularly. The only people which the Farm Workers Association counts as members are those who pay their $3.50 a month, every month. Farm workers who are committed can afford to pay $3.50 a month in dues, even though they have low incomes. Members commit themselves to the organization by paying dues regularly. Because they pay so much, they feel they are the important part of the organization; that they have a right to be served. They don't hesitate to write, to call, to ask for things—and to reaffirm their position in the association. Members enjoy certain concrete benefits and are offered assistance with social, economic, and legal problems which they might have.[13]

THE ACORN MODEL

Preparation for the Neighborhood Meeting

Before the first neighborhood meeting, the organizing committee is mobilized for two sets of tasks. First, the OC does contact work in the neighborhood with the organizer. Not only does this increase the labor power available to the organizing drive, but, as ACORN literature points out:

> Doorknocking in teams mutes the outsider role of the organizer and reduces the foreign experience of an organizing drive when you are using local people. Men and women teams are best, women teams second, and men teams third in neighborhood organizing. Having two people on the doors is also insurance against forgetting important things which need to be said.[14]

Members of the OC also do telephone contact work, address and mail letters, and distribute leaflets. Once again, this division of labor increases the labor power available and sets the tone for standards of membership participation in the organization.

Another aspect of laying the groundwork is in assisting members of the OC to prepare presentations for the neighborhood meeting. Here ACORN is in line with the Alinsky tradition: the organizer is introduced at the meeting, but all the upfront moving of the organizational agenda is done by the indigenous leadership.

The Neighborhood Meeting

The neighborhood meeting is the first tangible test of the organizer's ability to build mass organization. The model sets both qualitative and quantitative standards: "Most ACORN community organizing drives will net 15–25% of the list. Numbers are important because this is a mass organization directed at political power where might makes right."[15]

THE ACORN MODEL

The agenda for the meeting, conducted entirely by OC members, will include the following:

1. explanation of the history and role of ACORN;
2. discussion of the issues of the neighborhood;
3. naming of the group and selection of one issue (usually the one already targeted by the OC) for the group's first campaign;
4. formation of committees to conduct additional research on the problems in the area;
5. payment of dues by people attending the meeting who formally join the organization;
6. election of local temporary officers;
7. discussion of the date and scope of the first action.

Thus, in the first meeting a formal structure is established, and the group is committed to a specific action. This is a slight modification of the welfare rights Boston model, where the action was conducted on the same day that the organization was formed, and markedly different from the IAF, where as long as a year could elapse before the organization would conduct an action.

Collective Social Action

Within the organizing campaign, the first action is the group's baptism by fire: a mass of ACORN group members descend on a local target, usually a city official, and demand that a specific grievance be addressed in a specific way within a given time. The action allows the group to designate spokespersons, to flex organizational muscle, and—especially—to get its first negotiated concession: the "win." As ACORN organizers observe:

> An organized group can usually pressure a city traffic department to put up a needed street sign, and can

71

THE ACORN MODEL

usually pressure a city public works department to see that vacant lots are cleaned up. Those initial "wins" are often the first experience many neighborhood people have ever had of successfully fighting city hall or local institutions. By winning a stop light, people begin to understand the effectiveness of organization. Something tangible has occurred in their neighborhood and it has occurred because people got themselves organized and formed an ACORN group. The fact that you sometimes *can* beat City Hall, provided you are organized, is a critical lesson which ACORN members learn right from the start.[16]

Built into the ACORN model is the use of creative confrontation to polarize the interests of organized low-income people on one side and "monied interests" on the other. In its fifteen-year history, the organization's actions have lived up to the basic purpose of the activity—"a direct confrontation between a target and the entire assemblage."[17] ACORN's raucus style of confrontation has in itself been an issue to targets and the press, as illustrated by the following lead paragraphs in the *Arkansas Democrat* under the heading "MOB SCENE":

ACORN demonstrators came on like yahoos Monday at a Public Service Commission meeting called mainly in their interest. For people demanding a "utility consumers bill of rights," the ACORN-ites made a poor case for deserving anything better than a stiff lesson in minding other people's rights—not to mention the right of a public body to hold an orderly hearing.

Monday, ACORN wasn't only loud—it was rude, disorderly and intimidating and got away with it.[18]

Demonstrations are not ACORN's only form of action. An ACORN Community Organizing Handbook lists ten tactics for confrontation, seven for forcing negotiations, and eight for "maintenance actions." The last category includes letter-writing, "people's hearings," and lawsuits.[19]

Evaluation

Whether the action is successful or not, the model specifies that a collective assessment be made. John Beam, a former regional coordinator for ACORN, writes:

> In an adrenalin-soaked, action-packed, complex demonstration, the finer points of the negotiations, victories and defeats may get lost in the shuffle. If people are going to continue their involvement in the campaign, they need a clear sense of what happened. You can do it in the lobby, on the bus, back at the meeting hall or on the corner, but a de-briefing is invaluable. The leadership can review exactly what was said and what agreements were reached. Other participants can comment on how it looked from where they stood. Examples of strong, effective leadership can be singled out for applause. (Don't forget the silent leadership of the little old man who stood his ground when they tried to slam the door on him as well as the outspoken leader who wouldn't take no for an answer.)
>
> This is also the time to decide on the next step. If we won some concessions should we send a memorandum of understanding to the target defining our agreement? If we haven't won yet should we come back tomorrow? Should we take twice as many people to the next jerk up the ladder next week?[20]

After each evaluation, the group may redefine the issue and actually repeat some earlier steps of the campaign. *However, the structure of the local organization is built through the initial organizing drive.*

THE ACORN MODEL

Organizational Structure

In putting together local groups, the organizer attempts to put into practice the slogan "Organize the unorganized." ACORN members become involved in their neighborhood groups as individuals, not as members of some other organization. Moreover, the vast majority attend the first meeting of that group—the large community meeting that is part of the organizing drive—and thus they are, in a sense, "founding members" of that ACORN chapter.

Flowing out of the model, then, are three separate and clearly distinguishable components of the organizational structure: membership, leadership, and staff. Members participate in the organization by belonging (paying dues) to a local group, attending monthly meetings, and joining in local actions. Leaders operate on several levels. First, there are local group officers (chair, co-chair, secretary, and treasurer) who are responsible for developing local group issues. Next (depending on the stage of organizational development) comes a citywide board, then a statewide board, and finally the Association-wide leadership, with delegates and alternates from each state.

The staff is similarly structured. Local organizers are supervised by city or state head organizers. The head organizers are supervised by four regional directors, each covering six to eight states and all responsible to the chief organizer. The chief organizer, in turn, is directly responsible to the Association board.

On its face, the ACORN structure is both hierarchical and democratic, with clear divisions of labor. This description, however, leaves out a fundamental assumption about the nature of almost all community organizing: the leader/organizer dichotomy. One ACORN staff member was quick to note, "The Association is really run by the members, and the staff merely offers support."[21] Wade Rathke, when asked about the contention that ACORN members are manipulated by staff, snapped, "Wishdream—the establishment just can't bring itself to believe low- to-moderate-income people are capable of thinking and doing the things ACORN does."[22] Similarly, Madeleine Talbot, head organizer of Michigan ACORN, asserted,

THE ACORN MODEL

"We just organize the groups. The residents make decisions for ACORN."[23]

This is the standard line of most community organizers. But as Richard Rothstein states, and summarizes in Table 4 showing the differences between finished democratic organizations and real world organizations:

> The conventional model of a finished democratic organization has members, leaders and staff. The members debate and decide policies and actions. The leaders propose those policies and actions to the membership. The members elect leaders whose proposals are most often sensible, who speak well in public on behalf of the organization and who are trusted to make interim decisions on policy between membership meetings. When leaders in a finished democratic organization lose rapport with

TABLE 4. ORGANIZATIONAL STRUCTURE

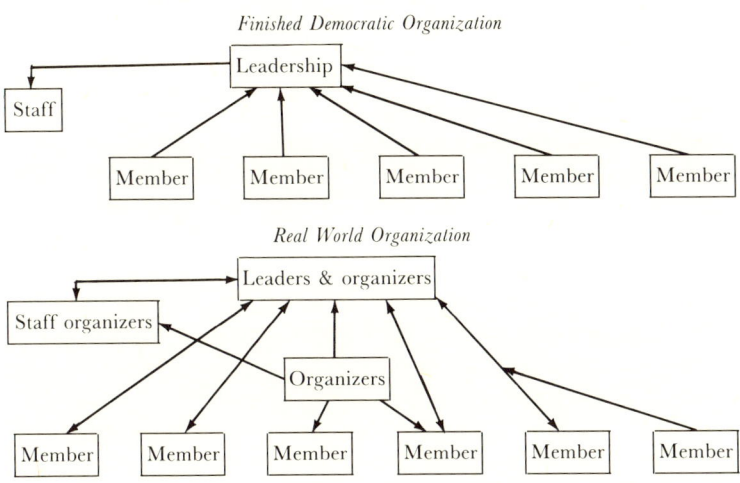

Source: R. Rothstein, "What Is an Organizer?" Midwest Academy, 1973, p. 8.

75

THE ACORN MODEL

> members and no longer make the interim decisions members would want, these leaders are defeated for re-election and replaced by those who know what policy initiatives members would approve.
>
> None of you has ever been in an organization like this, however, and most likely none of you ever will. . . .
>
> The members of real organizations have marriages or affairs, jobs and children; and problems with each. They may join an organization because, in the long run it *might* alleviate some of those problems, but in the meantime those problems accupy most of their time and energy. In real organizations, leaders are not just those with the best policy and action proposals (although that helps) but often those who are more willing and able than most to ignore their everyday lives.
>
> Consequently, real organization members never have the time or energy to think carefully about all the issues and actions their leaders contemplate. In real organizations, democratic debate is only partly a process whereby members instruct leaders; it is also a process whereby leaders get members to agree to proposals those members haven't fully developed.
>
> Real-world organizations not only have members, leaders, and staff; they also have organizers (acknowledged or not) whose function is to increase the active participation of members and to create the conditions in which strong leaders emerge.[24]

In other words an organization has a manifest and a latent structure; the actual, as opposed to the ascribed, power of the positions is not evident on the surface. It is ACORN's public position that local leaders develop issues and move the organization; in fact, the development of major issues, tactics, and political thrust is initiated at the staff level. The role played by the organizer within the context of the ACORN model is that of social reconstructionist.

Defining the Organizer's Role

Much has been written about the role of the organizer. Journalist and Alinsky-trained organizer Nicholas von Hoffman stated, "Organizers have single-track minds. They care only for building the organization. The organizer's first job is to organize, not to right wrong, nor to avenge injustice, and not to win the battle for freedom. That is the task of the people who will accomplish it through the organization, if it ever gets built."[25] Mike Miller, another Alinsky-trained organizer and veteran of the Student Nonviolent Coordinating Committee, writes, "An organizer doesn't like to do all the talking. He talks; he listens; he asks questions. He operates on the principle that the people in the streets, in the neighborhoods, in the fields, in the plants, on the unemployed lines, on the welfare rolls know better than he what they want and need—but they don't know how to get it."[26]

Richard Harmon, former director of the Industrial Areas Foundation, calls organizing teaching and the organizer a catalytic agent, teacher, and agitator,[27] while Richard Rothstein, writing for the Chicago-based Midwest Academy, observes that organizers are "those most concerned with promoting the organization's growth, who have the greatest vision about how to get from here to there, and who patiently try to organize their visions."[28] This is compatible with Grossman's notion (see Table 5) that the community organizer is a "militant activist," one who "does not seem to have a political position as such but advocates a set of distinguishing stances on power, organizing and tactics."[29]

In the ACORN model, the organizer is defined in terms of what she or he does:

> First of all, an organizer is responsible for putting together an organizing drive.... Once a local ACORN group has been formed, the organizer is responsible for [helping] the group develop campaigns, and issues, tactics, and strategy. The organizer works to develop skills

TABLE 5. INDIVIDUAL IDEOLOGY AND ACTIVIST ROLES

	Ameliorator	Reformer	Militant activist	Rebel	Revolutionary
Degree of alienation	Little or none	Sometimes antagonistic but approves of the American way (often anti-Communist)	Obscure—rhetoric condemns system but actions validate it	Totally alienated from system & quality of life	Totally alienated
Roles	Social workers	Activist professionals (academics—science, law, "rationalists")	Community organizers, single-issue activists (e.g., anti-nuke), union organizers	Students	
Concept of power	Power based on who has "legitimate authority"	Interest groups—"struggle in the political marketplace"	Most significant element of change (often confused with influence)	Anticorporate	Parties
Themes & change emphasis	Upward mobility for all	Continuous challenge to laws & institutions to "keep democracy alive"	Community organizations & unions	Building constant coalitions	Building cadres that will be "the vanguard"
The enemy	Mistakes or lack of knowledge; individual failure	Selfishness, shortsightedness, apathy, bureaucratic rigidity, inefficiency	Social welfare professionals	Corporate liberals, "the welfare state"	Capitalism—basically a system that exploits

	Ameliorator	Reformer	Militant	Rebel	Revolutionary
Types of social action	Policy improvement; building "democratic skills"	Issue-oriented pressure, theory-building, "helping the poor"	Large-scale organizations, mass mobilization	Small groups, political discussions, some "bore from within"	Small, highly structured groups
Concept of "democracy"	Meeting formal requirements for "an open society"	Democracy always imperfect—we need better programs	Most important factor is achieving different power balance	Letting the people decide; refusing alliances	People build & run their institutions to create the revolution
Values	Importance of individual rights; professional techniques	"Feasibility"—no absolute values—all can be traded	Building the "people's machine"	Hard put to compromise—will take "principled positions" in "significant formations"	Some bore from within; some recruitment of individuals; some critique of other groups
Attitudes toward other types	*Reformer*—unscientific, useful; *Militant*—posturer, exaggerates accomplishments, untrustworthy; *Rebel-Revolutionary*—dupe & enemy	*Ameliorator*—naive; *Militant*—appreciation & caution, hates all "manipulation"; *Rebel*—viewed fondly & paternally; *Revolutionary*—ready to use as ally	*Ameliorator*—insignificant; *Reformer*—dangerous; *Rebel*—unclear; *Revolutionary*—condescendingly friendly (many militants used to be revolutionary)	*Ameliorator*—dangerous; *Reformer*—right rhetoric, wrong action; *Militant*—appreciated but too manipulative; *Revolutionary*—varies—sometimes allied, sometimes written off	*Ameliorator* & *Rebel*—liberals to be manipulated but not trusted; *Militant*—major ally since they have the organizations; *Rebel*—primary source of recruitment

SOURCE: Adapted from L. Grossman, "Ideological Stances on Change in the United States," 1968 class handout, School of Social Welfare, University of California, Berkeley.

among the membership and . . . acts as a liaison between the local membership . . . and the support staff. If the group needs technical or legal assistance, the organizer arranges [this]. Finally, the organizer works with the Executive Board . . . on city-wide plans and directions.[30]

In my view, none of these descriptions, whether ideological, pedogogical, or functional, is entirely accurate. Much of the work that attempts to define the role of an organizer is the writing, largely unpublished, of Warren C. Haggstrom, an Alinsky cohort and mentor of the welfare rights movement through his role as director of the Community Action Training Center at Syracuse University in 1965; currently he is director of an experimental organizer training program at the UCLA School of Social Work. In a mimeographed paper distributed in 1966, in which he acknowledges the contributions of Fred Ross, Saul Alinsky, and Tom Gaudette of the Mid-America Institute, Haggstrom writes:

> The organizer lives in a world in which everything is called into question, subject to change, where half-perceived and complex structures constantly dissolve and re-form before him, a world of possibility in which he takes a hand to reshape the future. Philosophy, not political science, is the proper intellectual preparation for this work.[31]

To understand the organizer's role, it is first necessary to understand the context in which she or he works: the urban core. As William Appleman Williams explains:

> The capitalist metropolis is a social vacuum cleaner. It yanks people from their human place, time, space, and scale. Even more: the sustained and accelerating centralization within the metropolis distorts and even denies any sense—even memory—of a humane set of relationships. Capitalism does not create neighborhoods. Capitalism

THE ACORN MODEL

instead cements over grass for commuter stations on the main line to nowhere. Bluntly, capitalism destroys neighborhoods and communities.[32]

Within the context of this atomized space, the organizer molds organization. But how is the intersubjective dimension of the process best understood, and, more important, what is the meaning of organizing people in terms of residential patterns—patterns that Hognacki cautions can be mobilized for "defensive purposes employing institutions and organizations as defense mechanisms"?[33] Now, in this context, can the organizer be perceived as a radical or a progressive? Williams describes the tasks of the radical as follows:

> 1. A radical digs down to the roots of reality. A radical probes the sources to describe the actual—rather than the apparent—nature and ramifications of the political economy.
> 2. A radical develops a dynamic explanation of the relationships between the various aspects of reality.
> 3. A radical offers an alternative hierarchy of values.
> 4. A radical offers specific options, strategic as well as tactical, and engages in sustained people-to-people action to achieve those objectives.
>
> The definition clarifies the responsibilities. Dynamic, effective radicals must offer ruthless analyses; must imagine truly different alternatives; must practice citizenship as action to realize those alternatives; and must thereby set the terms of the public dialogue regardless of how long it takes to change the world.[34]

How does a community organizer fit this definition? By reexamining the ACORN Model in terms of the ability of the organizer to construct not only an organization but also an alternative view of social reality, I hope to explain the organizer's other role—that of constructing alternative and oppositional social relations and views of the world.

81

THE ACORN MODEL

It should first be pointed out that there is some confusion, especially among organizers themselves, about exactly what is meant by "organizing ordinary people for power." A common misconception, both within the organizing world and outside of it, is that organizing people for power is equivalent to mobilizing them to win a specific benefit (better streets, more welfare, lower taxes, etc.). This view focuses on "taking the people where they're at" and having them exercise their latent power in the system. In a recent discussion of whether or not people really objectively exercise power or subjectively feel more powerful when the group succeeds in getting a stop sign in the neighborhood, one organizer noted, "Hell, if all we'd wanted was a stop sign, we could have taken up a collection, bought a plastic one for $4.98 at Walgreen's, and tacked the damn thing up with a staple gun."[35] The organizer's point here is that the purpose of organizing is not to obtain a specific benefit—there may be easier ways to accomplish that—but rather to build the power of the group. As Bill Pastreich has often said, "The best campaign is one that you lose because you needed *one* more person, and everybody understands that."

An organizer's notion of building power is related both to a group's ability to achieve a specific *goal* and the *process* it goes through to achieve that goal. The ACORN Model is only one approach to community organizing, but it comprises tasks and objectives common to most CO models.

In the first stage of the ACORN Model, research and analysis, the organizer attempts to conceptualize the neighborhood and to define his or her role in the organizing process. Organizers, therefore, collect political and economic intelligence that "deals with all things that should be known in advance of initiating a course of action,"[36] as well as considering the quality of the relationship with neighborhood residents. This is common to most CO models.

In the process of the initial work, the organizer will make an assessment about the boundaries of a specific area—a community. There are many variables to consider. How, for instance, does one define "neighborhoods"? As Keller writes:

THE ACORN MODEL

Essentially, it [neighborhood] refers to distinctive areas into which larger spatial units may be subdivided. . . . The distinctiveness of these areas stems from different sources whose independent contributions are difficult to assess: geographical boundaries, ethnic or cultural characteristics of the inhabitants, psychological unity among people who feel that they belong together, or concentrated use of an area's facilities for shopping, leisure, and learning.[37]

Assessing these variables is both a research and an organizing problem. The organizer must be able to develop an analysis of a locality and, in order to do so, must enter into a dialogue with people who define themselves as part of the community. If that research uncovers the fact that the locality is too fragmented to constitute a community, it gives the organizer some sense of how much work needs to be devoted to building community as well as building power. Research also helps to determine appropriate scale of organization initially and what kinds of tactics the people feel most comfortable with.

One example of how basic research shaped the organizing approach is the case of the United Farm Workers (UFW). Arguing that the immediate entry into the economic (wage) arena was too threatening for farm workers to take on as their first issue, Cesar Chavez strengthened the group's social cohesion by setting up nonthreatening economic self-help structures (food- and gas-buying cooperatives) and by using the Catholic Church to develop the ideological base of La Causa. By the time the union entered the economic arena, there was already an infrastructure built on values common to most workers as well as a common experience. At that point there was a cohesive community, and the United Farm Workers were a viable organization.[38]

Even in communities where there is already a strong infrastructure and a high degree of ideological consensus, the conflicts present will limit the direction and scope of initial action. In order to define community, an organizer needs to be able to analyze structures of production-distribution-consumption, socialization, social control, social participation, and mutual support.[39] In addition, the organizer must be able to identify the predominant values of the community, the ways they are validated, and what potential contradictions in the value structure could be exploited. Finally, after looking at values and tensions, the researcher needs to identify specific problems within the community. (The talent for identifying institutional community infrastructure and ideological consensus is even more important in the IAF organizing model, which relies on existing [church] infrastructure as the base of the organization.)

It is irrelevant whether the organizer/researcher, working with indigenous leadership, decides to move on a specific local issue or initiate the building of an alternative institution. What is important is that the decision be based on analysis so that research informs the social action.

In ACORN's next organizational phases—the initial contact work and the organizing committee meeting—the organizer begins to share knowledge strategically in order to motivate people to act. To do so, the organizer must first gain access to community residents. There is an old adage in organizing: "It doesn't matter how tight the plan is if you can't get in the door."

Developing initial contacts has three objectives. The first is the creation of a *dialogue*. Organizers listen to and discuss with community residents their feelings about either the community (if the organizing takes place in a neighborhood) or a specific problem (if the organizing is with a special-interest constituency). These discussions help organizers and researchers to understand both the problems and the perceptual framework of the members and to cut through the problems of depersonalization and dehumanization that may be felt by the resident. The second objective is *validation*. The organizer offers encouragement and supports the notion of collectively analyzing and confronting problems. The third objective is obtaining some form of *commitment* to the organization. The resident might be asked to introduce the visitors to the next-door neighbor,

THE ACORN MODEL

to canvass the neighborhood at a later date, to hold a meeting of neighbors, to become a member of the area organizing committee, or simply to join the organization. This contact affirms from the beginning the ability of people to change their social reality through collective social action. *This is in and of itself an ideological position.* Not only do organizers transform individual self-interest into some form of collectivity; they also attempt to build a vision of the collective good.

About the next phase, the organizing committee meeting (another preliminary form common to most CO models), Mike Silver writes:

> The body of any housemeeting is the pitch. It excites people, it tells organizational success stories, and it communicates a vision of a better future. The organizer is the citizens' first contact in building the new social reality, the initial agent of resocialization. The role is to help create a "plausibility structure," an action- and idea-based pathway to a new reality of grassroots power. The main elements of the pitch are agitation, vision-making, and closure.[40]

In my view, however, the dynamics of the organizing committee meeting initially lend themselves more to the collectivization of individual perceptions. In this process, the role of the organizer is that of a facilitator who must direct the group to ensure that the meeting:

1. reinforces individual perceptions;
2. redefines and expands the notion of specific problems and the group's power to affect them;
3. develops some common tools for analysis;
4. involves community residents in the research/organization process;
5. begins to develop a group understanding of contradictions in dominant ideologies by focusing on a specific problem;
6. expands the base of the organization.

THE ACORN MODEL

At a house meeting attended by, say, eight to fifteen people, group members would hear one another's opinions on specific issues, thus both reinforcing and redefining their own perceptions. There is always a question as to why a particular problem exists. It is the organizer's job to help community residents analyze the social relations that cause the problem. Usually there is an assertion by someone in the group that "the schools are supposed to teach kids" or "the city is supposed to pick up the garbage." It is the organizer's job to encourage people to question those assumptions about the way things work.

For example, prior to a recent meeting on trash pickup in New Orleans, the organizer worked on a survey with community residents and a work-study student that showed that black, low-income neighborhoods got the worst service in the city; all the new, more efficient equipment was allocated to affluent neighborhoods. The survey expanded group members' perception of their problem by suggesting that the same problem also existed in other neighborhoods, thus redefining the notion of collectively and community. This led to discussion of the potential of working with other neighborhood groups.

Another major objective of the organizing committee meeting is defining the organizing campaign. Haggstrom writes, "Once at a meeting, an organizer concentrates on moving those attending into decision and action through whatever formal structure may exist. . . . He may ask action-oriented questions, or he may suggest alternatives by describing what other organizations have done in similar situations or on similar problems."[41] In defining the campaign, the organizer assists the group to

1. focus on an initial problem and discuss long- and short-range goals, a strategy for each, and the tactical steps that will be the building blocks of the strategy;
2. begin to define a process for group decision-making and group reflection;
3. determine which other groups are potential allies and which potential enemies, then develop a strategy to neutralize enemies and gain support from allies;
4. define research goals for the project;

THE ACORN MODEL

5. evaluate its own chances for success based on the its sources of power, its ideological position, its ability to influence third parties, and the availability of group resources: time, personnel, money, contacts, etc.

In the next phase, the neighborhood meeting, the organizer's task is to help the group articulate a structure and define its first confrontational action. Haggstrom writes:

> From the point of view of the organizer, the sole point of meetings is to prepare for action just as the sole point of organization is to provide structure through which action takes place. Thus, he helps clarify alternatives around concrete and immediate courses of action, makes certain that whatever process results in decisions is both legitimate (in accordance with the rules) and efficient (... likely to attain the objective intended or otherwise to build the effectiveness of the organization).[42]

The importance of the action itself—whether it be a demonstration, meeting, statement at a hearing—is secondary to its internal function of upping the ante of group participation and defining the group's collective experience.

The actions are by definition confrontational and will by their very nature generate a response from the dominant, established institutions.

> In a conflict situation the objective consequences of an act by one side or another, or the intentions behind the act, may be almost irrelevant. The act is one point around which conflict swirls, and a common interpretation may eventually be made as both sides, usually first really brought together by the conflict, begin to know one another better.
> At the outset, the people in areas of poverty have only two alternatives: to accept the interpretation of powerful

institutions and figures relevant to them, or to withdraw into their own alienated inactivity outside the major community. Through organization they acquire a third alternative: to participate through a conflict process in the creation of interpretations which fit the facts which they know and which are also held by the major community.[43]

After the action, the organizer initiates the most final and most important phase of the organizing campaign: the evaluation. As Mike Silver notes:

> The period immediately following a confrontation may find participants confused, unsure about the *meaning* of what took place. Although peers play a role in perception during confrontations, each individual's personal biases and unique cultural valuations of the event's components determine what is remembered. The fundamental purpose of reviewing the action is to develop a *consensus* definition of the experience. This is mainly a process of reality construction. The community worker's role is to elicit from as many participants as possible their subjective descriptions of what happened, and then to help tie the descriptions together into an objective reality that is mutually shared within the organization. Typical exploratory questions to initiate post-action discussion include: "What happened?" "What did their response mean?" "How do they see the problem?" "Are they going to help or hinder us?" "Did we get any meaningful concessions?" A major function of the review is to make explicit the gap between verbal and symbolic gestures of opponents and actual concessions.[44]

Evaluation not only reviews the assumptions that dictated the action but also questions the dynamics of the action. How were people treated? Why? Would more people have been treated the same way?

THE ACORN MODEL

Fewer people? Did the target really have the power to grant a concession? Does the group still want the concession? What is the group's source of power? Has that changed? Does it need to? Often, evaluations take as long as actions, since they provide the first real opportunity to examine assumptions critically. Good evaluations may redefine what the group perceives about the nature of the problem, which may in turn effect changes in goals, strategies, and tactics, as well as lead to reassessment of the group's source of power and potential allies.

The process, then, is continual: research-action-reflection-research. The point is not *just* to build a machine that can win concessions from this complex socioeconomic system. The real challenge is to create an institution that can collectively validate an alternative view of social reality and redefine appropriate behavior and collective action. A group's power is obviously related to what action it is willing to take based on its analysis of collective experiences. Clearly, the battle for power is as much a struggle for the interpretation of people's experiences as it is the winning of a specific issue. As the "radical" described earlier by William Appleman Williams, an organizer is fighting a battle to win not simply campaigns but people's minds. Given the fact that there are few structures through which the contradictions between the ideological construct of social reality and the actuality of the real world can be challenged, community organizers cannot afford the luxury of defining the consciousness of their membership as "false." Rather, organizers must use the process of organizing to expand the collective experiences of community residents and use organization to validate redefined collective perceptions of how the world works. In this sense, community organizers are social reconstructionists. Their role is to develop the ability of people to understand the world so that they can act in it.

No model always works, nor does the ideal role of the organizer as social reconstructionist always succeed in empowering people. An organizing model is a structured attempt to respond to specific historical moments by manipulating already existing social relations, both manifest and latent, and transforming their relative significance. To do so, it must reflect the experience and culture of the people it attempts to mobilize, as well as contain a commonsense notion of "how the world works" and a theory of social change.

This very often latent theory of social change is frequently evidenced in how the model organizes alternative, though not always oppositional, social structure. Models must address questions of how to mobilize human, financial, and communicative resources, as well as more subtle questions of the development of leadership, the role within the organization of a vanguard (if any), and the social composition of the organization.

The ACORN model demonstrates the ability to reproduce a set of social relations (a structure) over a variety of geographic locations and deliver tangible benefits to members of the organization. To assess whether ACORN can point out societal contradictions without creating contradictions of its own requires following the story of ACORN's development through the 1970s and into the present.

5

Expanding the Turf

> *ACORN will expand and organize in more cities and towns, perhaps leading to governmental takeovers similar to the Quorum Court . . . leading the organization even further past the bounds of what one would expect of a community organization.*
>
> —Internal Memo

> *At the beginning of 1974, ACORN received an award from the Jaycees for being an outstanding community-oriented, self-help project. By the end of 1974, after the lifeline campaign and the press hoopla around the Quorum Court . . . we couldn't even buy a ticket to a Jaycee Luncheon!*
>
> —ACORN Organizer

ACORN entered 1973 with considerable experience in a single state and a carefully worked-out organizational model. Over the next seven years it expanded dramatically, broadening its range of activities, entering new arenas, and taking on new adversaries. While ACORN's growth strengthened the organization, the rush toward expansion did have its costs.

EXPANDING THE TURF

Phase II: New Tasks, New Territory

In 1973 ACORN mounted successful organizing drives in Pine Bluff and Fayetteville, expanding the number of cities in Arkansas where it had local organizations. Yet its major accomplishments that year were statewide and even broader in their implications, as ACORN experimented successfully with new tactics and strategies.

White Bluff

The most creative effort was the campaign against Arkansas Power and Light's proposal to build a 2,800-megowatt coal-burning power plant near Redfield, Arkansas. The White Bluff plant was to cost close to a billion dollars, the single largest private investment ever undertaken in the state.[1] In addition to producing electricity, however, the plant would send 178,000 tons of sulfur dioxide per year out of its smokestacks, causing pollution to settle on farms growing rice, soybeans, and cotton—some of the richest, most productive land in the state.[2] While farmers were the constituency most immediately affected by the plant, rumors of unacceptable pollution levels began spreading to other groups. The Jefferson County Improvement Association, a local ACORN group, requested research from ACORN to discover more about AP&L's plan for Redfield. When that research uncovered the clear environmental problems in the proposal, ACORN, utilizing a 1973 study by Governor Bumper's Energy Forum, formulated a series of over one hundred questions concerning the need for more energy and the environmental and economic impact of the White Bluff plant.[3] Armed with their findings, the projected effects of the proposed plant on land productivity, ACORN organized farmers in the Plum Bayou, Ferda, Tucker, Wright, and England areas—small rural towns near Redfield—into two new ACORN groups: the Protect Our Land Association (POLA) and Save Health and Property (SHAP).

Taking a traditional CO view of "self-interest," ACORN organizers had initially assumed that residents of communities immediately adjacent to the proposed plant would have the most serious and vocal objections to its construction. This assumption, however, turned out to be incorrect. Because they'd been promised both an increased corporate share in the tax base and jobs for residents, the people who lived in White Bluff were actually less ready to organize than were farmers downwind from the plant. These farm communities would suffer all of the costs of the plant's construction in terms of pollution but would share in neither the (alleged) tax nor employment benefits.

To further sharpen the conflict, ACORN initiated local demonstrations against Arkansas Power and Light in Little Rock and, by releasing the organization's preliminary research findings and demanding regulatory action, motivated the Public Service Commission and state pollution and environmental agencies to "take a second look."[4] Amicus briefs filed by a number of environmental groups convinced the PSC that AP&L's environmental impact statement "failed to provide satisfactory evidence on the plant's long-term effects."[5]

The two farmers' groups had, meanwhile, embarked on their own course of action—they were beginning to confront the utility directly:

> A request delivered by a delegation of ACORN farmers and signed by over 1,000 area residents asked the company for a $50,000,000 "deposit in reverse." The deposit would serve as a guarantee against any damages suffered by the farmers from the plant's operations. AP&L, of course, refused to put up the deposit.[6]

It was this attack that disclosed the most interesting facts in the campaign: that AP&L was a subsidiary of Middle South Utilities, and that the largest stockholder in MSU was Harvard University.

After uncovering the "Harvard connection," ACORN farmers moved the battle over power-plant construction in Arkansas to

Harvard Yard. In a letter to Dr. Derek Bok, president of the university, the ACORN groups requested that Harvard use its resources to produce an independent environmental study of the plant's impact on Arkansas, and its position on MSU's Board of Directors to raise the question of sulfur controls. When Bok failed to reply, ACORN sent Bill Kitchen, a former staff member, to Boston to organize student and faculty support for the ACORN position. Working with Steve Kest, a Harvard student who had been an intern with ACORN the summer before and who was scheduled to return to Arkansas after graduating, Kitchen was able to generate a series of actions and stories in the *Harvard Crimson*. As a result,

> when Arkansas Governor Dale Bumpers, the standard bearer of the "New South," spoke at Harvard, he encountered unexpected, stiff questioning about politics back home. He responded by calling for responsible measures by AP&L to protect Arkansas from pollution by the White Bluff plant. The Arkansas press, aided by ACORN, picked up this news item and carried it across the state. The Governor eventually also supported ACORN's demand that Harvard undertake a systematic study of the plant.[7]

The university's Advisory Committee for Shareholder Responsibility publicly released a letter to Middle South Utilities urging the installation of sulfur controls at the Arkansas plant and underwrote a $5,000 "fact-finding" report by the Investor Responsibility Research Center in Washington, D.C.

Utilizing the Harvard pressure and the research center's report at Public Service Commission hearings, ACORN was able to cut the plant's proposed size by half and force AP&L to include pollution control devices in its plans. The plant, consequently, was never built.

The campaign was significant on a number of levels. First, it tested ACORN's ability to apply its organizing model to a new constituency—farmers. A Little Rock reporter, observing an ACORN meeting, wrote:

These farmers were no sharecroppers. Most of them were medium-well-off landowners, typical middle-class Arkansans. Very few were even in working clothes. They were the type who would go to their graves believing in the righteousness of racial segregation and who could afford to send their children to the nearby segregationist private school. Still, they sounded the typical ACORN themes: They were the underdogs, victims of powerful, self-serving interests; only collective action would get results; they were going to demand that their elected state and national representatives join with them in their cause or regret it come next election.

"It takes numbers. You've got to have numbers to make a showing," said one man.[8]

ACORN was now expanding its numbers all over the state and expanding its structure to accommodate them. The citywide alliances of ACORN groups made way for the next organizational building block: the statewide council made up of elected representatives from each ACORN-organized area.

The campaign against AP&L also extended the geographic and political terrain on which ACORN was able to do battle. Breaking with the localistic frame that had previously characterized community organizations and taking the struggle outside the the state's borders made the confrontation more than a fight between Arkansas farmers and an Arkansas utility. Rather, it was a struggle between a statewide organization that manipulated the media and used all its political intelligence and disruptive power to force concessions, and a major company replete with New York offices and ties to several elite universities: the haves versus the have-nots. Additionally, as Rathke was to note shortly afterward, for community organizing it was "the first time the source of local discontent had been explored to its corporate roots."[9]

A third level of significance was the campaign's effect on ACORN's ability to recruit staff. After White Bluff, a stream of Harvard radicals made their way south to ACORN. Steve Kest recruited Seth

Borgos, who succeeded him as research director, followed by Steve Holt, Meg Campbell, Mary Lassen, Zach Pollett, and Madeleine Talbot. All were recruited between 1973 and 1975 and all became lead organizers in ACORN's multistate expansion between 1975 and 1980. This core staff, trained in the hinterlands of Arkansas and living on $37.50 per week, cut their teeth on the ACORN Model and, after eighteen months' work in their respective areas, developed the skills necessary to move the model into nineteen new states in four and a half years.

The Quorum Court Takeover

The 1972 school board elections and the victory over AP&L had whetted the appetites of the ACORN staff and membership to test their mettle in the political arena. Staff research disclosed that a test of voting and organizational power could be mounted in a local government body: the Pulaski County Quorum Court.

The quorum court structure that ACORN attempted to take over in 1974 was based on a section of the 1872 Arkansas Constitution decreeing that there would be one justice of the peace for every two hundred electors. Although the decree was passed when there were only a few thousand people in the county, by 1974 the Quorum Court of Pulaski County had 467 seats, some of which remained empty for lack of candidates to fill the slots. The JP's who sat on the court were responsible for approving tax rates and the county budget. The court's main function was to act as a check and balance against the chief judge of the court, whose duties were more executive than judicial; the court fulfilled its function by meeting twice a year to rubber-stamp the recommendations of the chief judge. Further investigation of the court members uncovered the fact that many ran for election chiefly so that they could perform marriages and notary services for extra money.

According to John Beam, the organizer responsible for the Quorum Court campaign:

The low profile of the Quorum Court (twice a year meetings, rubberstamping duties), its low entry costs ($10 filing fee), and the low level of competitiveness for its seats provided a unique opportunity for an insurgent movement led by low to moderate income people whose interests were often ignored, particularly in the areas of property taxes and expenditures benefitting urban residents of the county.[10]

ACORN recruited 250 members and supporters (from the International Ladies' Garment Workers Union) to run in the May 1974 Democratic primary, and 195 were elected to the Pulaski County Quorum Court in June. In a body where the quorum was 234 of the 467 seats, 195 elected members looked, at the very least, like fighting odds. While the campaign had no publicity, once the takeover was complete the ACORN victory was characterized in a number of newspapers as everything from "subversive" to "a victory for grass-roots power."[11] The question of whether ACORN really had won power, however, remained to be answered.

It was the tradition of the Quorum Court's chief judge to hand out the county budget on the day of the Quorum Court meeting. ACORN's first order of business, therefore, was to get copies of the budget ahead of time so that members could study it and propose changes. By an interesting series of demonstrations, ACORN members, in their capacity as elected officers of the court, forced the judge to release the budget earlier. ACORN members then discussed their strategies for the first Quorum Court meeting and their concrete budget proposals: equal distribution of funds and service to low-income neighborhoods, controls over disbursements, and so on.

At the first Quorum Court meeting the ACORN faction moved to appropriate only one-sixth of each line item—enough to keep the county running until budget hearings could take place. The proposal was made from the floor by an ACORN spokeswoman with a bullhorn, and the issue was debated. But thanks to a bogus credentials fight (the first credentials check in the court's 102-year history) in which ACORN lost five to ten votes, plus some imaginative arithmetic on the part of the judge, the proposal was defeated 169–163—even though both newspapers covering the meeting, the *Arkansas Democrat* and the *Arkansas Gazette*, counted the votes as either a one-vote majority for ACORN or a tie.[12] Incensed by this treatment, ACORN members walked out in order to break the quorum. As one participant remembers the action:

> There was one item for $3,500 for a "machine" that no one knew what it was for. We wanted to pass only one-sixth of the budget for two months, until we could figure out where it was going. But the judge just wouldn't let us. He said the others won . . . and the assistant district attorney said, "arrest them!" But we just walked out.[13]

In spite of losing the first vote, ACORN reaped several benefits from the experience. During the next two years, the court became an arena in which such issues as revenue sharing and the budgeting process, became polarized. The ACORN actions also brought about the retirement of the incumbent county judge. The most important effect of the Quorum Court campaign, however, was structural: in a state constitutional amendment passed in 1976, the size of the Quorum Court was reduced from 467 to a streamlined 15 members. The implications are clear. Not only was the large court cumbersome; it was too accessible. Even when ACORN proposals were lost or (as in the case of the budget) stolen, the government as an institution was delegitimized to ACORN members.

ACORN managed to secure one seat on the smaller fifteen-member court, but the organization was not able to regenerate the dynamic excitement and participation of two hundred low-income people who were willing to walk out on the government if they were not taken seriously. Nevertheless, the experience prepared a number of ACORN leaders and organizers to consider ways of merging local politics with community organizing, a discussion that had serious consequences for ACORN's membership after 1975.

EXPANDING THE TURF

Arkansas and Beyond

The Quorum Court challenge had put ACORN on the map. The attempted takeover was reviewed in liberal publications, and much attention was given to the fact that ACORN had utilized a low-income community base to enter the electoral arena. It was the in-state expansion of 1975, however, that truly made the organization a thorn in the side of both established local government elites and bureaucrats in the corporate offices of Arkansas. Starting with local issues and organizers recruited from Harvard and other eastern universities, ACORN had opened six offices around the state by 1975, and the organization was able to mount statewide campaigns on three issues: generic drug pricing, "lifeline" electric rates, and property taxes. Clearly the Quorum Court challenge had defined ACORN as a new and different type of community organization.

The passage of an ACORN-sponsored generic drug pricing bill in the state legislature was no small accomplishment, but it was the lifeline and property tax campaigns that demonstrated the growing sophistication of the group. ACORN had, in fact, been involved in rate increase fights with the Public Service Commission since 1973, each time forcing the commission to cut the proposed increases in half. In attempting to approach the problem of rising electric rates once more, ACORN staff uncovered "an old law which gives municipalities the right to set the rates which investor-owned utilities are allowed to charge customers residing within the municipalities' limits."[14] Utilizing the legal handle on utilities regulations in much the same way that the "minimum standard" had been used in the NWRO furniture campaign, ACORN mobilized local group support and held simultaneous press conferences in nine cities to request that the city councils adopt lifeline rates, which would give low-income, low-volume users the same kind of rate breaks as large commercial users.

ACORN's expanded ability, permitting it to mount the campaign in nine cities, was instrumental in attracting the interest of the newspapers. The press conferences were followed by mass actions and announcements of church and labor endorsements, and in areas where the local municipality refused to hold public hearings, ACORN members took petitions to the streets.

> In Hot Springs, for example, the City Council refused by a 7–5 vote to even schedule a public hearing on the matter. ACORN members quickly began circulating petitions in the wards of two of the anti-public hearing aldermen, and after 1,500 signatures (out of 1,800 registered voters) were gathered in one of the wards, the Council quickly called itself back into session and voted 11–1 for the public hearing.[15]

In a 1976 initiative campaign, six cities where ACORN had gotten enough signatures put lifeline on the ballot. Although legal maneuvers by the utility company kept the measure off the ballot in four of these, the voters in Little Rock did approve the measure.

In the matter of property taxes, ACORN effected a similar strategic shift. Although the organization had initially campaigned for changes in the property tax breaks available to large businesses, as opposed to homeowners and small businesses, and had succeeded in getting some neighborhood reassessments, the 1975 tax campaign was aimed directly at the throat of the state's growing banking and finance industry. Discovering once again a useful state law, this one providing that intangible property—stocks and bonds and money in the bank—could also be taxed by county assessors, ACORN members obtained a writ of mandamus ordering the assessor in Lawrence County to begin assessing intangible wealth. ACORN ultimately lost the campaign, but its actions and demonstrations managed to accomplish two things: raise serious questions about the "impartiality" of governmental regulatory agencies, and earn ACORN the permanent enmity of the banking and finance industry throughout the state.

Mounting these two statewide campaigns in 1975 had seriously changed the way in which the organization was viewed within Arkansas. Meanwhile, its staff was testing the validity of the ACORN

EXPANDING THE TURF

Model in yet another way—by opening operations in two other states. Negotiations initiated by Congressman James Abourezk about the possibility of setting up a group in South Dakota had begun in mid-1974. Rathke and two other organizers, Tony Fazio from California and Dewey Armstrong from North Carolina, drove into Sioux Falls and, in early 1975, with the temperature hovering at minus ten degrees and a persistent foot and a half of snow on the ground, began to work the ACORN Model. Fazio remembers, "It was so damn cold and so damn boring, there was nothing else to do *but* organize!"[16] After an eight-month evaluation of that experience, ACORN sent Steve Holt and Meg Campbell, two soon-to-be-married Harvard graduates, into Dallas–Fort Worth. In December 1975 the "A" in ACORN had changed from Arkansas to Association, as the organization's tri-state board founded the new Association of Community Organizations for Reform Now.

By December 1975 an ACORN publication claimed sixty groups throughout Arkansas, regional offices in ten cities, and a membership service center in North Little Rock. With a total membership of 5,200 families, the newly formed association also boasted 200 families in South Dakota and 245 in Texas, with regional offices in Dallas and Fort Worth.[17] All these new members fit neatly into the established ACORN structure, which simply added a new tier as the top leaders from three states became the new Association's board of directors.

ACORN also established two spinoffs from its main local organizing thrust in 1975. The first of these, ACORN Associates, Inc., offered (for a fee) consultation, training, and technical assistance to other CO groups. Its purpose was to utilize the talent of ex–ACORN staff, scattered all over the country, to conduct training and to kick back the money to ACORN. The second offshoot, the Arkansas Institute for Social Justice (AISJ)—after 1978, simply Institute for Social Justice—was formed to offer week-long training programs in cities across the country to make money for ACORN and to set up an intern program through which trainees would receive stipends from the institute while learning community organizing in Little Rock.

Although their programs were similar, the purposes and operation of these satellite entities were different. The Associates program was as much an attempt to keep ex-staff in touch with the ACORN network, setting up organizing opportunities for expansion, as it was a fee-generating proposition.

The Institute's program, on the other hand, was intended, first, to provide ACORN with a nonprofit, tax-exempt arm, important for securing foundation grants. Second, it would serve as a means of organizer recruitment through both the training sessions and the intern program. Third, it represented ACORN's attempt to hegemonize the field of community organizing by offering training in "principles and techniques of community organizing, drawing particularly from the ACORN model of neighborhood-based organizing."[18]

The regional expansion and successful record of the organization was beginning to affect its relations with the press. By November 1975, its statewide organization with electoral potential, its multistate expansion, and the creation of the AISJ and ACORN Asociates led a number of local reporters to launch an investigation of ACORN. They unsuccessfully attempted to gain access to ACORN's financial records, which they claimed should be open to the public under the Arkansas "sunshine law" because ACORN was allegedly receiving government money. In an attempted "exposé" on 22 November 1975, accompanied by a banner headline worded "ACORN Tells Expansion Plans," a reporter from the *Arkansas Democrat* could only write that the organization "receives no money from the government" but had plans to expand into four additional cities in 1976.

It was not only in the press, however, that ACORN's image as the little David against the Goliath of corporate greed and incompetent, insensitive local government was beginning to break down. ACORN was getting big, and in the thinking of many conservative people in the rural South "big is bad."

On one side of the coin ACORN was gaining recognition. In an interview in early 1975, the former state prison commissioner noted that "ACORN had about as much clout as organized labor and couldn't help but get stronger."[19] On the other side, the organization was losing its motherhood-and-apple-pie appeal. As Larry Ginsberg remembers "At the beginning of 1974, we [ACORN] received an award from the United States Jaycees foundation for being an outstanding community-oriented self-help project. The three other organizations in Arkansas receiving the award were two community service centers and a child abuse reporting project. . . . By the end of 1975," he continued, "after the lifeline campaign and the action around the quorum court . . . we couldn't even buy a ticket to a Jaycee luncheon!"[20]

Phase III: Multistate Expansion

The year 1975 marked the beginning of the third stage of ACORN's growth. By 1976, using the increasingly efficient pool of organizers trained in Arkansas in 1973–75, ACORN began organizing efforts in New Orleans (February), St. Louis and Houston (May), and Memphis (July). The criticism leveled at ACORN had also intensified: in 1971 it had been chiefly tactical; by June 1976, State Representative Boyce Alford of Pine Bluff was calling the organization a "possible threat to capitalism and democracy,"[21] and the second exposé series in the *Arkansas Democrat* quoted Little Rock Mayor George Winberly's accusation that ACORN was "secretive," plus an ex-member's claim that "ACORN was always greedy to claim credit for its victories."[22]

Within the staff and leadership of the organization, however, there was a new aura of confidence as members began to evaluate its prospects. In a speculative article written for internal use, Rathke noted, in part, the future of ACORN was clear. "ACORN will expand and organize in more cities and towns . . . perhaps leading to governmental takeovers similar to the Quorum Court . . . perhaps ACORN would even up the ante at other levels of government . . . leading the organization even further past the the bound of what one would normally expect of a community organization."[23]

It was early in 1976 that ACORN began to consider seriously the potential of community organization to influence national electoral politics. The geographic expansion goal of "twenty states by

1980" was directly linked to an analysis of ACORN's ability to leverage power and money (federal campaign financing) in the electoral arena. The second significant shift in organizational thrust was ACORN's interest in going beyond the traditional boundaries of community organizing. In a memo dated 26 December 1976, Rathke wrote: "The primary thrust of ACORN has always been the community. The issues of everyday life are central. We concentrate on our share of the interest and time of low- to moderate-income people for 16 hours a day. We compete in these time spaces with the media, sleep, and church, among other things. We cannot beat sleep or church. Media may be something else though." He concluded, "Over the long haul, we have to impact with a heavier and more organized hand [on] other areas of membership concern."[24]

Rathke went on to outline two areas of development that would be both politically desirable and financially viable. First, his memo advocated the creation of a Little Rock–based, self-sustaining, noncommercial FM radio station that could feed into local organizing. Recalling that ACORN's purchase of the *Arkansas Advocate*, a small bimonthly, had resulted in the publication's folding after less than two years of operation because of failure to develop a sufficient subscription base, Rathke wrote that given ACORN's low- and moderate-income constituency, "I would think we are probably a lot closer to envisioning an ACORN radio network than we are an ACORN newspaper division."[24]

Second, he recommended the development of "independent unions" as a way for ACORN to penetrate other spheres of people's lives. Rathke argued that

1. independent locals would bring financial stability—the union membership would increase ACORN's dues-paying membership;
2. ACORN had the skills—an "almost one to one transference of all of our professional skills as community organizers to those of union organizers";
3. ACORN would be able to merge organizing activities with the union operation under existing overhead;

4. the unions would permit constituent expansion because ACORN could organize where there were no jurisdictional claims—among household workers, sugar cane workers, the armed forces, small farmers, fishermen, clericals.

Rathke also speculated that beyond increased membership dues, new funding could be mobilized for expansion in both these areas. This is actually not a small point. It reflects a truism of community organizing: that is, in order to continue raising money from liberal church and foundation sources, the organization must at least appear to be doing something new. Even successful efforts like ACORN cannot continually leverage money for "more of the same" work, however good. While it is unclear that by 1976 the art of community organizing had become "a growth industry," as a reporter for the *Des Moines Tribune* claimed,[25] it is certainly true that, as organizer and fund raiser Meg Campbell put it, "every year when you make the trip to the trough, *you may be selling the same produce but you'd better have a different wrapper.*"[26]

These ideas for organizing in new areas met with mixed reactions. Many members in Arkansas were already anxious about ACORN's rapid expansion in 1976 and projected goals for 1977. But Rathke countered: "Have we grown too fast? No, we simply did not have sufficient resources to develop a staff and membership which could produce these surges of growth even earlier."[27]

How was ACORN able to expand so rapidly? In part the answer lies in the replicability of the model and the recruitment of a skilled professional staff to implement it. Equally important was the fact that ACORN organizers could pretty much count on the same problems cropping up wherever they went. In every city targeted for expansion the tax base was being eroded by lowered corporate assessments, municipal services were being cut back, neighborhoods in central cities were being "redlined," and jobs were becoming scarcer.

Another aid to ACORN's growth was the fact that its reputation preceded it in many cities. In a number of instances, the organization was actually invited by groups or individuals with substantial legitimacy in their communities. For instance, Mary Ann Fiske, who had worked with Rathke in Massachusetts welfare rights, held a key position in the Colorado Peace and Justice Commission, an activist organization affiliated with the Catholic Church. In the latter part of 1976, Fiske set up meetings between ACORN organizers and the Denver AFL-CIO, Catholic Charities, and several church-based service organizations. With this assistance, Colorado ACORN was founded in July 1977.

Although the expansion plans worked well for the most part, ACORN's voracious appetite for new areas began to produce "maintenance vs. expansion" tension in both staff and leadership ranks. Should the organization have four or five organizers per city, or should one or two maintain the initial groups while four moved on to open new cities? (The decision was to train organizers in initial drives in cities with successful operations—Little Rock, Fort Smith, Dallas, and Houston—and then send them to new areas.) Should the organization as a whole continue to pursue a southern, rural contingency, or should the model (having proved its urban potential in Dallas and Houston) be tested in the Northeast?

In planning a long-term strategy for expansion, the organization operated from both strategic and opportunistic impulses. Strategically, ACORN had an interest in organizing in the South, specifically in the states immediately adjacent to Arkansas: Tennessee, Louisiana, Mississippi, Missouri, Oklahoma, and Texas. Expanding into these areas, however, required more than merely sending in a couple of organizers. Opposition to "outsiders" was best neutralized by an invitation from local people to come in and organize. Money had to be raised to support the operation for the first eighteen months—usually about $30,000 to support two organizers, an office, and overhead.

ACORN's image externally, among left/liberal journalists, academicians, and funders, was that of the populist South being reborn: a cross between the the grassroots constituency of the Southern Tenant Farmers' Union, which had united white and black sharecroppers in the South in the 1930s, and the Nonpartisan League, which had built an important socialist alliance of farmers in the

Dakotas in the early 1900s. Nevertheless, because funders often give money to start organizations or to replicate successful efforts, there was pressure from this sector for ACORN to "move the model north." Clearly, behind the urging was the promise of resources to establish local organizations.

The opening of the Tennessee offices in mid-1976 gave the press an opportunity to question ACORN's expansion plans and rationale directly. Twenty-six-year-old John Beam was asked point-blank by reporters in Memphis, "Who invited ACORN and how long does the organization intend to stay in Memphis?" In response, Beam displayed a letter signed by a number of local leaders, including two ministers, requesting ACORN's presence. He stated that ACORN expected to establish thirty to fifty groups in the state, and asserted that he expected the office in Tennessee to be a permanent one.[28] In the fall of 1976 a reporter from the *New York Times* interviewed Wade Rathke about plans for the future. Rathke, noting that fast growth had killed other organizations, asserted that the Memphis expansion was "the last one for several months."[29]

"Several months" ended in April 1977 when ACORN opened an office in Florida. The operation was, once again, rapid and successful. In July, the organization moved into Denver; in August, Reno; in September, Philadelphia; in October, Des Moines—increasing its total number of states to eleven (Arkansas, South Dakota, Texas, Louisiana, Missouri, Tennessee, Florida, Colorado, Nevada, Pennsylvania, and Iowa). As Rathke wrote later:

> On January 1, 1976, ACORN had 3059 paid family members in the three states with 86 per cent of the membership in Arkansas. On June 30, 1977, eighteen months later, ACORN has 9187 family members, a staggering increase of a hair over 300 per cent! Furthermore, looking at the transformation of ACORN from an Arkansas organization to the Association, only 46 per cent of ACORN's membership is now in Arkansas, despite the fact that Arkansas ACORN has also doubled in size over the last 18 months. Put plainly, ACORN has organized more

people in the last 18 months of its seven year history than it had over the previous five and one half years. Given the current growth rate of the organization (seven per cent per month net growth), ACORN can reasonably expect to have more than 12,000 family members by the end of 1977, especially given the expansion program coming on line for the next six months.[30]

By keeping in regular contact with its groups in all eleven states, ACORN was able not only to replicate its organizational model, but to use centrally gathered research on what has become standard targets—banks, utility companies, and specific federal regulatory agencies—in a number of localities. It was possible, for example, to mount almost the same campaign in Missouri and Arkansas against Southwestern Bell's proposed pay phone hikes, and the generic drug bill drafted by Arkansas ACORN in 1975 could be the basis for similar efforts in Texas and Missouri in 1977–78. Besides the advantage of centrally generated research, the ACORN organizing staff, with its rich experience in eleven states, began to contribute to a growing pool of research, tactics, and strategies for organization. Moreover, as Rathke wrote in an evaluation memo, "The day is swiftly approaching when we will be able to launch multi-state campaigns on simultaneous timelines."[31] Continuing in this vein, he asserted:

> ACORN will have the advantages of scale enjoyed by government and industry. We will be able to pick our fights and set the precedents and roll them into the more difficult campaign situations, which previously has been a strategic luxury never enjoyed by low to moderate income people. This will increase the range and depth of our effectiveness steadily. In other campaigns where we might have been fighting improbable odds, our efforts will be able to seek the points of vulnerability and hit the seams on more fronts and more quickly, since their tactical weaknesses and inconsistency will be exposed on broader

expanses: *an error in Des Moines could cripple them in Denver and kill them in Dallas* [emphasis added].³²

The idea of multistate campaigns was not new to organizing. Both the antiwar and the civil rights movements had successfully replicated tactics and utilized sympathetic federal agencies to pressure local governments. But ACORN's application of political intelligence gathered in one local campaign and used in another was the first articulation of an approach that was to systematically take advantage of structural weaknesses in both corporate and governmental bureaucracies. Although not until 1979 could ACORN truly mobilize local groups in a systematic national campaign, it was this strategic ability that allowed this organization to win lifeline electric rates in three states and to gain concessions in five cities on bank redlining.

Internal Dissatisfaction: The First Rumblings

The multistate expansion in 1975–77 was not without problems. Internal trouble emerged on two levels: staff and leadership. For the staff—mostly young, white, well-educated radicals—ACORN offered an opportunity to learn the organizing trade and to build progressive local groups. But the time and energy required for the organizing work was tremendous, and the salaries for organizers were low (by 1976 a raise had guaranteed organizers with four-year commitments $4,000 per year), contributing to the emerging problem of rapid staff turnover. Another organizational problem was directly related to the rapid geographic expansion: the degree to which the most experienced staff could give support and direction to new field organizers. In order to competently build statewide organizations, ACORN needed to create a supporting staff structure—a bureaucracy.

On the leadership side, a different problem emerged—the resistance of the older Arkansas leadership to sharing power on the multistate board. Arkansas leaders had come to view ACORN as *theirs*, and though the majority were interested in initiating other projects, the organization had been started by and was ultimately accountable to the Arkansas leadership. By December 1977 there was another source of tension: when two hundred black teenagers marched into the Memphis City Hall in an ACORN sponsored jobs action, some ACORN leaders were displeased by the rowdiness of the group. After similar demonstrations erupted in New Orleans and Philadelphia, board leaders in New Orleans and Arkansas questioned the validity of these disruptive demonstrations.

To soothe the local boards, meetings were arranged between teenagers marching for jobs and the older, more established leadership to explain the whys and wherefores of the action. While these meetings did help to quell the leadership's immediate anxiety, they pointed to two structural problems. First, organizing constituencies (as opposed to neighborhoods), particularly around the issue of employment, produced units that reflected a different segment of the low-income community, one that was difficult to integrate into the organization. Second, working with constituent groups could create split loyalty and accountability for ACORN organizers. This second problem was related to the internal dilemma caused by expansion: how could ACORN train, maintain, and support new staff, especially staff that was spread over eleven states and twenty-five cities?

While these problems were generally identified in late 1977, they were only partially addressed in the January 1978 annual Year End/Year Beginning meeting (YE/YB). Approaching the problem of staff supervision and support, ACORN initiated several changes. First, through a series of staff/board negotiations, the Association and Arkansas ACORN staffs were separated, both functionally and physically; in January 1978 the Association staff, now called the "Organizing Support Center," moved to New Orleans. Second, all research and publications were consolidated under the new Association structure. Third, all finances were centralized in the New Orleans office. Fourth, canvassing—a door-to-door method of soliciting funds previously unused by ACORN—was begun. Fifth, in 1977, ACORN had signed a $470,000 contract with ACTION, the federal agency, to train one hundred VISTA volunteers in ACORN statewide organizations.

While this contract guaranteed ACORN free organizers to support and maintain the expansion efforts, it brought its own contradictions and liabilities. While ACORN had previously utilized VISTA volunteers, under the contract the organization agreed to accept one hundred persons (more than doubling the staff) without extensive prior screening. During the contract period, therefore, over half of the ACORN staff was being paid—at a rate higher than regular ACORN staff—by a third party that was often a target of ACORN actions: the federal government. And there was an additional complication: as federal employees, VISTA volunteers were not allowed to take part in electoral activities, a restriction that caused ACORN special problems in its 1980 political campaign.

In attempting to address the concerns of leadership, ACORN created an Association Board structure with two members from each state and slots for representatives from each state into which the organization planned to expand. While the Arkansas leadership still dominated (Arkansas leaders were elected president and vice-president of the board), there was now an opportunity for new state organizations to participate in the policy-setting process. The second change in the leadership process was the convening of a "Futures Committee" in Arkansas, which had the responsibility for mapping out "contingency plans for organizational survival."[33] This committee answered two needs of the old Arkansas leadership: it allowed them an opportunity to plan the organization's future, and it gave them continued access to the Association's chief organizer.

The question of ACORN's constituency was much more serious and less easily answered. Because the organization had essentially been built around the ability of local neighborhood units to achieve "specific, immediate, realizable" victories, there was no political or ideological reason for Redfield farmers to feel solidarity with unemployed black youth in, say, Memphis or Philadelphia. Although in 1976 the *New York Times* called ACORN "the most potent organization of have-nots in this region since the Southern Tenant Farmers' Union grew out of eastern Arkansas in the 1930's,"[34] the New Orleans *States-Item* was to note that ACORN had increasingly aimed for a different constituency, "a broader, more middle-class base."[35]

This tendency was reflected in the types of issues that ACORN addressed between 1970 and 1976. In 1970–72, welfare, food stamps, health care, and public transportation in low-income neighborhoods were key issues. In 1973, ACORN began to involve farmers in the White Bluff plant struggle, and the statewide campaigns clearly organized a more moderate-income base, especially the property tax initiatives in 1975–76. In 1977, efforts to curb insurance redlining in Missouri, a property tax reassessment campaign in Houston, and picketing in Denver's Jefferson Park community to protest parking in the neighborhood during football games demonstrated an even more marked change from the low-income benefit campaigns of earlier years, accompanied by a shift in the groups with which ACORN worked. For instance, headlines in the Jacksonville-based *Florida Star* read, "Seniors, ACORN Hit Southern Bell Rate Hike Proposal."[36] As Florida organizer Dewey Armstrong noted, "We intentionally went after seniors to move the issue. Their presence gave us legitimacy and added clout on the issue."[37]

New Organizational Directions and Alliances

In 1978, ACORN set up new groups in three states: Michigan and Oklahoma (May) and Arizona (September). In addition, following up on his December 1976 memo, Rathke directed an organizing effort in New Orleans to organize maids into a Household Workers' Union—the first unit in ACORN's planned affiliated United Labor Unions (ULU). The contracts negotiated by the Household Workers in New Orleans were, for the most part, with individual employers, and the organization was funded in part by the Jobs and Justice Campaign of the Movement for Economic Justice (MEJ) in Washington, D.C.

That organization had been founded by George Wiley in 1972 and staffed by Bert DeLeeuw, an ex–welfare rights activist. The other major Jobs and Justice organizing project was located in Boston—the Workers' Alliance to Guarantee Employment (WAGE), and it was staffed by Mark Splain, Barbara Bowen, and Lee Staples, all of whom had worked on the Massachusetts Welfare Rights Organization staff (Splain had succeeded Rathke as director). In 1973 these three had started the Chelsea Organizing Project that evolved into Massachusetts Fair Share, a statewide organization with staff and chapters in every major urban area. After a series of meetings in 1977, DeLeeuw, Splain, and Rathke, all of whom had common NWRO roots, formulated a mobilization strategy that would organize youth to engage in local direct action to produce jobs.

The resulting Jobs and Justice Campaign initiated local demonstrations targeting the federal Youth Entitlement Services Program in four cities. Organizers in each city claimed at least some success, in both speeding up job placements and increasing the number of available jobs.[38] ACORN, however, reaped two even greater benefits when Splain, Bowen and Staples's project merged with the ACORN-initiated United Labor Unions, and the Movement for Economic Justice became the locus for ACORN's Washington, D.C. activities. In this way, ACORN obtained not only a pool of talented, experienced organizers but also a well-connected and knowledgeable advocate in the nation's capital Madeleine Adamson, the editor of the MEJ publication, *Just Economics*. This development also eased the tension between constituent and neighborhood organizing. Creation of the ULU and the jobs campaign defined a separate entity for labor organizing with which ACORN would have fraternal relations, often sharing staff, yet each would maintain its own identity.

Another part of the December 1976 memo was also activated by March of 1978: ACORN had begun to produce a bimonthly radio program, "People Take Action: ACORN and the Issues," on KXXA, a Little Rock–based country music station, and work had begun on getting ACORN's first radio station on the air in Tampa, Florida.

A third type of expansion, the affiliation of existing groups, was a by-product of ACORN's association with the Movement for Economic Justice. Two of the groups that affiliated with ACORN in the spring of 1979, Carolina Action and Georgia Action, actually had had earlier ties to ACORN. Dub Gully, an ex–ACORN organizer, started Carolina Action in 1973. Shortly thereafter, the group's growth and development was left to Jay Hessey, a VISTA volunteer who built a strong statewide organization; by 1979 it had expanded to form a sister organization: Georgia Action. While Hessey had no ties to ACORN, he was connected to the eclectic Movement for Economic Justice, which related to organizers from all of the major community organizing networks. It was through a series of meetings facilitated by MEJ that ACORN and Carolina Action staff and leadership began a negotiation process that was to lead to an organizational affiliation in 1979.

A third affiliation, with the Citizens' Action League in California, was a carefully balanced negotiation for both sides. Tim Sampson, one of the key leaders in CAL and another former welfare rights worker, was open to developing a relationship with ACORN, as was Mike Miller, a veteran of SNCC and key in a number of organizing projects in the Bay Area. CAL was interested in participating in national politics without giving up local autonomy, while ACORN was interested in CAL's local strength to leverage national politics.

The affiliations were not without problems, however. ACORN wanted the ability to control finances and move staff around to fit the needs of the total organization. All the new affiliates (and a good many of the ACORN-built statewide organizations) were much less eager to give up good organizers to a trouble spot. Surprisingly, it was not political differences or organizational styles that were most problematic in affiliation agreements; it was the sacrosanct tenet of community organization: local autonomy. Could these affiliates become part of ACORN and retain the ability to make independent decisions? And would signing an affiliation agreement truly make Carolina Action an ACORN affiliate? Jay Hessey has noted that organizational history and experience are the most important variables in making alliances work. "Had it not been for the commonalities in the organizational history of ACORN and Carolina Action," he stated, "all the ideological compatibility in the world would not have helped in the affiliation."[39]

EXPANDING THE TURF

Expansion: The Political Costs

By 1979, ACORN had begun to pay the social costs for its rapid development. Criticisms were no longer raised only within the confines of the organization's structure; *questions of ACORN's purpose, power, and tactics had been elevated to a more public forum.* The mayor of New Orleans demanded that ACORN be investigated by the National League of Cities, and articles in the *Houston Post, Denver Post, Arkansas Democrat,* and *Detroit News* were calling ACORN organizers everything from paid agitators[40] to "damn know-it-all yankee kids."[41]

In addition, whereas ACORN had managed to recruit, train, and socialize a relatively tight knit group of organizers prior to 1979, the VISTA contract brought a much larger and more diverse group of people onto the staff, some of whom had different ideas about community organizing. Immediately following the first training session in Little Rock for VISTA volunteers, one of them flew to Washington and demanded to be reassigned, stating, according to former VISTA staff liaison Andrea Kydd, "ACORN is really interested in power, not helping people. They may even be a threat to the government."[42]

If the turnover for regular ACORN-recruited staff was high, the VISTA turnover was even higher. Unaccustomed to working the long hours ACORN demanded—including nights and weekends—and uncommitted to "living my whole life for ACORN,"[43] as one volunteer put it, fewer than half of the nationally recruited VISTA volunteers lasted a year.

Further troubles emerged when, because of the political/electoral work the organization was engaged in, ACORN and other community organizations funded through VISTA's liberal director, Marge Tabankin (an ex-organizer and foundation director), were investigated by the House Appropriations Committee for using VISTA volunteers in political lobbying activities in violation of the Hatch Act. The investigation, which resulted in the cutoff of ACORN's national grant, also charged that ACORN had used VISTA volunteers to help organize the Household Workers' Union in New Orleans. The audits and charges did seriously affect both the organization's funding base and, to some extent, its fiscal credibility, since federal auditors cited ACORN with "a deliberate effort to conceal evidence of an organization with serious financial problems."[44] (Of more interest to both the *Houston Post* and the *Arkansas Democrat*, however, was ACORN's refusal to open its financial or membership records to Congressional investigators.) Declaring that ACORN had "religiously avoided federal money up until that point," Rathke, in a letter to Tabankin, asked that ACORN "not be considered for a national grant."[45] (In fact, however, ACORN continued to use VISTA through state grants right up to the end of 1980.)

The VISTA debacle also intensified the tension around staff salaries. When ACORN was started in 1970, Rathke was being paid about $8,000 from NWRO (as one of eight state organizers paid by a special grant) and I was paid $100 a week under a grant from the Children's Foundation in Washington, D.C. After the break with NWRO, salaries went down to $35 a week, and by 1978 the top salary (based on seniority) had inched up to the 1970 $8,000 level, with a starting salary of $3,600. Thus, as low paid as were VISTA volunteers (averaging about $6,000 per year plus full health coverage), they made more than many ACORN organizers, even those with seniority. This tension served to move forward the discussion of staff raises in 1979–80. As a result, salaries at the bottom of the scale were increased; a special incentive program for minority organizers was established; and a health plan guaranteeing maternity care was adopted. For many ACORN veterans who had worked in the early days for $200 a month, this was considerable progress. Others declared even the new beginning salary of $450 a month insufficient "for people who don't have middle-class parents to fall back on,"[46] and couples (a total of four) with children found the salary scale impossible unless one spouse got a "real" job to support the ACORN staff member.

A second major crisis that ACORN had to address in 1979 was one in the leadership. In a front-page story headlined "ACORN Official Barred from Meeting; Leader Resigns" in the *Arkansas Democrat* of 22 April 1979, Chairman William Brookerd of Nevada ACORN, having resigned his position, charged, "If the leadership at any level insists on pursuing their priorities over staff priorities, they are 'democratically' exorcised from the leadership." He continued, "I have become greatly disappointed in not having the slogan 'The People Shall Rule' materialize for Nevada." Pearl Ford, another board member, made similar charges: "The tactics sound good at first. They come into a neighborhood and ask if you need stop lights and your trash picked up," she said. "The next thing you know they get you involved in storming city hall and other things that I don't approve of."[47]

It was not, however, either the leadership/staff tensions or the congressional investigation that was to hurt ACORN's credibility with left/liberal allies. It was the decision to organize in Boston, stronghold of Massachusetts Fair Share—an organization with similar goals, if a different style of organizing and a different constituency.

The Boston Question

The expansion into Boston, making Massachusetts ACORN's twentieth state, did not follow the usual process. Normally, new states were reconnoitered by staff, and board discussions of the staff evaluations followed. The decision to organize in Boston, however, was made by the Association Board at an October 1979 meeting with no discussion or report from the staff—indeed, with no inkling to the staff that such a decision would be made.

There had been turf conflicts when ACORN had invaded territory perceived by other organizations to be theirs. Several such arguments had emerged in Texas with the Dallas-based Bois d'Arc Patriots, a local community group, and in Denver with the local organizing project of the Industrial Areas Foundation. Similarly, ACORN had butted heads with organizers from the newly formed Citizen Action Organizing Committee in Connecticut (which became the statewide affiliate of Citizen Action, the Connecticut Citizen Action Group).

The Boston situation, however, was different in several ways. First, it necessarily brought to the surface the uncertainties of alliance and reopened the question of ACORN's true intentions. ACORN had, early on, defined its task as "organizing as many people (for power) as we competently can," but by 1979, it had definitely overstepped the traditional boundaries of community organizing. When asked about ACORN's relationship to the Alinsky tradition, Rathke said of Alinsky, "He was a cheerleader for this business of community organizing. His work was of tremendous influence; however, the confrontation tactics adopted by ACORN come from a tradition as real as American history."[48] In an attempt to stem the tide of federal investigators, lawyers, and right-wing activists interested in ACORN (in 1979 when Ronald Reagan, in a radio talk show, called ACORN dangerous, a Denver-based member who also belonged to the John Birch Society called in to disagree), Rathke talked to reporters from the *Houston Post*, which stated,

> ACORN has no "plan or ambition" to organize in all 50 states, and said it would be "presumptuous to assume that clout" when he said ACORN also has "no plans" to affect national political campaigns.
>
> Right now, he said, he sees ACORN as being "into the mosquito stage—able to raise up a little bump and draw a little blood."[49]

The Boston initiative was to "draw a little blood" from both ACORN and Massachusetts Fair Share. The turf war was reported in *Mother Jones*[50] and *In These Times*[51] as well as whispered about among liberal funding sources all over the country. There was internal staff opposition to ACORN's move into Boston, as well, and while some of it was political, the other two arguments were that ACORN would make permanent enemies and that the resources for expansion were not available.

In a sixteen-page memo dated 18 December 1979, and entitled "Boston Decision," Rathke addressed these and other concerns. The memo is important not only because it was the final document for a key decision but also because it illustrated how Rathke defined the parameters for and context of the decision. After a meeting with Fair Share leadership, said Rathke, ACORN leaders commented that the Fair Share leaders were "good people, but that the organization was white and middle class. That is not bad but it is different."⁵²

> The direction and commitment of the organization there seems to have shifted from that of a community organization which sometimes gets involved in community issues (as does ACORN), to a consumer organization that sometimes gets involved in community issues with those chapters it has in local areas. On the bottom line it has been different from ACORN. *Some of its commitments to organizing low-income families seem to have been lost in its work with higher-income homeowners. Its commitments to organize multi-racially in different areas seem to have been filled with less than total resolve.* Its commitments to direct action seem to shift and shift with the canvass needs and the needs of the coalition building strategy they have adopted over recent years. . . .
>
> On the bottom line it has been clear that we are different. *Though they have been an outstanding consumer organization, they are in fact not committed as ACORN is to the same values and principles of community organization understood by leadership, membership, and organizers.* Their lack of a clear, replicable organizing model seemed to mean to me professionally that they were not prepared to organize seriously either in Massachusetts or in other states in terms that we would understand or applaud [emphasis added].⁵³

By moving into Boston, ACORN was encroaching on the turf not only of Massachusetts Fair Share but also of the newly formed Citizen Action Organizing Committee, a consortium of organizations loosely connected through the Midwest Academy, The Academy, probably the largest organizer training entity in the country, had begun an effort early in 1979 to consolidate organizations from six states (Illinois, Ohio, Massachusetts, Connecticut, New Hampshire, and Indiana) into first a network and, potentially, a national organization. A series of memos regarding ACORN's possible participation in Citizen Action had flowed between Rathke and Midwest Academy Director Heather Booth, ending in ACORN's withdrawing if, in Rathke's words, "19 states didn't equal 19 votes."[54]

Although there was always underlying tension between ACORN and the Citizen Action affiliates, the tension was based on strategic as well as organizational differences. By 1973, Heather Booth had formed the Midwest Academy, which was to play a major role in initiating community organizing efforts in five of the six states which would come together to form Citizen Action Network in 1979.

Boston, then, through Massachusetts Fair Share, represented a significant piece of the Academy's attempt to consolidate its training efforts into a national network.

From ACORN's point of view, there were a number of factors that influenced the decision to use the people already in Boston working on Jobs and Justice issues to initiate an ACORN chapter. First, there were political differences between ACORN and Fair Share. The ACORN staff and board did view Fair Share as a different sort of animal, more involved in coalition work than in grassroots organizing in low-income communities.

A second factor in the decision was personal. Since Massachusetts Fair Share had grown out of the Chelsea Organizing Project, which was supported by George Wiley and later Bert DeLeeuw of the Movement for Economic Justice, it was therefore perceived by organizers in the old welfare rights network (which had produced Rathke, Deleeuw, Splain, and Bowen) as part of the welfare rights "orbit." In 1974, Fair Share, under financial pressure, merged with the Boston Community School, which was directed by Michael Ansara, an ex–SDS activist and close friend of the organizers of the Midwest Academy. Under the merger, Ansara assumed the role of executive director of Fair Share, and Mark Splain remained head organizer. The power struggle that ensued over decision-making and organizational direction resulted in Ansara's retaining control over the organization; three of Fair Share's founding organizers, Mark Splain, Barbara Bowen, and Lee Staples, left to begin organizing unorganized workers in Boston before they were recruited by ACORN.

EXPANDING THE TURF

A third factor was that ACORN had access to skilled organizers already in place in Boston—people who had numerous connections in the city and were chafing at the bit to develop an "ACORN presence" in the Northeast.

Which of these factors most influenced the decision to go to Boston? Rathke's carefully defined organizational differences were not, in my view, the real issue ACORN had never *not* organized in a locality simply because there was an existing organization. Personal factors were certainly important, particularly in an organization where high value is placed on personal loyalty. Mark Splain and Barbara Bowen were capable organizers, had worked with Rathke on numerous occasions over the preceding twelve years, and were highly respected in the organization. It was the matter of resources, however—the fact that the organization already had personnel in Boston—that made the expansion into Massachusetts a foregone conclusion. Given all the other variables, if ACORN had not had the staff in place, the discussion might have been moot.

Despite the strong staff sentiment for the move, John Beam (regional director for the southern states), Charles Koppleman (director of ACORN's training institute and former regional director of a national foundation) and I (coordinator of the 1980 platform campaign; see chapter 6) argued against it. Beam and I contended that the move potentially pitted ACORN against allies who could be important to us in the upcoming political campaign. Koppleman asserted that the costs to ACORN in the funding community, where it already had a reputation for not working in coalition, would be tremendous, especially at a time when the organization was attempting to develop overtly political alliances. Following a four-hour debate, however, the sentiment of the statewide head organizers and national staff was unchanged. ACORN would move into Boston.

The first ACORN organizing began in Boston in the spring of 1980. The move did indeed negatively affect ACORN's ability to raise money from liberal foundation and church sources, and to build alliances with labor leaders who had relationships with the Citizen Action network. Now, five years later, ACORN and Fair Share have separate neighborhood organizations in Boston. While there is no

EXPANDING THE TURF

love lost between the staff and leadership of the two groups, there does not currently appear to be a turf war. Was the decision to move into Boston correct? "That depends," replies a former ACORN staff member, "on whether your view is that you are part of the movement or you *are* the movement."[55]

The question of ACORN's relationship to a larger movement would become more apparent in the organization's next political project: a campaign to influence the direction of the Democratic party in the 1980 elections.

6

Jamming the Democrats

> *The real question is whether we'll come out of this as a national organization or as three hundred local groups winning the hell out of stop signs.*
> —Jay Hessey, Organizer, Carolina Action/ACORN
> (on the bus to the 1980 ACORN Convention)

Organizing campaigns implement what organizers call the three I's: identify the enemy, isolate him, and ice him. This appears to be a simple set of principles and, on a local level, they brought ACORN and other community groups a high degree of success in dealing with local government officials, state and federal bureaucrats in regulatory agencies, and representatives of local and national corporate entities. But could these principles, and ACORN's model as a whole, be applied successfully at the national political level?

In 1976, ACORN initiated an effort to consolidate itself as a national organization by waging a protracted confrontation with the Democratic Party, exploring how its organizing approach would fare against a national political party that claimed to represent the same constituencies.

Unlike many local community groups, ACORN had always been involved in politics. In 1971, ACORN leaders in Arkansas had registered as lobbyists (see chapter 5), advocating a poor people's platform that called for a public defender system, expanded collective bargaining, free health care, and a lowered voting age.[1] The 1972 election of a Little Rock school board member marked an extension of the platform to local demands for "free textbooks, abolition of school fees and targeted additional funding in low-income areas."[2]

Until ACORN's experience in the Pulaski County Quorum Court in 1974–75, however, the organization's attitude toward the role of government was consistent with the strategic thrust of the National Welfare Rights Organization: the government could be manipulated on two levels.

First, the state could be held fiscally responsible for all benefit programs; therefore organizing efforts were directed at increasing benefits through welfare reform and expanding state benefit programs to larger constituencies. Consistent with this thrust, known in organizing circles as "breaking the bank,"[3] ACORN's first non-welfare campaign (1970) used the federal government to force the North Little Rock School District to provide free or reduced-price school lunches to the non-welfare poor.

Second, the state could be held accountable for fairly enforcing the law on behalf of poor and working-class people. In line with this thrust, ACORN published a table of comparative assessments in low-income and downtown neighborhoods that forced the county to reassess properties in low-income neighborhoods. This direct action approach demonstrated that the state could be held accountable, whereas without an organization of the poor, it would be more responsive to other class interests.

However, a shift in thinking within ACORN occurred in 1975: the Quorum Court experience showed both staff and membership the difference between forcing a state institution to be accountable and actually controlling the institution. As organizer Steve Kest wrote: "The state might be dominated or even controlled by powerful economic institutions, but if the low- to moderate-income majority is ever able to take control of the state, there's a good chance that the lines of power between the state and the economic institutions will begin reversing themselves."[4] This potential was enhanced by ACORN's transformation from an Arkansas organization with operations in nine cities to a multistate association with new organizations in Sioux Falls, South Dakota, and the Dallas–Fort Worth area in Texas.

The Proposal

In 1976, Wade Rathke produced an ambitious document entitled "The 20/80 Plan."[5] On six single-spaced mimeographed pages, he made a series of arguments for expanding ACORN's organizational base from three to twenty states over the next four years, focused in part on expanding to states that held a Democratic primary or statewide caucus. Rathke argued that it would be possible to use the "event" of the presidential campaign to build ACORN's national power and prestige. If ACORN were to run a presidential candidate in 1980, the organization could capitalize on the following four opportunities.

1. *Campaign financing*: $5,000 raised in each of twenty states (hence the twenty-state goal) in contributions of less than $250 would trigger a matching grant from the Federal Campaign Commission. "The feds would pay for the 20/80 plan."
2. *Voting Rights Act*: skilled use of the act would allow ACORN to influence the votes of a million newly registered people.
3. *Delegate selection*: there was potential for ACORN to win caucus states, where the "entire ball game is based on organizational strength," if there was an ACORN operation already in place in those states.
4. *Platform*: if ACORN succeeded in electing delegates to the Democratic Convention, the organization might be able to influence both the candidate selection process and the Democratic Party platform.

The campaign plan would therefore require expanding ACORN to twenty states by 1980, with an emphasis on caucus states; creating an ACORN platform; and running delegates for the Democratic Convention—a campaign aimed directly at provoking issues and candidates within the Democratic Party. Rathke, ever the organizational man, argued that such a campaign offered a focus and timetable for ACORN's organization-building over the next four years; an opportunity to break down the localism of ACORN organizers and leaders and begin building some ideological coherence; and a chance to transform ACORN-the-organization into ACORN-the-social-movement of low- and moderate-income people. "ACORN has an organizational and professional responsibility," Rathke added, "to demonstrate the potential of community organization as a mechanism for social change."

The significance of the idea outlined in this speculative, internal document can be neither ignored nor underplayed. In defining a new direction for ACORN, Rathke was breaking with the "hands off electoral politics" position taken by most community organizations in the Alinsky tradition and many others. He was redefining not only the future of ACORN but the shape of community organization in this country.

Openly recognizing the problems of mounting a political campaign, however, Rathke also listed—with what turned out to be deadly accuracy—the potential liabilities of such a campaign.

1. A membership split might occur: ACORN had organized people around economic self-interest, and the group was politically mixed; Republican members would have trouble with a totally Democratic Party strategy.

2. ACORN would risk being seen as a political party rather than a community organization.

3. ACORN would be red-baited.

4. The selection of local ACORN candidates from within the organization could create intraorganizational conflict.

5. The campaign would not only cost the organization a great deal of money but probably involve significant "social costs" in terms of staff loss.

6. ACORN would be harassed by the Internal Revenue Service.

7. If successful, the campaign might bring ACORN into conflict with as many allies as it would gain, given the fact that the Democrats had to some extent enfranchised women, minorities, and labor.

8. Generally, repression of the organization from corporate and state sources would increase.

A demonstrator in ACORN's "human billboard" anti-inflation campaign in Memphis, 1979.

ACORN members put the Democratic Party on notice at the 1978 mid-term convention in Memphis.

Squatters descend on Washington, D.C. for a confrontation with the administration in the summer of 1983.

An ACORN member gets ready to "hit the bricks" at the 1980 convention in New York City.

ACORN delegates from 30 cities prepare to march on the Democratic Convention and "draw the line" in New York, 1980.

ACORN supporters unfurl "Alliance for Justice" banner at the site of the 1984 demonstrations at the Republican National Convention in Dallas.

Detroit youth march for jobs in ACORN campaign to get preference for city residents in city hiring.

JAMMING THE DEMOCRATS

Internal Differences

The memo met with mixed reactions. John Beam—a veteran of the Quorum Court campaign who was at the time a regional organizer in Jonesboro, Arkansas, and later became a regional director of six southern states—remembers:

> Although we were definitely on an organizational upswing, there was some opposition to the idea based on what some people felt was our inability to even maintain the organization that we had at the time. I was opposed to the idea myself, but more because I thought that entering the electoral arena might permanently change the direction of the organization—might point ACORN in a direction that I did not think was in the interests of our constituency, given the Democratic Party's unwillingness to respond to the needs of our constituents.[6]

But Zach Pollett, a new organizer in 1976 and now also a regional director, recalls, "I thought it was exciting as hell. Clearly the Quorum Court campaign had demonstrated the potential for us to get state power on the local level, and I thought if all the campaign allowed us to do was duplicate that effort, it would be worth it."[7] Mary Lassen, former Texas head organizer, was interested in the campaign's potential for alliances with "other progressive forces—labor, women's groups, minorities. I saw the campaign as a means to build some meaningful alliances for the long haul."[8]

Even some organizers and leaders who supported the 20/80 plan, however, were concerned by the potential for intraorganizational conflict. In response, Rathke developed the following guidelines: (1) ACORN's platform would be forged from existing and common organizational issues (borrowing from the Non-Partisan League);[9] (2) ACORN would "run the organization rather than candidates"—in other words, its people would run on ACORN's record in each of its states. Moreover, since there was still internal opposition, it was agreed in early 1976 that the 20/80 plan would be evaluated at

131

the end of the year against two criteria: an analysis of the 1976 presidential campaign, and the progress of ACORN's state expansion plan.

In a memo issued in December 1976, Rathke concluded that Carter's campaign was a successful example of the "running against government campaign" that he had suggested as a tactic a year earlier. He also noted that the "Right to Life" efforts demonstrated that federal matching money provisions were indeed flexible enough to be manipulated by issue-oriented groups, and that whereas the caucus process could not be as easily manipulated as he had initially posited, certain states could be targeted. He also pointed out that where an incumbent had the convention nomination locked up (as Carter likely would in 1980), issues could become extremely important.

In exhaustive staff discussions in December 1976 and January 1977, a number of key senior organizers continued to oppose the 20/80 campaign, arguing that it would be too great a resource drain and that "taking over the Democratic Party is not the business of a community organization." Essentially, there were two factions supporting this view. Most of the opposition argued for "maintenance over expansion," reasoning that if ACORN's ability to mobilize resources were to remain constant, the campaign's financial and personal drain within the organization would necessarily lower the quantity and quality of organizing throughout the Association. Others contended that electoral politics, given the existing party structure, was strategically incorrect because no amount of work would reform the Democratic Party; the very process, they argued, could potentially co-opt ACORN leadership. These points of contention were not resolved, and questions of resource mobilization and potential co-optation continued to be debated as the campaign evolved over the next four years.

One initial concern about internal conflict was quelled with an amended plan (January 1977) to run uncommitted delegates to both the Democratic and the Republican conventions. In addition, ACORN leadership decided to frame the campaign totally in terms of the issues of low-income people rather than to endorse a candidate.

These decisions reflected concessions to internal staff and leadership factions as much as ananalysis of the strengths and weaknesses of the Democratic Party and ACORN's ability to make an impact on its decision-making. Moving against the Republicans and running uncommitted delegates were concessions to those who worried that ACORN might be perceived as the "loyal opposition," as well as to Republican ACORN members concerned that the campaign would not involve *them*. The decision to address the issues with which ACORN groups had experience reflected both an adherence to the organizing principle of not going outside the experience of the membership, and a strong reluctance to develop positions that might be termed "ideological."

ACORN's front-end analysis of the Democratic Party was fairly sketchy. In 1976, the organization's only experience with the party had been local. Although based on an assessment of the party's successful presidential campaign, Rathke's analysis of party vulnerability did not examine the crosscurrents of organizational self-interest within the party. His sense of party porosity at the local level was correct. It was, however, the relationship of the local party to both the candidate campaign efforts and the national party that would determine ACORN's ability to implement a national agenda.

Memphis: Setting the Stage

Although ACORN had expanded into and was working in twelve states by the end of 1978, it was still seen by most activists as a southern organization. Clearly, then, it was essential to establish ACORN as a "player" in national politics. As a first step, the leadership, deciding to challenge the Democrats in their Memphis midterm convention brought together 1,200 members and supporters from twelve states to march on the convention—in a freezing rain—in December 1978. Foreshadowing the 1980 campaign, ACORN members demanded platform changes and representation for low- and moderate-income people.

The Memphis action helped to concretize the 1980 campaign by demonstrating ACORN's ability to mobilize people from all over the country and by bolstering internal organizational spirit. The Memphis action was also the occasion of the first ACORN national convention and the first opportunity for many members to meet members from other states. As Elena Hangii, former state chair from Arkansas (elected Association board president in 1983), put it: "It was our first chance to really see the potential of the organization. We were surprised at how much the same we were even though we were from all over the country.... The other thing that was really great about Memphis is how all the Democrats were falling all over themselves to speak at our convention."[10] Further, the Memphis action was the galvanizing impetus for ACORN to develop another expansion strategy: affiliation agreements with three statewide community organizations—Georgia Action, Carolina Action (North Carolina), and the Citizen's Action League (California). By February 1979 all three had agreements with ACORN. Another set of negotiations had earlier brought *Just Economics*, a national magazine for organizers, and its talented editor, Madeleine Adamson, under the aegis of the tax-exempt Institute for Social Justice, ACORN's education and training arm (see chapter 5).

It was the affiliations with these groups and (in December 1979) with the Jobs and Justice staff in Boston that allowed ACORN to reach its organizational goal of operating in twenty states without overextending its own staff and financial resources (the affiliation strategy was therefore viewed as a concession to the maintenance faction in the expansion/maintenance fight). In addition, the 20/80 campaign permitted ACORN to define a realizable goal that was attractive to the other statewide community groups, which—although all on friendly terms with ACORN—almost certainly would not have affiliated outside the context of the campaign.

Although the twenty-state goal was in sight by January 1979, ACORN was beset with problems. The expansion into sixteen states in four years had indeed taken its toll. Many key organizers were tired and emotionally drained. There were staff turnover and related conflicts in a number of states. Both staff and leadership were pushed into positions of heavy responsibility that they had to fill adequately or drown, and many did not make it.

Additional difficulties emerged from the centralization of the growing organization. It was not clear, for instance, how much direction ACORN head organizers, much less staff and leadership in "affiliate" states, would take from the national Association staff. And expansion had brought on other troubles. First, there was wide variation in the quality of work performed in ACORN cities, the result of the newness of local organizations and the issues tackled, plus an organizing staff that had worked relatively well in small autonomous units but had little experience in large-scale coordinated efforts. Second, while many senior staff members had come through the Quorum Court experience, this experience had not been successfully communicated to ACORN's membership outside of Arkansas. Third, many ACORN campaigns reflected local conditions, and victories in Sioux Falls on redlining did not necessarily build solidarity with members with the same problem in Dallas.

In a memo prepared in the summer of 1978 entitled "20/80 (Apocalypse or Long March?),"[11] research director Seth Borgos and Steve Bachmann, head of the organization's legal staff, asserted that the campaign was a necessary next step—an opportunity to use both the Democratic and Republican conventions as forums for raising the issues of low-income people. Reasoning that presidential election years are times when "issues are on the people's minds," Borgos and Bachmann asserted that ACORN could use the election year to identify crucial national issues; to present its vision of a worthwhile America; to raise the nation's consciousness about power relationships and what organized people can achieve; and, by these means, to enhance ACORN's impact.

The memo's emphasis was on the strategy and tactics of raising issues at the Democratic National Convention, with an optional scenario for running ACORN delegates either sub rosa or as "outfront uncommitted." Sidestepping the expansion/maintenance argument, Bachmann and Borgos asserted that while "local organizing will continue to be the bare heart and soul of the campaign . . . a street scene is something that Walter Mondale and Walter Cronkite can always ignore; [therefore,] the central strategic problem in the 20/80 plan is how to get as many delegates as we can onto the floor of the convention—by comparison, everything else is easy."

By 1979 other oppositional forces were showing interest in electoral politics. In New York a group of left/liberal foundation people considering a third-party effort invited ACORN and the New York–based Women's Action Alliance to discuss the potential of a "citizens' party." Representing ACORN, Rathke was asked to write a memo exploring the tradeoffs between two options: "building a party (an organization) versus developing a campaign (running a candidate for President)."

In his response, entitled "Notes toward an Organizing Plan for a New Party,"[12] Rathke first noted that "there is no way to escape the realization of where we stand today. There is no party pre-existing. There is no clear constituency base. There is no mass movement from which our candidate and organization springs." Without an organized constituency, running a candidate would imply a top-down national campaign that would be forced to make compromises based on the candidate's need for alliances and support. Rathke also pointed out that, in view of the nature of American politics, more money would be spent for publicity than for building organization. Further, since running a candidate would require matching the opposition's strength, the new party's candidate would necessarily have to be a "big name" and necessarily "non-indigenous." A "party-first strategy," on the other hand, would offer the advantages of organizational permanence, indigenous leaders, local issues, local alliances, and a concentration of resources based on the likelihood of success. Such a strategy, Rathke concluded, would allow the building of a mass base, while a candidate strategy would have to be based on individual decisions that might not even reflect or symbolize a mass base, much less organize one.

In the subsequent meeting, the Citizens' Organizing Committee elected to move forward and establish the Citizens' Party, with Barry Commoner as its candidate; ACORN and the Women's Action Alliance elected to organize their respective campaigns locally.

The People's Platform

There were a number of reasons for ACORN to develop a platform, most of them internal. While it is true that the organization wanted to generate a concrete position from which to criticize the Democrats, conventional party wisdom assumes that the platform is traditionally a throwaway to the liberal/radical wing of the party; the platform, therefore, is always more radical than the actual program. Thus, even if ACORN were able to win platform concessions, it was assumed that these concessions would mean little to the candidate because they would in no way be binding.[13] Why then initiate a process for the development of a platform?

For one thing, the membership's experiences with the organization were disparate: for instance, some groups in Arkansas were all black and some in South Dakota all white; the ages and relative strengths of statewide operations were very diverse; and since local ACORN groups had initially organized around different but basically economic issues, many social issues were beyond their organizational experience. The process through which the platform would be developed could be used to consolidate and collectivize the membership's positions on key social issues, thereby beginning to forge an ideological unity within ACORN.

A second reason for a platform was that the process would, if successful, force nonprogressive elements to either take progressive positions or leave the organization. Third, the platform development experience would give the staff and membership of the organization an opportunity to familiarize themselves with issues on which they had not waged local campaigns. Fourth, the platform process would escalate the expectations of the organization's membership: ACORN would be taking responsibility for creating social programs instead of just demanding accountability from already existing programs.

There were two limitations to achieving these objectives. First, in following the community organizing principles of "not going outside the experience of people and starting where people are at," ACORN restricted its platform planks to nine areas in which it had experience—including taxes, jobs and income, energy, and health care—but these were not the areas in which special interests, especially racially based and women's groups, were spending their energy. Nevertheless, although the community at large was discussing such issues as quality education and women's rights (specifically the Equal Rights Amendment), ACORN elected to concentrate on issues that, while they might cause political disagreements within ACORN groups, would seldom touch on macroeconomic or social issues. The second limitation on platform development was time. With the Democratic National Convention as the eventual target, the platform had to be conceived, discussed, and ratified in six months in order to be used as a tool to build ACORN's alliances during the fall of 1979.

The initial platform positions were developed by staff members, whose background papers on each of the issues included a general definition, places where ACORN had worked on that issue, and a series of related questions. These questions ran from the most general ("If we were to put together a health care system that was really run by and for the people, what would it look like?") to fairly specific ("Should a percentage of all people who sit on governmental regulatory boards be low-income? How should they be chosen?").

These papers were sent to organizers in all cities where ACORN had local groups; there they were duplicated and distributed to local leadership for discussion by area boards and later at neighborhood meetings. Comments and suggestions from local group discussions were funneled directly to the Association staff in New Orleans, to be consolidated into preliminary versions of the platform—noting which planks came from which states—and sent out for further discussion. This cycle took place three times before ending in statewide platform conventions in which state bodies recommended final versions of the platform.

As with most attempts to initiate and implement a participatory democratic process, there were many problems. One was the reluctance of organizers, who usually function only as low-key facilitators, to initiate discussions. Another was that, background papers notwithstanding, many organizers and leaders did not feel sufficiently knowledgeable to conduct discussions on certain topics. There was also some outright resistance to the platform process. One organizer wrote: "This platform stuff is a waste of time. It takes away from my time on the streets and it won't do a goddam thing to move Democrats in this state. What we need here is more organization and less talk. . . . Why don't you all just write the platform and we'll sell it."[14]

Still, the variety and range of suggestions generated by the platform development process, despite the reticence of some organizers, cannot be ignored. Louisiana members proposed the creation of a "community housing corps" to put unemployed residents to work providing housing in their own communities. Philadelphia groups suggested that corporations making "big profits" should be required to hire unemployed people to do meaningful work. North Carolina affiliates recommended that "local communities should have the power to veto nuclear plant construction within their boundaries." Detroit groups argued that low-income community residents, rather than real estate investors, should be given first priority for HUD foreclosures. Arkansas groups wanted public financing of all elections, postcard voter registration, and 70 percent of the membership of all regulatory and corporate boards to be low- and moderate-income people. Of course, not all the suggestions were progressive: from Arizona came a recommendation for sterilization of welfare recipients after the third child, and members in Florida voted to "protect our interests in the Panama Canal."

If one of the purposes of initiating the platform was to "smoke out" unprogressive elements in the organization, on at least two occasions it succeeded. In an Atlanta neighborhood of the newly affiliated Georgia Action, a member who was upset with the local organization's stance on increased banking regulation took the group's position and its affiliation with a "socialist" ACORN to local newspapers and produced substantial debate on a local call-in radio show; as a result ACORN lost seven members of the local group and later had to totally reorganize the neighborhood. As staff coordinator of the platform development, I was personally involved in a second incident in Denver, where one of the local ACORN leaders who was also a John Birch Society member became convinced that ACORN had taken a wrong turn. In one meeting she presented me with a copy of the right-wing bible *None Dare Call It Treason*, suggested I read it, and told me that she was bound and determined to make sure Colorado ACORN never backed any of these outrageously communist ideas. Fortunately, she was outvoted. There were similar manifestations of contradictory political tendencies in Florida, Texas, and Louisiana. The only states where the platform did not produce at least some conflict were Arkansas and Pennsylvania.

Interestingly enough, while ACORN was at least philosophically prepared for the dropping out of less progressive elements, it was not prepared for the ability of organized progressive groups to enter into the platform process and influence the planks. In Houston, for example, leftist elements were consistently successful in advocating more radical positions in the areas of health care, housing, and banking. However, the most organized penetration of an ACORN group took place in Sioux Falls, South Dakota, where members of the local Farmers' Union openly joined the organization and proceeded to agitate for income parity with nonfarm wage earners, tax deferrals for small farmers, and antitrust legislation to break up the monopolization of agricultural marketing. Dewey Armstrong, the state's first head organizer, commented, "We'd been working with the Farmers' Union for years in South Dakota . . . in fact our Huron group was mostly composed of members of the local Farmers' Union. It was not until ACORN initiated the platform process, however, that they really organized their input in terms of ACORN's political direction."[15]

The culmination of the platform process was the 1979 ACORN Convention in St. Louis, where 2,000 delegates from nineteen states gathered at Washington University to finalize the platform. The three issues that generated the most intense conflict in the organization were the planks on guaranteed income, nuclear power, and rights of workers.

The guaranteed income plank read as follows: "Guarantee a minimum annual family income at a figure equivalent to the current Bureau of Labor Statistics' medium living standard." The plank was developed in Arkansas and advocated by organizational old-timers who were present when ACORN was still an experimental project of the National Welfare Rights Organization. It was on this issue that the tenuous coalition of low- and moderate-income people on which the organization is built was most seriously challenged. Advocates of the plank (mostly black and low-income members) argued that all families were entitled to a basic income, health care, and housing; opponents of the plank (the most vociferous of whom were also black but more moderate-income) argued for income based on employment.

This conflict, which culminated in a plank struggle in St. Louis, was the result of a fundamental difference within the ACORN constituency: the division between low-income members who essentially argued for guarantees from the welfare state, and the working class who were for individual access to resources without guarantees. The division was based not on race but rather on the differences between urban and rural constituencies with different organizational experiences and different values.

Other divisions were based on the relative age of statewide organizations. The older ACORN groups were dominated by low-income people who had fought for welfare and Medicaid reform; the newer ones were more likely to comprise homeowners and blue-collar workers. This difference was especially prevalent in the ACORN affiliates in California, North Carolina, and Georgia, where the lowest-income elements were the senior citizens' groups.

Although the guaranteed minimum income plank did pass, it was not without bitter feeling on both sides. There were similar divisions on the "right-to-work" question. Labor union advocates were pushing for a plank that would extend the right to organize, streamline union elections, and broaden the National Labor Relations Act to cover all workers. Not surprisingly, a strong anti-union tendency emerged from the right-to-work states within the Association—North Carolina, Louisiana, and Georgia—and was supported by the more conservative elements in Colorado and Arizona. The anti-union (right-to-work) position was essentially advocated by a coalition of very low-income people who had never been in unions and by some of the relatively more affluent members who ran small businesses. Once again, the plank passed, but not without considerable internal struggle. In North Carolina, the anti-union position was prevalent throughout the organization because of the local stand of the AFL on the third key issue at the convention: nuclear power.

Nuclear waste disposal was a major issue in North Carolina, Arkansas, and Louisiana. Moreover, the Three Mile Island incident had motivated significant support on an antinuclear plank from Pennsylvania, Tennessee, and Michigan. While there were no strong pronuclear groups within the Association (only Arizona and Colorado had refused to approve the antinuclear planks in the state conventions), ACORN groups in Missouri and Michigan, where there were strong union ties, advocated a more moderate stand. On the morning of the vote on the complete platform, the president of the North Carolina AFL-CIO, a staunch supporter of Carolina Action, addressed the convention, strongly urging that reference to nuclear power be deleted from the platform. Another member of the North Carolina delegation reiterated the merits of the antinuclear plank and demanded a vote by acclamation for its inclusion. Association President Steve McDonald, sensing the gravity of the situation, directed state chairs to count the ballots of their delegates. The measure passed three to one.

In all three of these areas, different factions struggling to move their agendas through the ACORN platform process created polarization and conflict within the organization. While it is true that each conflict resulted in a strong position on a key social issue, these positions cannot be accounted for by the general progressive nature of ACORN's national leadership. Rather, the victories can be attributed to the strong leadership roles of *local* leaders on *specific* issues. Those who had had experience in addressing a given issue were clearly, in the context of ACORN, the authorities on that issue. Therefore, while few individual leaders are necessarily progressive, socialist, or even left, their experience on specific issues gave them both the perspectives and legitimacy to push the organization to take a progressive stand.

The process did develop the knowledge and skills of both members and staff. It was no insignificant step to get low-income people to speculate on how banking *should* be regulated or how a national health plan conceived in their interests might work. ACORN members were given the opportunity to start with their own experience and expand the scope of their vision through a collective process— which culminated in a progressive social product.[16] However, in terms of advancing ideological unity within the organization, the platform was at best a starting place; at worst, it represented a hodgepodge of progressive notions with no underlying ideology. Sidestepping some major social issues, it allowed ACORN members in Memphis to be strongly in favor of local control of school spending while avoiding the issue of busing. Similarly, members in Texas could support requiring big corporations to include working-class and low-income representatives on their boards and support basing renewals of bank charters on the bank's performance in the community, while they opposed Mexican immigration and the Equal Rights Amendment.

Like many populist organizations, ACORN had opted to preserve class unity by developing an anticorporate political program that did not directly address salient issues of race and sex. Moreover, the platform demonstrated both the experience of ACORN locals in specific areas, and an ambivalence between anticorporate populism and the social-democratic state. This confusion is reflected in the poetic preamble to the ACORN People's Platform, which defines the ACORN constituency as "the majority, forged from all minorities" that vows to "fight until the American way is just one way, until we have shared the wealth and won our freedom" and demands as the American birthright "the chance to be rich, the right to be free." ACORN, then, was able to advocate one of the most progressive policy platforms written by any group, yet unable to accommodate the differences within this majority of minorities. And surely a more succinct statement of the ideology of laissez-faire capitalism than "the chance to be rich" could not be formulated. It is this ambiguity that allowed ACORN President Steve McDonald to say, "We're not trying to take over. The establishment has a right too. But we want our fair share."[17]

JAMMING THE DEMOCRATS

Grassroots Mobilization

Almost immediately after the St. Louis convention, ACORN members began to mobilize on four fronts. First, local chapters were urged to tie the positions taken in the national platform to local campaigns and to have members with other organizational affiliations (labor, church, Democratic or Republican Party) seek support for the adoption of the ACORN People's Platform by the Democratic Party. The purpose of this tactic was to develop grassroots ownership of and familiarity with the newly adopted platform; it was achieved by a "pledge campaign" in which members of the ACORN People's Platform Committee (APPC) would ask church, labor, civil rights, and women's groups for endorsements. Once a local organization had endorsed the platform, it might also be invited to support a local ACORN campaign around redlining or the equitable distribution of Community Development Block Grant (CDBG) funds.

This effort was necessary to move on the second front: the allied mobilization, in which ACORN began forging local coalitions in order to run ACORN-affiliated but uncommitted delegates to the Democratic National Convention. To support this effort, ACORN moved to public questioning of both the regular party platform development process and the rules through which delegates were chosen for the Democratic Convention. Members also explored the possibility of gaining acceptance of ACORN platform planks by the Democratic Party. In attempting to do so, ACORN adopted an inside/outside strategy. The inside strategy was one of co-optation: ACORN organizers and leaders were encouraged to talk with sympathetic party delegates, opportunistic candidates, and members of the Democratic Socialist Organizing Committee (DSOC), who, after years of hard work, had managed to capture a quarter of the seats on the Democratic platform committee. DSOC was helpful in ascertaining where there might be support for the ACORN platform and in assessing the Association's ability to elect delegates to state and local conventions.

The outside strategy reflected movement on the third front. Using the campaign tactics mentioned at the beginning of this chapter,

ACORN would identify, isolate, and ice (the three I's) uncooperative party members. Since the inside strategy was not available to ACORN in the Republican Party, the fourth front employed the politics of confrontation there as well, in an effort to maintain the avowed bipartisian nature of the campaign and secure representation at the July 1980 Republican convention.

One key factor in mobilizing platform support and polarizing the issues within the Democratic Party was ACORN's relations to other interest groups with more party clout, particularly labor. In a memo entitled "Building the Union Component into every ACORN Campaign," Danny Cantor, ACORN's head organizer in St. Louis, observed, "The more that labor realizes it doesn't really have power on the hill, and the more they realize that capitalism ignores OSHA [the Occupational Safety and Health Act], then the more they are driven back to the grassroots level where militant stands might be taken." Citing his own experience with an ACORN right-to-work campaign in St. Louis, Cantor noted, "We published one editorial and did one two-person action against the electric company for contributing to the right-to-work people. Labor appreciated the endorsement—but absolutely flipped out over the action." Pushing the point even further, he argued:

> These are not revolutionary times, so neither the unions nor ACORN are revolutionary organizations . . . though labor is heavily invested in the mythology of labor/ management cooperation, the labor movement is objectively on our side. We cannot do away with their worldview but we can . . . create situations that change the way discourse is conducted by opening things up for our own membership and theirs [in a way] that moves both organizations to a more radical plane. Gortz calls it pushing for non-reformist reforms, and it means raising demands and programs that do not accommodate themselves to the capitalist system, though their implementation does not in itself mean the downfall of the system. Pure lifeline is non-reformist since it predicates a utility

rate structure based on something other than capitalist rationality, anti-redlining campaigns are reformist as they don't really challenge control of investment . . . etc.[18]

Cantor's memo is interesting for several reasons. First, in the example he uses, ACORN was not the major actor but a supporter of another organization's campaign. Second, this was one of the few memos other than Rathke's that actually addressed movement-building as opposed to organizational development. Third, it has openly leftist overtones, including its reference to Gortz, a Marxist theorist. Fourth, it criticizes—though lightly and indirectly—some of ACORN's victories as reformist while defining some new standards on which to evaluate campaigns. The ACORN staff found the memo useful as nuts-and-bolts guidelines for building alliances with labor; the points it raises, however, will be at least as useful in evaluating the totality of the campaign.

Shift in Strategy

In attempting to carry out the platform mobilization strategy, ACORN ran into some unexpected difficulties. While the campaign was in part designed to consolidate the organization through the development of a national focus, there also had to be concrete gains. Prior to the fall of 1979, the goal was to win platform concessions from the Democratic Party and claim any changes as an organizational victory. Such concessions would legitimate ACORN and any fights it might make for future concessions.

By September 1979, however, two other factors had emerged that had not been initially taken into account. First, Ted Kennedy decided to run. Since the platform strategy hinged on the assumption that Carter was a relatively solid incumbent and that as a candidate forum, the primaries would prove fairly boring, Kennedy's announcement posed problems: not only was the drama of the campaign refocused on candidates as opposed to issues, but many of

ACORN's constituents favored the Kennedy candidacy and were interested in an ACORN endorsement.

The second unexpected development was an even greater problem: the Democratic platform committee was chaired by one of ACORN's chief nemeses, an ex-UAW organizer who had allied himself with General Motors in his rebuilding of Detroit: Mayor Coleman Young. Young and ACORN had already locked horns on many issues, especially during the 1979 struggle around the expansion of General Motors into an ACORN neighborhood, when Young and his deputy, Richard Simmons, had labeled ACORN organizers "outside agitators." The local group had been successful in that instance in winning its demands for relocation help and adequate compensation for homes lost to GM expansion. The organization's continued opposition to any Detroit "revitalization" that did not include the interests of low-income people earned ACORN Young's personal and permanent enmity.

Faced with the Kennedy candidacy and the intractability of Coleman Young in regard to any ACORN-initiated platform changes, ACORN convened a meeting in October 1979 to consider a new strategy. Jon Kest, head organizer in Philadelphia, suggested that the issue on which to base the campaign was representation of poor people on the delegate ballot. Utilizing a passage in the party rules (discovered by ACORN's research department) that prohibited discrimination "on the basis of race, sex, color, national origin, religion, ethnic identity or economic status," Kest argued that the language of the rule gave ACORN a tactical means of organizing its members and other groups to push for the increased representation of low-income people in the party.

Specifying the direction of his proposal, Kest recommended a shift away from platform or plank approval to the creation of a special commission within the Democratic Party to facilitate greater participation by low- and moderate-income people. Veteran organizer Mark Splain, cofounder of Massachusetts Fair Share and regional director for ACORN's northeastern states, backed the commission idea as a viable and desirable alternative to the platform plan; he argued not only that this strategy would give ACORN access to the party but that the success or failure of such a commission could "set the party up" as a target for further actions. Dewey Armstrong, head organizer of Florida ACORN and a strong supporter of the idea, pointed out that, given the splits within the party, a commission was one way for disenfranchised Democrats of both the Kennedy and the Carter camps to support party reform in an area where all factions seemed to agree—the inclusion of more low-income people in the party. The key rationale for the strategic shift, however, was provided by research director Seth Borgos: "Fighting for a commission for our people to be represented within the Democratic Party is both consistent with ACORN's politics and within the experience of the members of the organization—people are less sure about their right to demand seats on corporate boards [a plank in the ACORN platform] than a seat in the government that's supposed to regulate that corporation."

The proposal drew majority support at the October meeting, and the decision was to up the ante on the allied pledge to an "ACORN Commission": to make the commission a demand at all meetings with Democratic Party officials, and to attempt to secure support from "potential delegates and anti-Carter forces within the Party."[19] The strategy had all the requisites of a good campaign. The commission was an immediate, specific, winnable demand; it was within the experience of the Democratic Party to grant such concessions; and the ACORN membership could be mobilized for something they were truly interested in: their ability to influence Democratic Party politics.

Following up on this strategy shift, Dewey Armstrong was moved to the national office in New Orleans to coordinate the commission thrust, and Judy Meredith, a Massachusetts-based lobbyist with four years of experience in Democratic politics, was hired to woo Kennedy and Carter to the commission bandwagon. By February of 1980, the stepped-up pledge campaign to support the ACORN Commission was opening up an organizing opportunity that had not, at least earlier, been seriously considered: the chance for ACORN to win victories in local units of the Democratic Party.

In a *Village Voice* article entitled "It's Now or Never in Iowa: Door to Door with ACORN," Alexander Cockburn and James Ridgeway noted that ACORN had collected 2,000 pledge cards and could produce six hundred people at the primary caucuses in Des Moines and Davenport.[20] Similar stories in the *Valley Tribune* (Nevada), *Tulsa World* (Oklahoma), and *Telegram* (Bridgeport, Connecticut), plus the triumph of Detroit ACORN in controlling a significant percentage of the votes in Coleman Young's back yard, led ACORN to be more assertive about the commission.

These victories, coupled with Kennedy's, McGovern's, and Maynard Jackson's endorsements, made the commission a definite possibility for adoption at the August Democratic Convention. The general disarray of the Democratic Party also helped to advance the commission. A series of local actions aimed at embarrassing prominent Democrats—including the planting of ACORN's "planks" on the lawn of a prominent party official in St. Louis, a sit-in in the office of Democratic National Committee chairman John White, and interruption during Rosalyn Carter's speaking engagements in Arkansas and Connecticut—caused sources within the DNC to claim that "ACORN could have had the damn Commission in November of '79—if they had only promised not to embarrass the national Democratic leadership." A Kennedy campaign source said "Commission, hell, we were ready to do some real horsetrading, but ACORN wanted us to endorse their Commission without endorsing our candidate."

The DNC's hindsight had not been reflected in the July 9th meeting of the Democratic Rules Committee. Dewey Armstrong, the ACORN '80 campaign coordinator, described that meeting:

> The greased pig (slippery from being passed around from the Democratic National Committee's Task Force on Membership, Rules Committee, and various operatives from both the Carter and Kennedy campaign camps) finally ended up at a rules committee meeting where Task Force chair Paul Tipps who is also a Carter supporter tried to line up the Carter supporters to help him figure out the cleanest way to butcher it. . . . five hours

later the ACORN Commission sailed through the committee and Tipps actually made the motion. The actual turning point was the lunch break when Kay Thomas, a Carter rules committee member from Florida (and a staunch ACORN supporter) was able to "convert" Tipps as well as demonstrate sufficient support for the commission among other already-organized Carter delegates. This demonstration of support, coupled with the already organized Kennedy delegates who made up a third of the committee, secured the necessary votes on the commission.[21]

Clearly, the insider strategy paid off: by early July the commission was almost in ACORN's hands.

The Republican Strategy

Not being in a position to pursue an inside strategy with the Republican Party, ACORN applied tactics similar to those used on Democratic Party officials. Republican officials were embarrassed all over the country—without benefit of the backroom organizing that had both persuaded and smoothed the ruffled feathers of the Democrats.

In addition to the almost totally confrontational nature of ACORN's Republican campaign, there was an interesting difference related to the principle of "political payback." Since the Republican Convention was to be held in Detroit, ACORN used the event to embarrass the organization's old enemy, Mayor Coleman Young. In a public letter to the mayor written in July 1979, a full year before the convention, ACORN demanded to know:

> —What efforts will be made to see that some of the convention dollars make their way into the low- and moderate-income neighborhoods of Detroit?

—About 2,600 police will be used for security during the convention. Will police be drawn away from the neighborhoods for convention duty?
—Convention delegates will use Department of Transportation buses to get from place to place. Will regular public [buses] be taken off their regular routes during the convention?[22]

Two weeks later, on 31 July 1979, thirty ACORN members stormed into the Detroit Convention Bureau to dramatize their demands.

ACORN's Republican options were fairly bleak at first, however. A letter to Republican National Committee Chairman Bill Brock had received no reply, and the disruption of a September 1979 Republican fund-raising meeting in Memphis had produced only the promise of a meeting—which never materialized. Then, at an ACORN executive board meeting in October 1979, the idea of getting Republican delegates to "tour the real Detroit" emerged. Board members from nineteen states voted to send as many as three hundred ACORN members to the convention and to arrange for liberal Republicans to tour Detroit's worst neighborhoods "to point out the need for action on our platform planks."[23]

After disruptions and demonstrations against prominent Republicans and at Republican Regional Platform Committee hearings in Philadelphia, St. Louis, and Davenport, Iowa, ACORN secured a commitment from Senator John Tower (Texas), chairman of the Republican platform committee, that ACORN would be able to address the committee in Detroit. This success was coupled with the much-publicized tour of the "real Detroit" in which fifty Republicans, twenty-five ACORN members, and thirty reporters were given a view of the city's worst neighborhoods and an estimated cost of neighborhood rehabilitation compared with money spent on the convention. The tour was reported by the *New York Times*, the *Oakland Tribune*, the *Detroit Free Press*, and both wire services, and ACORN leaders from the Detroit area were interviewed on local television and radio and on the *Today* show. Thus, the same convention that nominated Ronald Reagan also aired the ACORN platform and was the means to national publicity specifying the contradiction between Detroit's fiscal policies for the Republican party and the policy imposed on its own low-income residents.

On the Democratic side of the ledger, by July 1980, ACORN had elected forty-two delegates and alternates to the Democratic Convention in New York, secured support for the ACORN Commission from thirteen state delegations, and mobilized its membership for ACORN's own convention, scheduled for New York a few days before the Democratic National Convention.[24]

The Democratic Convention and Its Aftermath

As predicted, the ACORN '80 campaign, with its mobilization of 1,500 ACORN members, 200 staff people, and 150 supporters, put tremendous strain on the personnel and financial resources of the organization. Although ACORN had held national conventions in Memphis in 1978 and in St. Louis in 1979, the expenses for them had been offset by two factors. First, they were held in the South, in cities where ACORN had organizational bases; therefore, travel costs could be minimized, and local "in-kind" resources such as food, housing, and telephones could be secured. Second, both conventions were supported in part by foundation grants, and local fund-raising helped pay delegates' expenses.

ACORN's 1980 convention had neither of these advantages. Having no organizational base in New York, ACORN was forced to split the advance operation into three units operating out of the Downtown Welfare Advocacy Center in lower Manhattan, Riverside Church in upper Manhattan, and Fordham University in the Bronx. In addition, financial sources within the foundation world had already contributed to the two ACORN conventions, and this fact, combined with the attempts of many groups to raise money for New York counter-conventions, made foundation and church sources slim pickings. The financial strain was exacerbated by ACORN's struggle to get the DNC to implement a recommendation of the McGovern

Rules Commission that 8 percent of the money spent for the convention be reserved for low-income delegates. Paul Tipps, chair of the DNC's study committee on the commission, promised that the DNC would "do its damnedest" to get funding, but the money never materialized.

Outlining this bleak financial situation in a memo three weeks before the New York convention, Rathke noted that transportation alone would cost between $92,000 and $115,000, while operating expenses in New York could run another $40,000. In a move to avoid a predicted $65,000 shortfall, he cut staff salaries an average of $100 per organizer per month. Balancing the potential of staff disenchantment and financial hardship against the possibility of some members being unable to attend the convention, he wrote, "It is clearly more acceptable in my view that 200 staff would be adversely affected than that 500 members would be potentially disaffected."[25]

This financial strain notwithstanding, ACORN planned to go to New York with two demands to be made on the Democratic delegations of twenty-four states: (1) that the delegations support the rules committee report that would establish the Commission on Representation of Low- and Moderate-Income People; and (2) that the commission be fully implemented and operational by November of 1980.

Experiencing two bus breakdowns and ninety-five-degree heat, 1,500 ACORN members arrived in New York on August 10 and took up temporary residence at Fordham University in the Bronx. Remembering the thirty-six-hour bus ride from New Orleans, Terry Sheehan, a young organizer originally from Boston, stated, "Many people had never even been to New York. The spirit on the bus was tremendous—everybody felt that ACORN winning representation from the Democrats was a big thing."[26] Western Regional Director Mike Shea had another view: "Logistics in New York City was bound to be crazy—we were already 90% sure of the Commission being passed—the key question was, could we take credit for it and get the hell out of New York without losing our shirts?"[27] Jay Hessey, veteran organizer of Carolina Action, had a different concern: "Will this action really consolidate the organization?" Riding the bus from Durham, Hessey had no doubt that the North Carolina contingent was heavily supportive of the commission and the platform. "The *real* question," he continued, "is whether we'll come out of this as a national organization or three hundred local groups winning the hell out of stop signs."[28]

ACORN's agenda for the three days in New York was simple. ACORN would have its own counterconvention, complete with speeches from New York City Councilwoman Ruth Messinger, Ruben Bonilla of the League of United Latin American Citizens, and Bill Lucy of American Federation of State, County, and Municipal Employees (AFSCME); ACORN would march on the Democratic Convention from the ACORN Convention Center in the Roseland Ballroom; and ACORN members would use the Roseland Convention Center as a base from which to sally forth and confront delegates about supporting the ACORN Commission.

Despite the logistical problems, the financial strain, and the ever-present humidity of a New York summer, on August 12 the Democratic National Convention voted to establish a commission to provide for the participation of low- and moderate-income people in the Democratic Party—the ACORN Commission.

After pushing the Democrats to agree to a commission, the next trick was to get the party to put enough resources and power into it to permit ACORN to move an agenda through the party. By March 1981, campaign coordinator Dewey Armstrong had delineated three primary demands that ACORN would attempt to wring from the party through the commission:

1. establish quotas for lower-income representation ("minimum standards") at party conventions and on central committees at all levels;
2. create Party Organizing Councils with authority in the party structure, directly representing organized groups within the low- to moderate-income constituency that would otherwise remain underrepresented;

JAMMING THE DEMOCRATS

3. once and for all, decisively remove all financial and procedural barriers that deny equal participation in party affairs to low- and moderate-income people, as called for in principle in the party charter for nearly a decade but still unfulfilled in practice (in other words, implement the 8 percent travel fund, hold weekend/evening party meetings and filing hours, etc.).[29]

The commission was to be chaired by Congressman Mickey Leland, a young black progressive from Austin, Texas, who had spoken in ACORN's behalf at the 1978 Memphis mid-term convention. It was the organization's hope that Leland's sympathy, coupled with ACORN's ability to continue to raise issues of low-income participation, would result in making such participation in the party meaningful. Leland, at ACORN's request, set up field hearings in Detroit, Little Rock, Houston, Los Angeles, and Chattanooga. It was at the Little Rock hearings in January of 1982 that he vowed to "fight like cats and dogs for solutions to the problems we've heard."

Two months later, the cats and dogs had been eaten by a hungry lion: after almost two years of agitation, the Democratic National Committee voted on 26 March 1982 to reject the recommendations of the commission (which were essentially ACORN's demands) and, instead, accept the recent recommendations of the Commission on Presidential Nominating Rules and the DNC's Executive Committee to add 548 uncommitted delegates (14 percent of the total convention) who were party regulars to the number of convention delegates. This DNC vote killed the ACORN Commission.

Adding Up the Score

The ACORN campaign was initiated in order to expand the organizational base of a community organization from three states in 1976 to twenty states in 1980, and to consolidate the local bases through a protracted confrontation with the Democratic Party. It was also intended to increase the ideological unity of the ACORN membership and break down "localism"; to build alliances with other groups—community, labor, minority, and women; and to bring about meaningful change within the Democratic Party.

It is clear that ACORN was successful in achieving its expansion and consolidation. This success was indicated not only by the presence of ACORN in twenty states in 1980 (now twenty-seven) but also by national press attention during and after the campaign. ACORN "arrived" enough to merit mention in the *New York Times*, *Wall Street Journal*, *Newsweek*, and *In These Times*; journalists in New Orleans, Houston, Colorado, and Oklahoma were initiating "investigative" feature stories on the origins of the organization. Even more important, ACORN's self-image had changed. The national staff was no longer an amalgamation of ex–lead organizers and hotshot researchers; it was a mature, battle-scarred operation that had coordinated delegate fights in over six hundred precincts in twenty states. Following the '80 campaign, the three statewide affiliates voted to add their ACORN affiliation to all their literature, and multistate campaigns are much more common now than they were prior to 1980. In the words of board member Mary Ellen Smith, "The issues we're fighting are bigger than our neighborhoods or even our cities, so it's definitely necessary to coordinate and plan our actions on the regional and national level."[30]

While the emergence of regional campaigns contributes to organizational unity, it does not necessarily help develop ideological unity. Work on the ACORN platform did foster internal debate and increase membership knowledge about a wide range of issues, but the platform remained an ideological hodge-podge. Still, the ACORN platform is not the only gauge of the organization's ideology. Embedded within the process of ideological development is the interrelationship of action and analysis. Seth Borgos, ACORN's research director, pointed out, "Over the last thirteen years we have increasingly targeted corporate sources directly instead of demanding regulatory intervention. Moreover," he argued, "we are tactically much more militant than other community organizations, in the South as well as the North."[31] While it is clear that tactical militancy does not necessarily relate to or translate into a progressive ideology, ACORN's recently launched multistate squatting efforts, in which low-income people in twelve cities are taking over abandoned houses, certainly demonstrates the organization's *attitude* toward private property and translates the attitude into action.

In building alliances with other organizations, ACORN was most successful with labor and church groups and, to a lesser extent, with local Democrats—although these groups were unhappy with ACORN's refusal to endorse a candidate. A top UAW official in Missouri was alternately miffed and mystified by ACORN's position on endorsements, remarking, "We were ready to go for the commission—but we were also committed to Kennedy."

Indeed, one has to question whether, in fact, by not endorsing a candidate, the organization truly took advantage of the presidential campaign to build ACORN. As coauthor of a memo that advocated a Kennedy endorsement, I'm satisfied that ACORN's support of Kennedy probably would not have had a significant effect on moving the organization's agenda, especially in the early stages of the campaign. The strategy on endorsements, however, is one of tactics rather than of principle; while it is true in the purest sense that issues should define and motivate the way people vote, the fact is that they largely do not. It may well be that an organization allied with the incumbent presidential candidate would have had a stronger hand at the initial rules committee meetings.

The factor that ACORN most miscalculated, however, was emerging trends within the party. ACORN tried to utilize vulnerable spots at the bottom—the local level—to dictate policy at the top at precisely the time the party regulars were attempting to close the openings created by the McGovern rules changes of 1972.

As for alliances, the nonendorsement strategy limited ACORN's ability to hold allies—especially labor—to working agreements; in St. Louis and Compton, California, UAW and Machinist locals pulled out of the uncommitted coalitions and attempted to run Kennedy-union slates. (In both cases, union candidates were defeated, and ACORN—in California, the affiliated Citizens' Action League—delegates won the convention seats.)

JAMMING THE DEMOCRATS

Some groups refused to ally with ACORN at all (most explicit was the statement from the Texas Women's Political Caucus, which initially chose not to support ACORN because the ACORN platform did not support the ERA),[32] and others that were organized around minority and women's issues did not support the ACORN platform. Therefore, while it is true that the ACORN '80 campaign built working alliances with many groups, and expanded its allied base significantly (probably 200 percent), it did not reach groups that ACORN traditionally did not have contact with. The ideological stance of the organization vis-à-vis issues of race and gender limited alliance, as did the nonendorsement of candidates.

As for bringing about meaningful change within the Democratic Party, ACORN won the first round by moving the commission, but it clearly lost the major struggle in the Democratic National Committee. There were at least three reasons for the loss. First, ACORN was swimming upstream against an overwhelming current within the party to block the infiltration of "outsiders" that had begun, many party regulars believed, with the McGovern rule changes. This current was actually supported by both Douglas Fraser and Lane Kirkland, presidents of the UAW and AFL-CIO, who approved the DNC recommendation for increased control by party regulars. The second reason has to do with the state of national politics: with Reagan's domestic and foreign policies adversely effecting low-income and minority groups, many organizations and individuals were running to embrace the Democratic Party, no questions asked. Third, though many members of the DNC were not opposed to the commission recommendations in principle, they were opposed to giving in to ACORN. Madeleine Adamson, ACORN's Washington, D.C. representative, noted that in her conversations with commission staff, the message was clear: "ACORN's demonstrated on us, maneuvered us and attempted to hold us hostage—we will not, therefore, give in to these demands."[33]

ACORN's inside/outside strategy of co-optation and confrontation did accomplish press coverage and led to the organization's obtaining a position from which to negotiate demands. But in the final analysis, it did not have either the external power to force the party to support its membership and allies or the internal status of an important "team" player to whom concessions might be granted in exchange for expected future favors.

Of course, another overriding reason for the commission's failure was that ACORN's demands were, in and of themselves, threatening to entrenched party regulars. Income quotas are tantamount to class quotas, and party organizing councils "directly representing organized groups" would have the potential to shift the balance of power within the party. In a meeting of the ACORN executive board in Washington, D.C., on 17 April 1982, Ron Brown, deputy chairman of the DNC, assured the board that ACORN had won a victory:

> For the first time low and moderate income people were singled out for special attention in the party by-laws. . . . A special task force will be appointed to monitor the participation of low and moderate income people and there will be a requirement for party outreach in the low and moderate income community. . . . A strong foundation was laid for assuring the participation of low income people in the party. . . . ACORN will see tangible results in sixty to ninety days.[34]

But Wade Rathke, ACORN's chief organizer, had a different evaluation of the situation: "The party was attempting to give ACORN the fast shuffle. . . . While we did get some language which will be useful in future actions on the party, we are clear that our interests were sold down the river to accommodate the new balance of power within the party."[35]

Internally, therefore, ACORN was able to use the campaign to develop organizationally, creating a unifying national focus, consolidating itself as a national organization, and making its regional and national actions more interesting to both the mainline and progressive media. The campaign did not, however, elevate ACORN into a movement.

JAMMING THE DEMOCRATS

Implications for Progressive Organizations

The achievements and failures of the 1980 campaign can be relevant to the future planning of many progressive organizations. First is the matter of emphasis. While ACORN had, in prior years, successfully elected local candidates, there was strong feeling within the staff and leadership that support for a presidential candidate would not build the power of the organization. This nonendorsement policy did allow ACORN to work with both Carter and Kennedy delegates, but since the party structure encouraged alliances based on candidates rather than issues, ACORN's nonendorsement strategy brought the organization minimal support, especially from the Carter delegates. In addition, most labor allies, the UAW in particular, were less ready to "go to the wall" with ACORN, given the organization's reluctance to endorse.

ACORN's approach to political parties, completely in line with its approach to other targets, was to create or uncover policy handles, then identify the enemy, isolate him, and ice him. This strategy was effective against both the Democratic and Republican parties to a certain extent. Besides mobilizing more than 10,000 people in the primaries, ACORN mobilized an equal number to picket, demonstrate, disrupt, and generally raise hell. Clearly the slot at the Republican Convention was due not to ACORN's power to pull Republicans to the polls but to its ability to embarrass key Republican figures— and the same is true of the Democrats. ACORN gained visibility at both conventions, and its demands were given at public airing. Pulling the campaign out of an arena where party politics controlled the rules of the game and where "third party actors" (allies and the media) could influence decision-makers was a key ingredient in advancing the campaign for the commission. At the bottom line, however, these tactics were not sufficient to wring more than symbolic concessions out of either party.

How could ACORN have been more successful? A more informed analysis of the Democratic Party would have helped at the beginning of the campaign, coupled with more experience in rules committee meetings. Possibly, though not necessarily, a Carter endorsement

JAMMING THE DEMOCRATS

would have been useful in the early stages but would not have been a factor by the time of the vote at the 1982 midterm convention.

In my view, the failure of the commission's resolutions in the Democratic National Committee was probably a blessing in disguise. ACORN had sufficiently penetrated the party apparatus to polarize the issue of low-income reprsentation into a "we (ACORN)—they (Democratic Party regulars)" adversary relationship that served to delegitimate the party in the eyes of the ACORN membership; it opened up the possibility of more militant action against the party in the future or more interest in participating in third-party efforts. A "win" in the DNC, on the other hand, would have reopened the question of party legitimacy and created the potential for co-optation of ACORN members.

To demonstrate to the organization's membership that their efforts were legitimate, ACORN's leadership had to claim a victory. To claim a victory—that is, to claim the commission—in the initial campaign was in some sense to legitimate the party, something ACORN certainly did not want to do. Yet the chances for co-optation were fairly small as long as the demonstrations and electoral work to gain the commission were still fresh in the minds of ACORN members. Had the commission's resolutions been passed by the party, however, the question would have become more complex: to what extent could ACORN really increase the power and influence of low-to-moderate-income people within the Democratic Party?

ACORN's real goals—and victories—in this campaign were internal; it served to consolidate the organization and test its ability to work in political alliances. At no time did ACORN expect to influence the outcome of the 1980 election. However, ACORN demonstrated the ability to be a significant player in national Democratic politics and that ability was a remarkable accomplishment for an organization only a decade old.

But the 1980 campaign was only the first step. ACORN's continuing efforts in recent years suggest some further important conclusions about the capacity of community organizations for political action and influence, as I'll examine in its 1984 campaign when it reversed its candidate-versus-issues position to support Jesse Jackson.

7

Cooperation in a New Political Climate

On the horizon we see more organized people, better campaigns, bigger victories, larger dreams, a more effective machine, a broader movement. These are the elements of ACORN's past, and they will be the driving force of our future. ACORN will either have it that way, or no way at all.
—ACORN Organizing Handbook, 1977

ACORN has been the Lone Ranger of the Left too long. . . . Unions, political allies and church support are all essential. We have developed the capacity to build these alliances but we have tended only to do so when we were up against the wall and knew we either had to have them with us or face the consequences. . . . We need some friends out there.
—"ACORN's Role in These Times"

Following the 1980 political campaign (which actually culminated in 1982), ACORN began an assessment of that campaign, the radically changed political climate, and its own organizational role vis-à-vis the development of a large-scale social movement. A major part of this evaluation was a look at the organization's relationship with other groups.

ACORN's tendency to work with some labor and church groups but to shy away from close ties with other community organizations

163

had political as well as "professional" roots. In an article, Wade Rathke quipped that organizers from other networks might characterize themselves as highly skilled, yet be "as conservative as Attila the Hun, as paranoid as Richard Nixon, as parochial as George Wallace, and as narrow as your grandfather's Hitchcock belt."[1] Rathke also criticized what he felt to be low standards and self-indulgence in other organizations:

> One still hears of people who have "burned out" in some mystical process that presumably sweeps our profession in epidemic fashion. Are our opponents so weak, or our victories so easily won that they only require short bursts of our energy rather than consistent work, month after month, year after year? Not only do we not confront that phenomena [sic], we do not even differentiate between organizers who work versus those who are retired; between those who work for organizations and those who work for themselves; between those who speak from a base and those who speak from bull. A false equity is not the "movement," it is only an operating hypocrisy. And worse, it waters down our work, allows seepage in our standards, and drowns our principles.[2]

Rathke's critique of conservatism and low standards did, in fact, reflect ACORN's view of many other community organizations, and this critical stance justified ACORN's "right" to expand into whatever geographic areas it deemed important without addressing the concerns of already existing groups. In 1978, ACORN's answer to the question of mutual interest was clear:

> And they cry "organizational arrogance" as if they weren't talking to themselves. And they cry "secrecy," as if any of us believed you were supposed to do a press release on every plan. And they cry "cooperate" as if they didn't mean affiliate. And they cry "coalition," as if that

COOPERATION IN A NEW POLITICAL CLIMATE

isn't an organization, or as if all of us had forgotten that one joins coalitions to borrow power, not to loan it. And they cry "for the people," as if they organized them. And they cry "what's the ideology?", as if they preferred rhetoric to the record of an organization's work and a people's struggle. And, when they cry, the best they should get is Kleenex, never consent.[3]

When ACORN was asked to join the Citizen Action Organizing Committee, Rathke's response to Heather Booth of the Midwest Academy stated that (1) the proposed organizing committee could not resolve problems of autonomy, independence, and internal accountability sufficiently to act as a national organization; (2) the formation was premature in terms of broad individual and organizational interests; and (3) the very agenda of moving toward a national organization will not move organizations or networks that have not yet come to see the importance of such a vehicle for their membership.[4] In this same vein, a memo by Rathke and Larry Ginsberg (of the ACORN research department) indicated that coalitions in general still did not seem to be a path to power for ACORN. Coalitions should be seen differently only when ACORN-led and developed.[5]

Because ACORN decided to organize in Boston—a stronghold of Massachusetts Fair Share—in 1979 and has since begun organizing efforts in Ohio and New York (amid considerable controversy in the left/liberal media and funding communities), ACORN has defined organizational differences in strong language. As Rathke writes, "Obviously in organizing, you can't claim anything but what you can organize; and if you can organize it or have it already organized you don't even need to bother claiming it. If your eyes are bigger than your stomach, somebody else will eat your lunch."[6] Having eaten twenty lunches by the beginning of 1980, ACORN was beginning to suffer some of the political consequences of its uncompromising expansion: it was developing a reputation for being "sectarian and difficult to work with."[7]

COOPERATION IN A NEW POLITICAL CLIMATE

Toward a More Ecumenical Approach

Chief among the factors that changed ACORN's approach to dealing with other groups was a reassessment of the political climate and ACORN's ability to mobilize and allocate resources. In a March 1980 memo, ACORN's staff argued that the only successful campaigns imaginable in the next several years were those targeted to issues common across the country. It noted that (1) the impact of energy development was producing fundamental social dislocation in the western countryside in the same way that it produced neighborhood dislocation in the cities; (2) the ACORN constituency was trapped in the secondary labor market; (3) anger was moving issues into the streets; (4) racial politics were in confusion since the election of black officials had not mitigated urban dislocation.

> Over the longer run we do not believe people's struggles against rising odds will be containable.... This localism cannot be allowed to remain provincial. The constituency must be educated to understand the full dimensions of the smallest stop sign campaign and its relationship to shrinking public services, the regressive tax base, and the voracious demands of downtown developers. Organizers are at first going to have to work close to home, but at the same time they are going to have to organize with their eye on the whole constellation of city, state, region, and nation.
> On the bottom line, we've got to believe that given the existence of the issues and the anger, even on low heat, *the eighties will ultimately boil* [emphases added].[8]

In a followup memo in June 1980, Rathke contended that after ten years of practice, ACORN dominated community organization. "It is true that we have not yet acquired hegemony over many currents of change (but) with continued growth, multi-faceted activity ... this hegemony would be achievable." He concluded, "*The first run is being part of the agenda. The next step is setting the agenda"* (emphasis added).

Within ACORN, then, two questions became important: what was the shape of the emerging movement, and how could the organization ride the crest of the new wave of discontent? Steve Bachmann, one of ACORN's attorneys and a political strategist, developed an early evaluation of the Reagan victory in December 1980. Citing Tom Hayden's assertion, published in the *Wall Street Journal*, that liberals had "lost god, the flag, national defense, personal safety and tax relief to conservatives," Bachmann echoed Hayden's question: "Why should they be entrusted with the authority to govern?" Noting that the New Right had won the election not so much by converting new people as by organizing and directing an existing constituency, Bachmann argued that the left in general and ACORN in particular needed to build their base, using a sprinkling of Jeffersonian rhetoric wedded to a measure of Old World organizational discipline. In sum, Bachmann reasoned, the bad public policy of the Reagan administration might produce a good organizing climate—so ACORN should solidify its base and get ready to move.[9]

In an early attempt to take advantage of Reaganomics, the Association board voted in October 1981 to initiate campaigns concerning community development cutbacks, housing, health care, AFDC cutbacks, and education cutbacks. ACORN managed to initiate local fights around community development and to raise questions about national housing policy through its squatting campaigns, which culminated in a four-day tent city in Washington, D.C., in the spring of 1982 that was reminiscent of the Poor People's Campaign. However, while exploration of these issues could have national impact, none of them had the potential to change the scope or image of the organization. The issues outlined in 1980's speculative memos that might have changed its image—a massive welfare rights campaign and a Latino civil rights campaign in the Southwest—were conspicuously absent from the issue lineup endorsed by the Association board in October 1981.

Looking at the rise of social unrest through 1981 and the first part of 1982, however, Rathke produced a memo that equaled the bold sweeping strokes of his 20/80 plan of 1976. Entitled "ACORN's Role in These Times,"[10] it provoked discussion about the possibility that ACORN might play a pivotal role in movement consolidation.

The document begins with a survey locating and defining four tendencies: (1) Reagan's role in precipitating mass social dislocation; (2) the rise in antiwar activity as well as the heightened pace of antinuclear mobilization; (3) the disarray of the left, "a scramble of voices without bases, ad hoc outfits without ongoing programs and agendas, often leaderless and anti-organizational and, as always, ambitions and unaccountable"; and (4) ACORN's increased ability to pull large numbers on well-defined campaigns. Arguing that "we have witnessed people mirroring economic uncertainty" and declaring that ACORN has been the "Lone Ranger of the Left for too long," the memo goes on to mark a shift in ACORN's external relations on two levels: the organization's alliances and its role in a broader movement:

> Though we have an organization, I think it is probably time we build a network. I am *not* arguing that we have been hurt by the thinness of our alliances, but neither have we been *helped* as much as we might have needed from time to time from campaign to campaign. Certainly, where we have spent the effort during 20/80 and on other campaigns to put together the extra pieces with strong alliances, we have improved our protection and legitimacy, even when it didn't necessarily make the difference between winning and losing. At the least we have learned that *politically* and *financially* our operations with broad-based friendships, alliances, and networks of support, have been stronger than our organizations with a narrower base of assistance. Unions, political allies, and church support are all essential. We have developed the capacity to build these alliances, but we have tended to only do so when we were up against the wall, and knew we either had to have them with us or face the consequences. Where we have not had an immediate, organizational

COOPERATION IN A NEW POLITICAL CLIMATE

need, we have tended to allow these relationships to atrophy too often, and have sometimes lost the strength they can lend because of our own transitions and lack of maintenance.

We need some friends out there among the array of independents. We already have some, but we involve them little to none. We could be helped by having other organizations involved in the community development effort, the squatting campaign, perhaps even in the 84 activity within the Democratic Party.

Recommending a series of exploratory meetings locally and nationally to signal this changing policy, as well as some participation in events the organization would normally have ignored, Rathke also suggested proposing a major joint organizing campaign with other networks for 1983.
Assessing the organization's internal ability to mobilize around antiwar concerns, he wrote:

> (1) the work of the religious community has focused and legitimated concern for these issues where they worship, (2) our Hispanic membership is more interested because they (and we) are more familiar with the issues and commonality of people in Central America than was true for the Vietnamese, (3) our people are understanding more clearly the increase in military expenditures under Reagan with the cutbacks in social programs, and (4) the increasing domestic unpopularity of the El Salvadoran war effort is coupled with fears that the draft will as always call our people heavily to serve and die, if intervention increases. True or false, we would have to cut the actions and campaigns in such a way that we were sure of our constituency first, and mobilizing others secondly.

Although he noted that there were significant external barriers to movement into antiwar or disarmament organizing, including the potential structural clashes over consensus decision-making within the antinuclear movement and general suspicion of ACORN, he concluded, "Clearly we are going to find a mainstream within this movement where we can speak the same language and move in a concerted fashion." As to the other movement-building ventures, Rathke asserted that ACORN is on strong ground organizing around budget cuts as well as moving the ACORN constituency closer to efforts in minority and women's organizations.

In summary, the memo argued that ACORN should be in the vanguard of movements for social change in the United States, should reshape its program around building alliances both inside and outside community organization, and should develop a strategy of specific campaigns and direct action tactics, including a plan for the 1984 presidential election.

> Strategically, I think one contribution we make as a player in building a network of broader movements is in fact making the issues, strategy, tactics and demands more real, specific and concrete, thereby increasing their appeal not only to our people but to all people, making the fight more winnable, which after all is part of what it should be all about.

Internal organizational conditions also contributed to the decision to develop positive relations with other groups. First, the pace of ACORN's 1976–80 growth had been both fast and grueling, and after 1980 the ACORN staff had to recommend a slowdown in the expansion process. ACORN was having difficulty maintaining organizers in some cities: in 1983 a number of offices were unstaffed for months. Contributing to this difficulty were the gradual exit of organizers who had joined ACORN just for the 1980 push; the cutoff of the VISTA contract, which at its height had paid the salaries of one hundred volunteers; and a slowdown in the recruitment rate as fewer young college students were eager to join up and "put out" for ACORN.

COOPERATION IN A NEW POLITICAL CLIMATE

The gap in resources was exacerbated by the loss of several key senior staff people. Seth Borgos, research director and important political strategist, left after over ten years with ACORN. Madeleine Adamson, ACORN's Washington political operative, left after seven years. Regional director John Beam, political director Dewey Armstrong, former St. Louis organizer Danny Cantor, and comptroller Sue Bissenden—with eight or more years' experience each—left the organization between 1982 and 1984. Though many of the vacant positions have been filled with competent people, the loss of so many experienced staff has had a negative impact on remaining staff, lessened the organization's ability to function coherently, and externally raised questions about ACORN's stability.

None of these staff people claimed to leave for reasons of political difference with ACORN. John Beam, now working with solidarity groups in Latin America, wrote "I wanted an opportunity to actually *see* somewhere where they'd had a successful revolution.... I was also getting stale and thought I needed a different experience."[11] Danny Cantor sees his new job as director of the National Labor Committee in Support of Democracy and Human Rights in Latin America as an opportunity to work with the same constituency on different issues. Madeleine Adamson and Seth Borgos have finished a book on social movements in which ACORN is prominently featured. Though there are no hard feelings, the organization's capacity for effective action has been at least temporarily reduced by the loss of these staff people. ACORN's failure to sustain cadre staff after the 1980–82 political peak may indicate a need for internal restructuring.

Another area of internal concern has been problems in relationships with groups that "merged" with ACORN during the 1980 campaign, partly because each one had slightly different roots, styles, and emphases. Staff of the California Citizen's Action League (CAL) and Georgia and Carolina Action had developed different perspectives on the issues of wages, and hours, and fund-raising; they had developed a sophisticated canvassing procedure that supported over 80 percent of their expenditures. This meant that the canvass staff would, at times, dominate the political direction of the organization because they raised the money. ACORN, on the other hand, although it attempted to institute a canvass in every area possible, placed the burden of local fund-raising (between $600 and $1,000 a month) on the organizers, in addition to their organizing responsibilities. The emphasis on membership dues figured in terms of a per-organizer quota per month was unacceptable to both CAL and Carolina Action, as well as to a number of regular ACORN organizers. In addition, since the quotas were not strictly applied to "national" staff, tension emerged between the Association staff and local organizers.

1984 and Beyond

Given these problems and its expanded political vision, how has ACORN been able to develop in the 1980–84 period? The organization may well have sacrificed some local effectiveness in order to become a "player" on several national fronts. In the 1984 election campaign, for example, ACORN not only endorsed Jackson and joined the Rainbow Coalition but actually ran the Jackson campaign in New Hampshire and played a key role in the Arkansas and Michigan campaign efforts. ACORN also worked actively in voter registration efforts in all 27 states where it has organized. Its participation in the Jackson campaign was partly a direct result of the organization's interest in developing more solid ties with other groups: as one organizer pointed out, "The Jackson campaign has mobilized a significant segment of the black community and ACORN could work with these new constituents to move on issues and build relations with existing black organizations."[12] A second reason for ACORN's work in the campaign was clearly the recruitment of members. ACORN will attempt to follow through on the electoral campaign to recruit members to local ACORN groups.

An example of national coalition building has been the ACORN-initiated "Alliance for Justice." Originally conceptualized as ACORN's bid to initiate a "dump Reagan" campaign, the Alliance— which was endorsed by over 150 local and national union, church, civil rights, women's, peace, and environmental organizations—

COOPERATION IN A NEW POLITICAL CLIMATE

evolved into a series of actions focused on the Republican National Convention in Dallas in the summer of 1984, including the erection of a tent city of low-income people in Dallas, a mass rally in opposition to President Reagan's foreign and domestic policies, a coordinated voter registration canvass, and a protest march to the official opening of the convention. These drew national media attention and were reported in the *Los Angeles Times*, the *New York Times*, and *Time* magazine. Capitalizing on the organization's role as the only visible opposition to the Republicans in Dallas, ACORN was able to develop local and national support for the effort, which "registered over 12,000 new low income and minority voters."[13]

Mike Shea, who coordinated the Dallas actions, noted:

> While it was significant that we registered opposition to Reagan's policies and we were successful in getting endorsements and registering voters, there are still many problems in this type of coalition. . . . Not the least of these included the condescending attitudes of many people in the peace movement towards ACORN's membership and the major hype out there in the whole voter registration game. For instance, one local group, which I won't name, got a lot of press coverage and free tickets for a registration effort scheduled to take place outside of a Michael Jackson concert. As part of the local Rainbow Coalition, eight ACORN members turned up to do some registration—three people from the organization that initiated the registration effort turned up, late, and all in all, we registered about seventy-five people in an hour. The next day their press release, which never mentioned ACORN, claimed that they'd registered 2,500 people. Unfortunately, that's typical—everybody's taking credit but few are doing the work.[14]

Voter registration, direct candidate endorsement, coalition-building—how did these activities become the major thrust of

ACORN's 1984 political efforts, and how effective were these strategies in reaching the organization's avowed goals? It is obvious that nobody dumped Reagan in 1984—but internal memoranda make it clear that ACORN's 1982 assessment of the political situation was that "only a miracle could unseat Reagan."[15] Why then, did the organization focus on a mobilization at the 1984 Dallas Republican Convention? As in 1980, the reasons were more internal than external. In 1984, however, ACORN entered the political arena with an analysis and strategy that were markedly different from those of the 1980 campaign.

First, the organization owned up to the fact that presidential campaigns are essentially centered on personalities and that ACORN did not have the capacity to make the campaign respond to issues, especially if the Democratic contender chose not to do so. Second, both staff and board ageed that ACORN should "endorse a candidate and work for who[ever] we endorse." Third, the massive anti-Republican rally in Dallas was seen as an opportunity to build a coalition against Reagan and to move with the coalition, no matter what the outcome of the election. Finally, the voter registration campaign was viewed as more than an opportunity to register voters. In concert with other national voter registration efforts, ACORN's agenda was to make registration into local campaigns in which barriers to low-income registration were uncovered and local ACORN groups could target voter registrars for direct action.

Has ACORN's three-pronged strategy for building the organization worked in the context of the 1984 campaign? Yes and no. ACORN's Alliance for Justice has secured individual and organizational endorsements and developed working relations around specific actions. However, consolidating those endorsements and actions into a national organizing agenda will prove much more difficult. Many of the peace groups, in particular, don't really have a developed constituency, and there are economic issues on which the components of a progressive coalition-minority and women's groups, unions, church and community organizations—simply have not reached agreement. The dump-Reagan movement may have been the necessary glue to form an initial coalition of progressive forces, but it is not sufficient to actually keep the coalition together and move an agenda.

ACORN's endorsement of Jesse Jackson was important internally and externally. Internally, Jackson was the overwhelming choice of the organization's membership, and many members were thus able to work in concert with both ACORN and other local organizations they belonged to (mostly church or civil rights groups) on registration and rallies. Externally, ACORN was able to join forces with a number of national black organizations, and as one of the first organizations to endorse Jackson, it had access to the Jackson camp on the way basic issues were framed—"although," Mike Shea notes, "Jackson was great on most of our issues even before the campaign."[16] ACORN was least able to realize direct organizational benefits from its efforts to register voters and get out the vote, and as part of a macro strategy to win the presidential election for the Democrats, clearly that campaign was a failure.

New Ties to Labor

An area where ACORN has made strides in improving relations with other groups is in labor organizing. In 1979, ACORN developed local efforts in New Orleans, Detroit, and Boston aimed at organizing low-wage workers in a variety of occupations, including fast food restaurant and hotel employees. Four years of organizing produced one union contract for cafeteria workers at Tulane University. (In a number of cases, Detroit and New Orleans especially, large union-busting firms were hired to thwart unionization efforts.) Nevertheless, the unionization campaigns were significant to the organization. First, they were initiated by Wade Rathke, which meant that the energy of the organization's most experienced organizer and ablest strategist was available to the union effort (correspondingly, his energy and talents were less available to ACORN). Second, they changed ACORN's relations with organized labor. The overall unionization efforts were developed under the name United Labor Unions (ULU), and some of ACORN's AFL-CIO supporters were initially leery of what they perceived to be dual unionism. To counter this charge, at least in New Orleans, Rathke built a coalition effort called TEAM (Teamsters ACORN Engineers Movement) that was sanctioned by both the local teamsters and engineers unions, who also agreed to contribute resources, though the bulk of resources and organizing was provided by ACORN. TEAM functioned the same way as the Citizens for the Abolition of Poverty, which had institutionally neutralized possible supporters of Arkansas's liberal Republican Governor Winthrop Rockefeller in ACORN's first campaign. In both cases, potential opposition was organized into an ACORN-controlled structure and neutralized.

With its unionization efforts, ACORN had two distinct operations and at least two ways to organize the same constituency: in the workplace and in the community. Interestingly enough, it was ACORN's expertise in the political/electoral arena that opened the doors to developing direct political ties with some unions. Coalition work in local campaigns often put ACORN on the same side as labor. These ties were strengthened by the work of Gerry Shea and Bill Pastreich, both ex–welfare rights organizers who had been founders of the initial organizing efforts of the Service Employees International Union (SEIU) in Boston. Shea set up a series of meetings and negotiations through which ACORN's ULU groups in New Orleans, Detroit, Chicago, and Boston became independent locals in SEIU. In the merger, ACORN's new Local 100 in New Orleans took over the jurisdiction of SEIU's already established locals; each of the other three cities was granted a three-year subsidy, and Mark Splain, a long-time ACORN organizer, joined the national SEIU staff in Washington, D.C. The merger, according to Rathke, allows ACORN the resources needed for effective union organizing. Bill Becker, a union ally of ACORN and president of the Arkansas AFL-CIO, noted:

> ACORN people are good organizers but this doesn't do any good unless you can service the people that you've organized. You have to know how to negotiate a contract and there has been no evidence that ACORN can do

COOPERATION IN A NEW POLITICAL CLIMATE

that. SEIU is good in the field and ACORN's affiliation with them is a positive step and shows good judgment on their part.[17]

Since 1980, ACORN has broadened its strategy and tactics considerably. It has entered new arenas, built alliances with groups it had previously been unable to work with, and become a significant though modest national force. This is a positive record in a period dominated by the Reagan administration and the upsurge of new conservative forces in American politics. The question now is whether ACORN's coalition, merger, and alliance strategy will help it make a qualitative jump from its history as a community organization to a future as part of the leadership of a major social movement.

8

Internal Organization and Social Structure

In our cities, in our states,
We're the ones that pay the freight,
But the rich folks go rolling along.

Keep us divided, whites from blacks,
Moderate and poor on different tracks.
And the rich folks go rolling along.
—ACORN Marching Song (to tune of the Caison Song),
ACORN Songbook, 1982

To assess ACORN's prospects, it is necessary to examine its internal organization, its staff/leadership/membership relations, its choice of issues and means of achieving its goals, its ideology, and its resources—and to observe how, in these various aspects, it interacts with the dominant external social structure.

The Social Composition of ACORN

In most community organizations, the roles of members, leaders, and organizers are markedly different. When asked to differentiate between group leaders and community organizers, Zach Pollett, regional director for six ACORN states, smiled: "Why, leaders lead and organizers develop leaders."[1]

INTERNAL ORGANIZATION AND SOCIAL STRUCTURE

Indigenous Leadership

Most of the CO literature is in agreement on a number of points regarding the role of leadership. First, leadership should be indigenous, composed of people from the neighborhood. Second, leaders are not born but developed, usually by organizers. Third, leadership is not structural; it is a function. As Meg Campbell writes in "The ACORN Maintenance Model":

> Leadership is something you do rather than a position or title you hold. It is something that happens in a group, not a particularly designated person with certain qualities. Leadership, then, is responding to the current needs of the group in such a way that the group is helped to go on with whatever task it has and to have its own needs met at the same time. A person is a leader when s/he offers help or services to a group in a way the group can receive.[2]

Within this short definition lie all the problems and contradictions of the organizer/leader dichotomy. The organizer who creates a formal structure with definitive participatory roles may then render the formal structure irrelevant in a particular situation by defining the terrain of discussion or steering the group toward a particular issue. "Responding to the current needs of the group" is, of course, a matter of judgment, and implicit in Campbell's statement is a notion of who has the real power to determine the appropriateness of a specific response: the organizer.

The organizer training schools are unanimously agreed that developing indigenous leaders is the toughest task of the organizer. Mike Miller has written that organizers find leaders by discovery (listening to what other members of the community say about a particular person) and observation (watching leaders in meetings and while working within the group).[3]

"Leaders are developed through experience, mainly the experience of action," maintains Mark Lindberg of the New England Training Center. Therefore, he continues, the organizer should

(1) give potential leaders a job;
(2) create obligations for potential leaders;
(3) when possible, let people's peers convince potential leaders to act;
(4) when necessary, manipulate the situation;
(5) to get people into action, heighten their emotions;
(6) when possible, pick a leader who is directly affected by the issues;
(7) graduate leaders to new levels of experience.[4]

Steve Max of the Midwest Academy adds, "Developing leaders is like teaching singing, acting or painting. You can't create talent where none exists, but you can shape and develop what talent there is."[5]

None of the literature minimizes the importance of training leaders; in fact, it takes special care to define leadership development as the most important part of an organizer's job. Neil Gilbert, for instance, writes:

> Recruitment is a singularly arduous chore in a professional movement aimed at the poor; not only are the organizers outsiders, but the individuals they are seeking to enlist are predominantly nonparticipants. The task is difficult, but not insurmountable. Indigenous leaders may be uncovered and trained; and less articulate and less motivated members of the target population may be stimulated to participate. This process, however, is long-range, involving a concentrated commitment of time and energy, with no guaranteed payoff.[6]

What happens when leaders do get "developed"? One example of a seasoned leader is Willard Johnson, former chairman of Arkansas ACORN, a retired railroad blacksmith whose "enthusiasm for socialism," according to a *New York Times* interview, "is about as deep as Barry Goldwater's."[7] After becoming a member of the Quorum Court in 1974, Johnson won a seat on the Little Rock Planning

Commission. While he did talk out of one side of his mouth about the importance of the free enterprise system, in an interview I conducted with him in July 1979, he also talked about how his position on the Little Rock Planning Commission has allowed him to keep a freeway from being built through the center of town, and to make sure that residential neighborhoods were not down-zoned for commercial interests. Johnson is very clear about his blue collar status: "I'm the only peasant down there at City Hall. . . . My background is different; most of the other commissioners have had an educational advantage that I haven't had—they move in different social circles."[8]

Paul Cox, an ACORN leader in New Orleans and a tugboat captain, was moved to work for lifeline utility rates "because the company is a damn monopoly."[9] And in Bridgeport, Connecticut,

> Tom and Cathy Leehy of Remington Street said they have been fighting by themselves to no avail for better traffic signals and more signs in their neighborhood after their child was hit by a car. "At least we'll attempt as a group," said Leehy.
> "Before ACORN we all used to sit in front of our TVs at night and wait for something to happen."[10]

The good stories of leadership development are plentiful enough, yet clashes between staff and leaders have also affected the dynamic of developing the organization. For example, Bill Brookerd, former chair of Nevada ACORN, resigned in 1979 because he claimed he never had access to copies of the ACORN organizing model or financial information. Similarly, R. Walker, a former ACORN member and currently a Pine Bluff, Arkansas alderman, recalls having floor fights with organizer Madeleine Talbot over access to membership lists and dues receipts. Both of these incidents were coupled with charges of "organizer manipulation."

Barbara Friedman, a former ACORN trainer, remarked: "Manipulation can be an unrealistic hangup. A good professional organizer can tell early on who would make the best officer. We use common

INTERNAL ORGANIZATION AND SOCIAL STRUCTURE

sense and try to be sensitive to the feelings of the members, but we don't agonize and torture ourselves."[11] Friedman's approach is eminently practical, but how does it merge with the official line that "members run the organization"? It is clear that organizers play a role in choosing and developing group leaders; in selecting potential candidates, they look for specific skills such as the ability to talk to people in the neighborhood, being articulate, having time and energy and demonstrated ability to accomplish tasks. Because of ACORN's organizing approach, however, prior leadership of a community group, (as opposed to a labor or church organization) might actually rule out a candidate as an initial leader of an ACORN group. Extensive experience with a left political formation that had a "developed" ideological framework would almost certainly eliminate a neighborhood resident as an ACORN organizer's (and almost any community organizer's) candidate for a leadership position in a new ACORN group because of the possibility that such a leader would be pushing another organization's contradictory agenda. As a result, ACORN leaders with little or no prior leadership experience of any sort are very often voted into office by ACORN members.

This is both a plus and a minus for the organization. It is a plus because the leaders are truly indigenous grassroots people who can usually be developed effectively within the ACORN structure. It is a minus because very often such leadership brings no close connection to an existing infrastructure, and because people without previous organizational experience are less likely to challenge the assumptions and assertions of ACORN organizers, at least initially. Thus, while it is true that members do run the organizational meetings and take part in decision-making, it is equally true that the parameters of these discussions are set by the organizers. Given their experiential base, indigenous leaders are not in a position to challenge these parameters.

This rather obvious tension in the organization has manifested itself in several ways. First, seasoned ACORN leaders have repeatedly questioned the organization's commitment to hiring and training indigenous leaders as organizers. Rathke and others have articulated the hope that the sons and daughters of present members would choose to become staff organizers, but thus far ACORN has not achieved this goal. The problems of recruiting members as organizers include low staff salaries, class and racial differences that are actually exacerbated by the leader/organizer role relationship, and the inability of the organization to provide a social and cultural support system for non-white and low-income staff.

ACORN's difficulty in this area is not unique. In the context of another community group in Pittsburghs, Neil Gilbert observes:

> As organizers, nonprofessionals are often better equipped than the professionals for recruiting low-income participants, securing their trust, and activating their will to cooperate. The crucial factor is not the hiring of indigenous leaders, but the capacity in which they are employed. In Pittsburgh, the philosophy and structure of the program dictated that these individuals be skimmed off to expedite services rather than to organize a movement. As a result, *whatever time and effort went into recruitment and indoctrination were quickly dissipated* [emphasis added].[12]

While ACORN is unlikely to hire members to expedite services, it has occasionally—conscious of the need for constituent representation on the staff—precipitously thrust leaders into staff positions when they were neither technically nor ideologically prepared. The resulting level of friction was not simply over questions of access to information, manipulation, or even recruitment. These are, of course, vital issues. But more fundamentally, there are class and race differences between organizers and members that are generally not successfully overridden by any unifying, comprehensive ideology.

Scholar-activist Tim Sampson has written of "the need of the professional to define him or herself as of the people they are working with rather than a breed apart,"[13] but the predominant tendency in the world of community organizers, and particularly in ACORN, is to apply a rigorous division of labor. CAP leaders in Chicago, interviewed by Joan Lancourt in 1976, observed:

> The organizers did not speak in public, did not get their names in the paper . . . did not speak at meetings. [They] did the preparation work . . . research, getting the fliers out, arranging the meeting place . . . making sure people were coming . . . getting there early to set up the chairs. All that kind of stuff. Gradually, in the better CAP organizations more and more of that was transferred to the leadership.[14]

In my own interviews with ACORN leaders, I ran into an interesting set of perceptions. When asked to describe the staff functions, all eighteen leaders talked about "technical assistance and/or resource development." Yet when pressed, all but two admitted that virtually all the ideas for tactics and strategy in their last organizing campaign came from the organizer. Within ACORN, as within most large community organizations, organizers do in fact call the shots in terms of organizational direction; the organization has in fact become a staff oligarchy. That development is understandable: with greater size and complexity, increased specialization, and departmentalization, it is simply not possible for all members to possess enough of the relevant information for informed decision-making; therefore, communications increasingly flow from the top down.[15] Why, then, the ideological commitment to "the people decide"?

The history of community organization shows that, for the most part, there was no leader/organizer dichotomy in the early days of either the labor movement or the civil rights movement. The twin roles were actually developed in the early community organizations to address the question of the role of "social work" professionals in ghetto communities. The question surfaced anew in the civil rights movement when the need arose to define a principled role for people outside the constituency immediately affected: progressive whites. The role dichotomy was further reinforced in the merger of the

Alinsky-founded IAF with the Chicago SDS in the Citizen Action Program, where former SDSers felt compelled to define separate roles for organizers and leaders.

Within ACORN, the problems of class and race differences between leaders and staff also exist, but the leader/organizer role separation has defined interaction in an acceptable manner. In a frank moment, however, one organizer reflected, "It certainly is true that the organizer-leader thing is somewhat of a game—but it's a game that forces me to remember who I am and where I come from, a game I know how to play. Anyway, until I hear about another set-up that doesn't completely allow organizers to run roughshod over people, it's the only game in town."[16]

Given this situation, a fundamental question about the staff/leadership structure is this: has the indigenous leadership ever made a transition to exercising real political power, either through the formal leadership role or through taking over staff positions? For the most part, leaders who have joined the staff have actually had less power in the organization in their new positions. Very often the power of leaders is based on their relationship with a particular group. Joining the staff negatively affects that relationship. Becoming "paid staff" instead of "first among equals" in the community can set up real barriers between leaders-turned-organizers and their former constituents. Moreover, power on the ACORN staff is based on a number of other variables: seniority, the demonstrated ability to produce organizational victories, the ability to articulate a position or organizational direction and organize the staff to pursue it, and, perhaps most important, political proximity to the staff leadership.

Leaders joining the staff, with few exceptions, have been unprepared to deal with multilevel nuances, direct argumentative style, and protracted (often three-day and -night) meetings. While leaders have been able to push issues and agendas on a local level, no one leader has had a significant impact on the organization without the direct collaboration and support of the senior staff. This is not to say that ACORN's leaders do not influence the organization's direction; an example of a member/leader groundswell was the Jesse Jackson endorsement. However, even that endorsement—though initiated by activist leaders—was discussed, planned, and operationalized by the staff.

This observation points to an underlying structural fact: organizers, given their background, have had, in the words of the ACORN People's Platform, "the chance to be rich" and have chosen instead, at least temporarily, to work for what most members consider "beer money." Part of the ideological contradiction is that middle-class organizers who have rejected the organization's avowed goals of gaining economic benefits cannot blatantly direct low-income members who in fact enter the organization to make the system work in their interest.

In part, this motivational rift stems from the fact that some ACORN members are uncomfortable with the organization's tactics. On a more basic level, however, the cleavages between leaders and organizers are a reflection of differences in class, race, and sex between ACORN members and staff.

The Staff

ACORN's 50,000 members are 70 percent black and Latino, 70 percent female, and almost all from the working class (or reserve labor). In contrast, the 150-member staff is almost all white, about half female, and for the most part, from upper-middle-class families. Most organizers have college degrees, about 15 percent from elite institutions. While these statistics do not, of themselves, reveal anything but a contrast between the backgrounds of the staff and members, closer examination of the 1982 staff reveals that: of the nine field operations directors, all are white and two are women; four (all men) graduated from Ivy League colleges; three of the four directors of project categories—national operations, campaign operations, internal operations, and the United Labor Unions—are men, and all four graduated from elite institutions, two from Ivy League schools.

In small group discussions in the 1979–80 year-end/year-beginning meeting that included over 120 ACORN staff members, the primary reason given for working for ACORN, at salaries of $4–8,000, was that the kind of organizing ACORN was involved in really worked. In keeping with the ACORN line "mouth—good; action—better," organizers came to ACORN to be part of something that worked.

But how long do organizers stay? ACORN recruits some sixty to seventy-five per year, most of them fresh out of college. The majority, probably 70 percent, don't make it through the first three months, often being surprised by the sheer amount of work, the discipline, and the number of times people will assure them that they will "definitely be there" for a meeting and then fail to appear. Those who progress through the first drive usually begin to reevaluate their commitment again at six months. This time the question is more likely to be: "Can I really become an organizer?" About four out of five trainees who make it through three months will stay through their first year's commitment. After a year, the major question becomes: "Do I really want to organize with ACORN?" Unfortunately, once again, the fallout at this stage is great: almost half of the remaining trainees will leave, usually to work in social-change jobs "where the money is better and the hours are fewer."

There are, of course, other career junctures in ACORN. The decision to have or expand a family may influence an organizer to resign, while the recent decision of three key staff people to "take a break" after ten years reflects the pace and constant demands of the organization. In sum, the rate of turnover, especially initially, is quite high.

Nevertheless, ACORN has probably produced more trained local organizers than any other network of community organizations, and many continue to do social-change work. Ann Lassen, a former ACORN recruiter, explained, "We look for people who are right out of college who want experience, or people who don't like traditional jobs and are searching for something more creative." When asked about the ability of ACORN to recruit people from low-income backgrounds, Lassen admitted problems. "But it isn't just the money," she added. "The work schedule, collecting money from members, the level of responsibility required of new recruits is fairly intimidating to everyone—people with little experience with that kind of time and energy commitment to work usually don't last."[17]

INTERNAL ORGANIZATION AND SOCIAL STRUCTURE

What kind of people do last through the rigorous recruitment and training process? Kopkind writes:

> The organizers come from out of state, for the most part: Steve Holt and Meg Campbell, for instance, went to Harvard and Radcliffe, and both taught in Massachusetts before settling in Arkansas. Barbara Friedman went to the University of California at Berkeley, heard about ACORN in a Vocations for Social Change publication, and came to Little Rock to check it out; she stayed. The out-of-state organizers seem to have come with no heavy ideological baggage. They are not radical intellectuals who see their work "among the people" as direct steps to a predictable revolution. They clearly express a radical sensibility; most are recognizable children of the movements of the sixties, but not adherents to particular sects. Perhaps they are the kind of people who would have been Peace Corps volunteers in 1963. But the social history of the last decade has given them a different political context for their interest in community development.[18]

Examples include Phil Moore, who used to work in Boston but moved to Detroit to put his planning degree to better use; Val Orselli, who came to work for ACORN after reading about the organization in *Working Papers*; and Terry Sheehan, who came as a VISTA volunteer and stayed on "to do some real organizing."[19] While the managing editor of the *Pine Bluff* (Arkansas) *Commercial* has called ACORN organizers "damn Yankee know-it-all kids who would come in and tell us how to run things,"[20] Denver city councilmen Sal Carpio says, "They're pros—they really push to keep everybody on their toes."[21]

In part, this push comes from the example set by ACORN's thirty-six-year-old chief organizer, Wade Rathke. Rathke is a native of New Orleans, where he attended Benjamin Franklin High School, a public school that caters to children with IQs of at least 120. His mother, a junior college administrator, holds a Ph.D. in English, and his father is an accountant for a large oil company. Rathke fits the profile of the young radical. While he did spend two years at Williams College as a member of the local SDS chapter, he also worked as a draft counselor, rock band manager, and journalist. Lanky and red-headed, with a prominent Adam's apple, Rathke is prone to pithy, down-home proverbs and cowboy boots. While many activists describe him as arrogant and obnoxious, even his enemies in the organizing world will grudgingly admit his accomplishments. Faith Evans, former director of the Commission on Racial Justice of the United Church of Christ, calls Rathke "arrogant but effective,"[22] while Andrea Kydd, former administrator and trouble-shooter in the VISTA program, through which ACORN received grants, and current director of the Youth Project, a national foundation, views Rathke as "the only organizer from this period who ever really built something substantial."[23] As Cockburn and Ridgeway write, "To an outsider, ACORN's politics seem relatively limited. Rathke himself has the organizational reputation of being a kind of loner, playing the world of citizen politics rather in the manner of a general in a Pentagon war room."[24]

Military, gawky, arrogant—all these adjectives describe Rathke. He has also been called by other activists "piercingly analytical," "an organizational genius," and charismatic."[25] When asked to describe in terms of his own roots his future vision for ACORN, Rathke will point to an eclectic concoction: his admiration for the populist Non-Partisan League, the Southern Tenant Farmers' Union, and Huey Long's Share Our Wealth clubs, as well as his own involvement in the welfare rights movement and George Wiley's new majority: the Movement for Economic Justice. His politics? Like most community organizers, Rathke avoids labels. On various occasions he has claimed to be "just good at what I do—moving an agenda for low- to moderate-income people to take back what's rightfully ours." When asked what is rightfully theirs, Rathke smiles, "Why, everything!"[26] On the question of ideology, Rathke has said, "Our membership aren't out there in the clouds somewhere saying this is the way the world should look in 100 years. Our philosophy is very closely related to our membership's daily life experience. There's no ideology that instructs what we do. People make decisions and they start moving."[27]

The question of who makes decisions to move whom is clearly a subject of debate. In my view, ACORN reflects the shortcomings of an organization that is controlled by white middle-class male progressives. These shortcomings are evident and may be analyzed in two areas: the development of issues within the organization, and the recruitment, development, training, and advancement of other than white male staff.

Issues and Infrastructure

Issues ACORN has addressed include redlining, school closings, taxes, utility rates, housing, and welfare, all of which have a fundamentally economic dimension. However, with a constituency that is 70 percent women and 70 percent black and Latino, the organization has purposely avoided issues that reflect other than economic inequalities—questions of gender and race. One consequence of this choice is that the organization has been unable to develop a staff infrastructure supportive of women and people of color.

Women's Issues

ACORN is quick to point to the obvious—the prevalence of women in key leadership and staff positions. The number of women leaders is not unusual, however: most community organizations, indeed most progressive organizations, are composed predominantly of women. As Komarovsky writes:

> The home is regarded as primarily the sphere of the woman rather than of the man. Consequently, when a rent increase or a deterioration in services impinges on the home, it is usually the woman's task to deal with it since it lies within her sphere. This pattern holds true

> more frequently in working-class than in middle-class households because of the greater separation of the roles typically found there. Building organization mobilization is commonly based on a network of social ties within a building which women, whether employed outside the home or not, are much more likely to form.[28]

Along the same lines, Rubin adds, "Building organizations, like PTA's, provides an acceptable avenue for social action, since activities outside the home are seen as threatening by a significant minority of working-class husbands."

Although ACORN does follow this pattern, it has not addressed the issues that are raised by progressive women's organizations: day care, equal wages, reproductive rights. When asked about this gap, Rathke replied, "It's never come up. If a local group wants to take up the issue of abortion, that's their prerogative. We have had a group in Memphis address the question of rape—in a public school situation where a young woman was raped, we went after the principal on how he dealt with her."[29] Subsequently, ACORN has initiated anti-rape campaigns in Boston, New Orleans, and Detroit. While this direction is important, it still remains the exception rather than the rule in ACORN. Seth Borgos, responding to the question of why ACORN has not been active around reproductive rights issues, answered, "It might split our constituency—many of our black members are not for it."[30] While both Rathke's and Borgos' explanations sound reasonable, they do not take into account the fact that many issue campaigns are developed by the ACORN research department and "sold" to organizers in various locations. Moreover, it is important to note that ACORN did not, for instance, endorse the Equal Rights Amendment until it was clear that without such endorsement the Texas Women's Political Caucus initially would not back the ACORN People's Platform.

On the staff level, women who were once organizers argue that the atmosphere within ACORN was relatively unsupportive to women—or to men with families—and that while many women had titles of power within the organization, none had serious control of major decisions.[31] Former ACORN staff member Madeleine Adamson writes, "The turnover rate for all organizers is high. For women, it appears to be even higher. The reasons are varied but a few stand out. They have to do with lifestyle—the difficulty of integrating any other interests in life with organizing, particularly having a family, and with the difficulty of competing in what is still a male-dominated field.[32]

ACORN has a significant number of women organizers. As in many cases, however, numbers do not tell the full story. In my view, the assessment of the former organizers is correct. While women do have a semblance of power within the organization, they do not in fact have power on the staff: on a staff of over 150, fewer than five women have access to major decision-making. Male dominance in ACORN, therefore, is expressed two ways: first, structurally, in the issues it chooses and by not supporting the ability of people with families to work within the organization; second, informally, through the "old boys' network" that does make decisions.

Racial Issues

ACORN has a line: "Rather than organizing around racism, we involve our members in campaigns that affect all low- and moderate-income people, building solidarity." Echoing the line, ACORN leader Willard Johnson notes, "There's something about ACORN . . . it doesn't make any difference what a person's skin is. That's one benefit I think I've gotten out of ACORN. Our people have common problems and they try to help one another, not kick them in the butt because they're black or Catholic or something."[33] Former organizers Meg Campbell and Barbara Friedman have argued:

> We could have gotten hundreds more members with a racist position, but we kept it what it was, political and economic. After all, the issue never was "integration."
> We don't cut issues racially where that isn't relevant. There's no point is constructing rhetorical enemies who

193

cannot be defeated. Short of race warfare, black people cannot triumph over whites; but whites and blacks can win against real estate agencies or real estate boards, and they do. Winning is what is important in organizing, and it's almost an obsession with ACORN.[34]

ACORN's approach to issues of race is exactly in line with the rhetoric of the Alinsky organizations. Lancourt writes:

> The closest the black organizers came to using the racial issue itself as a rallying point was in their tactical use of rhetoric to awaken black pride. Specific contests were most often defined as community control versus outside control, or lack of institutional accountability. That outside control and institutions were white was implicit, but issues of racism were acted upon in the context of more and better jobs, education, or housing rather than solely black versus white.[35]

In fact, in an interview in *Just Economics* in 1979, IAF director Ed Chambers advocated getting minority organizers working in white communities "because they never really integrate all the universals until they understand the majority culture."[36]

But ACORN, IAF, and Citizen Action do not always simply merge race and class; they avoid racial issues. In one early campaign, notes Martin Kirby:

> ACORN issued a 19-point list of questionable aspects of the highway situation. Only two points were concerned with race. It was pointed out that the highway would "slash through neighborhoods and increase busing." The question was also raised as to why a paragraph in a preliminary draft of the project's Environmental Impact Statement had been stricken from later versions. The missing paragraph said that the highway at one point would "penetrate an area in which intensive efforts have

been taken to produce a racially integrated neighborhood." Such intrusion could very possibly result in the complete disruption of these efforts, resulting in the complete isolation of all-black neighborhoods.[37]

To ACORN's credit, the organizing staff did support the 1979 effort of a group in Star City, Arkansas, to desegregate a laundromat, but that action was initiated by black leaders and members in a town that had no organizer.

The avoidance of racial issues within the organization has both internal and external implications. In avoiding issues of race, ACORN has been unable to form linkages with single-issue minority groups organized around desegregation, police brutality, or saving vital services. This position has also had its effects on the recruitment of staff:

> For young Blacks, if you want to get into what's happening in your community, an ACORN or a Fair Share is not the place to do it. People still do not, in the Black community, believe that the primary reason for discrimination is economic or class; they believe it is racial. People will join ACORN but when you talk about what young Blacks want to organize, they want to organize something that deals specifically with racial issues as sort of the focal point for the organization.
>
> Second, the organizations are inadvertently racist. . . . I don't mean they're anti-Black or anti-Hispanic but what they do is they treat everybody the same way. If you don't take into account the fact that there are real differences culturally you're going to have problems. For instance, for any white person who comes on staff, there are natural social relations. If a Black orgnizer comes on a staff where there are few other Black staff, the social relations have to come from that very small group or from the constituency and that messes with the whole organizer/leader dichotomy. That causes role confusion

for people. They get confused about who they are, what they're doing, because the hierarchy is reflective of essentially what society is; it's all white and mostly male.[38]

Within the ACORN staff, formal decision-making takes place on several levels. Approaches to local campaigns are discussed between local organizers and their regional directors before options are presented to local boards. In setting national priorities, a prerequisite to action is the development of a written memo presenting the pluses and minuses of a proposed action, a set of organizational options, and a list of proposed first steps. While demonstrated ability to articulate the plan and proximity to key staff play a part in an organizer's ability to get a memo discussed at a national or regional staff meeting, it is my experience that, once on the agenda, the plan usually gets thorough discussion, and staff will take some action. Still, though these discussions tend to be reasonable forums for airing ideas, they also tend to be most accessible to those who have the experience in the organization and the developed conceptual skill to write, organize, and fight for a particular direction. Structurally, the people in the society and in the organization who are in the best position to operate in this context are white males.

It should be noted that although my discussion of the disproportionate percentage of white males in positions of power centers on ACORN, this situation reflects the reality of most left/liberal organizations. Within ACORN a number of attempts have been made to address the problem, including salary differentials and other incentives for minority recruits. The most successful initiative, however, has been the recruitment of young minority organizers to the affiliated union staff, where the hierarachy is less developed and the variety of work sites available for organizing allows for the development of many organizing approaches.

While all the large CO networks have attempted to initiate recruitment programs to remedy the small proportion (less than 10 percent nationwide) of minority organizers on their staffs, they have done so without attempting to address their fundamental assumptions that (1) economic issues subsume issues of race and gender;

(2) organizers must be trained in the dominant culture even to work in their own communities; and (3) the structure of the organization need not change in order to successfully bring in people of color. Until these assumptions are questioned, such efforts will continue to be unsuccessful.

With regard to issues of both race and gender, ACORN and the other community organizing networks replicate and reproduce the values of the dominant society and culture. In fact, with the exception of the explicitly political demands ACORN has made on the Democratic Party, the organization is susceptible to the criticism of economism—to reducing all issues to their lowest possible denominator: money or benefits. This reductionist tendency carries over from the way in which issues and campaigns are framed into two other areas of internal development: internal solidarity and ideology.

Internal Solidarity

Internal solidarity is a key variable in predicting the ability of any organization to be successful and to survive. Solidarity or *esprit de corps* may be thought of as the development of feeling among members on behalf of the organization resulting in a sense of common identity, the development of in-group/out-group relations, and general commitment to defend the group.[39] It is important to note, for example, that there appears to be little difference in the socioeconomic status of members and leaders. The majority of ACORN's twenty-six-member board are neither college-educated nor employed in white collar jobs.

Amitai Etzioni has observed that two factors predict the difficulty in socializing members into an organization: the selectivity of the organization's recruitment process, and the degree to which the organization's values and norms are concomitant with society's as a whole.[40] Lancourt, noting that the Alinsky citizen-action organizations, at least, are fundamentally system-affirming, writes, "The major socialization tasks appear to have been making the existing

INTERNAL ORGANIZATION AND SOCIAL STRUCTURE

social values of participation and democratic decision-making operative."[41]

I do not agree with Lancourt's conclusion that community organizations are fundamentally system-affirming. Struggles over the allocation of urban space, service cutbacks, welfare, and housing put community organizations on the front lines of battles for state-controlled resources. Moreover, community organizations create a contradictory system of social practices that validates oppositional behavior.

In addition, I would argue that the membership selection process is an important factor in building group solidarity. Mancur Olson's influential book, *The Logic of Collective Action*, argues that a group will not reach its full mobilization potential unless its members are provided with "selected (material) incentives."[42] As economistic as I've conceded ACORN's approach to be, the recruitment of stable leadership in the organization points to, if anything, the opposite conclusion: people join and maintain connection with the organization because of nonmaterial feelings of solidarity with other members and because of an identification with the collective actions of the organization.

My own experiences with this issue may illustrate the point. When first organizing in a new neighborhood in Little Rock, I discovered that people on the south side of a specific street had a tremendous drainage problem: when it rained, their homes were flooded. This problem was discussed extensively at two house meetings prior to the first neighborhood meeting, where I expected a large turnout from among the families affected by the flooding. On the evening of the meeting, the group did indeed choose to work on drainage as one of their initial issues; however, of the sixty-odd people in attendance, only eight were from the affected blocks. The issue was actually raised and carried by an elderly black man, elected vice-chair of the group, whose own home was not at all affected by the flooding.

After the meeting, Mr. Higgins, the new vice-chair, invited me to his home for coffee. Sensing my disappointment over the turnout of people affected by the chosen issue, he explained to me that "sometimes people aren't able to do for themselves, even if they know what's right . . . in those times it's the duty of people like you and me to help them out if we can." Mr. Higgins's comments, especially significant to a young organizer who had been beaten over the head with the notion of "self-interest," make my point. Certainly there are people who join ACORN to gain a direct benefit. Those who stay and particularly those who go on to become leaders, however, do so more from a sense of solidarity with other low-income people and with the organization than for the potential material benefits the organization may bring them.

Another, less altruistic reason for joining and maintaining connection with the organization is the recognition members and leaders receive, both internally and externally. Very often, ACORN members do not get positive reinforcement for their ideas or efforts in the society at large. ACORN provides a forum where they may develop leadership skills and receive recognition. As the organization's current national Board President, Elena Hanggi, notes: "Empowering the majority of people in the U.S. to exercise control over every facet of their lives means having poor people in positions of power."[43] To train ACORN leaders to develop the skills necessary for actually exercising power, ACORN has developed a formal structure described as follows in a recent report of the New World Foundation:

> Issues to be addressed by a neighborhood chapter are decided on by that chapter. For city-wide issues, the city board and the local chapters will both discuss them. If there are favorable responses to a city board proposal at the local chapters, the board will then set strategies, agendas, and time-lines. National decisions are made via a similar two-way flow of information, proposals, responses and action.
>
> Each ACORN chapter's chair becomes their representative to a city board. If ACORN is in more than one

INTERNAL ORGANIZATION AND SOCIAL STRUCTURE

city in a state, chapter representatives make up the State Executive Board, which, in turn, selects two delegates to the National Association Board. If ACORN is only in one city in a state, the city board will perform the same functions as a state board.

The National Association Board defines the national organization's policies and sets priorities. It meets twice a year and selects an Executive Committee which meets an additional two times a year. The Executive Committee is composed of regional representatives and the Board selected officers of President, Vice-President, Secretary, and Treasurer. The Association Board also has a Subsidy Committee selected by the President to oversee local budgets and allocate canvass funds.[44]

A monthly leadership publication, *¡Vamonos!*, is distributed to leaders and staff, and quarterly newsletter, *USA* (the United States of ACORN), is mailed to members. In addition, cultural solidarity is developed through the self-consciously organized social efforts that take place at state and national conventions, and the writing, singing, and distributing of ACORN songs by group members. Three themes generally recur in the songs: the growing power of ACORN, the solidarity of "the people," and the definition of the enemy. These examples are chosen from the ACORN Songbook of 1982:

ACORN ANTHEM (to the tune of Yankee Doodle)

> The politician woos my vote;
> He promises perfection.
> The vows compiled are neatly filed
> Until the next election
>
> We belong to ACORN now;
> We're alone no longer.
> All of us we'll raise a fuss
> Our voices stronger, stronger.

ACORN ORGANIZING SONG

> Aren't you tired of seein' the way that your own country's being run?
> For the sake of Monster Profit, they would even steal your son.
> And if you think it's bad, well, buster, you can bet it will grow worse.
> So you better start to organize, or empty out your purse!

ACORN MARCHES ON (to the tune of "Battle Hymn of the Republic")

> Mine eyes have seen the glory when the people stand as one.
> We have scattered all the bureaucrats and put them on the run.
> But even with our list of wins our work has just begun.
> The ACORN marches on.
>
> There's Republicans, there's Democrats, I don't know which is worse,
> Cuz the elephants they kill my job; the donkeys kill my purse.
> Well, it's time to take those fossil groups and pack them in a hearse
> As ACORN marches on.

Many of the forty-two songs reflect the organization's struggles with utility companies, politicians and corporate elites, but these are not the only "outsiders." Until very recently (with the 1984 Alliance for Justice coalition effort), part of the ACORN family's self-image was that of the only legitimate representative of low- and moderate-income people. While externally, this perception may have been rightfully interpreted as organizational arrogance, internally the belief ACORN was the only legitimate, multiracial, low-income organization with a tactically militant stance has been a prevalent and, I would argue, sustaining factor throughout most of the organization's existence. This sense of organizational integrity is integrally linked with the most elusive element in the glue holding the organization together: ACORN's ideology.

Ideology

ACORN's formal ideology is eclectic and populist: the chance to be rich; the right to be free. The closest ACORN has come to spelling out an ideology is in the set of organizing principles articulated by Rathke in 1978, which list ACORN's responsibility to "(1) organize the maximum number of low- and moderate-income people possible; (2) organize whatever individual and multiple constituencies possess the maximum ability to win change at any given place or at any given time; and (3) win the maximum amount of political power possible to be exercised by our constituency and their organization."[45] As opposed to pure ideology, then—which Schurman defines as a set of ideas designed to give an individual a unified, conscious world view—ACORN has developed a practical ideology, "a set of ideas designed to give individuals rational instruments for action. It provides the norms or rules which prescribe behavior. In offering a prescription of 'how to get there from here,' the practical ideology has direct action consequences."[46]

In describing the operation of such a developmental, practical ideology, Perlman writes, "Each victory on each issue may not be earth-shattering, but the cumulative picture is one of ongoing progress. . . . Even . . . where the achievement may only be temporary . . . people are beginning to understand the issues, to see how power and politics operate, to grasp both the potentials and limitations in collective action and to feel a new sense of self-esteem."[47] And ACORN training director Meg Campbell has written, "This *idea of being organized* in a constituency-based organization . . . is more important than the particular issue we work on. Again, we might lose or we might win, and still the *need to be organized* remains."[48]

The question, then, is how does this practical ideology shape

INTERNAL ORGANIZATION AND SOCIAL STRUCTURE

organizational development? Are democratic principles, an internal commitment to power, and an organizational commitment to organize "anything that moves" sufficient? The commitment is certainly necessary. Many groups reach a low level of political access; co-opted leaders or organizers are bought off, and the organizing stops. Nouveau populists, including Harry Boyte and Lawrence Goodwyn,[49] would also argue that these populist commitments are sufficient for building a class-based movement, while Piven and Cloward's *New Class War*[50] pictures a battle between capitalism and democracy, with democracy vaguely depicted as the focus of populism.

ACORN's contribution has been to concretize a number of left populist ideas, mostly related to the socialization of basic goods and services, coupled with a strong dose of radical democracy as evidenced by the platform's references to representation on regulatory and corporate boards and by the organization's consistent involvement in the electoral process. On a local level, this approach has certainly worked. Father Blitz, an ACORN supporter and director of the Office of Peace and Justice for the Catholic diocese of Little Rock, notes, "When Wade [Rathke] first started in this state, ACORN was a real threat to the system. They went through a stage of being called communist etc. You don't hear that much any more. Many of the people that criticized ACORN initially are now supporters."[51]

ACORN's avoidance of formal ideology is related to another factor in its potential to survive and to be successful in the political arena: the ability to mobilize resources.

Resource Mobilization

In social science literature, discussions of resource mobilization deal with many of the areas already discussed in this chapter: internal solidarity, ideology, and the means employed by "resourceful actors" to effectively garner resources.

As has been illustrated, ACORN's tactics often draw fire from the press as well as adversaries. In fact, since the tactics of confrontation have become routinized, some adversaries have used an

ACORN-initiated action to attack ACORN. An example of this occurred at the 1975 hearings on lifeline utility rates in Arkansas:

> Les Hollingsworth, a black city councillor, introduced the ACORN proposal. Mayor Wimberly took the microphone to argue against it. His earlier friendliness vanished; the color rose in his cheeks, and his hands shook. "This public hearing would only serve to give this organization a platform. And who are they? I have never seen a group so secretive. They refuse to tell where their money comes from. Those who set it up bring papers for others to read. In seven years, I have never known the real leaders of ACORN to come forward and make a statement.[52]

The question raised by Wimberly reinforces the explanation of the leader/organizer dichotomy and in addition raises the question of finances. The organization's survival depends on ACORN's ability, each year, to raise a high percentage of its budget by internal means—a budget which, between 1975 and 1981, rose from $250,000 to $2.3 million. Over that six-year period, the percentage of internally raised money increased from 27 percent in 1975 to 62.4 percent in 1981, with the dues per organizer per month averaging $379.

There are three sources of internal financing: (1) membership dues, which account for 45 percent of the organization's income; (2) grassroots fund-raising activities in the form of raffles, bake sales, community fairs, etc.; and (3) door-to-door canvassing—essentially, soliciting funds in more middle-class neighborhoods to support ACORN's work on specific issues, thus broadening the organization's support base without recruiting middle-class patrons to the membership ranks and/or leadership positions. ACORN's ability to finance itself internally is far from the norm for movement organizations, and its finances have occasioned much external comment and concern.

In 1984, 85 percent of the budget came from internal finances. ACORN has also initiated an allied business operation that is currently involved in selling paper to nonprofit organizations in 3 cities,

INTERNAL ORGANIZATION AND SOCIAL STRUCTURE

and is looking into the possibility of setting up housing and heating oil–buying cooperatives. Formally, membership is involved in the budget process through monthly local board budget meetings, the preparation of budgets by city and statewide budget/fund-raising committees, and an evaluation by a national subsidy committee. Since some areas project a surplus, some a balanced budget, and others a deficit, the subsidy committee, in this relatively new system, determines

> how to allocate canvass income which comes from canvass campaigns conducted by separate canvass staffs in non-ACORN neighborhoods. Income raised through canvasses doesn't go to the locals that raised it, rather, it goes into a national pool distributed by the subsidy committee. The delegates must defend their states' financial performance to the other delegates. If local leaders find themselves with a shortfall in the course of the year, they must go to the subsidy committee seeking either an emergency loan or a revised subsidy.[53]

This process is quite important for ACORN, not only because national foundations are shying away from grassroots organizing as a priority but also because ACORN's receipt of government funds made the organization a ready target for the New Right. *Conservative Digest* listed ACORN as one of "175 leftist groups that get your money"—that received government funds in 1981 ($231,370 in fiscal year 1980–81, according to an ACORN financial report dated 7 January 1981). The *Digest* objection to ACORN, however, was less its source of money than its political philosophy of using "food-buying clubs to build the necessary social bonds for people to struggle in the political and social arena."[54] While the magazine did list every group with even vague political leanings—including the American Bar Association and the National Wildlife Federation—ACORN's name on the roster and its featured place in the exposé suggest that as the organization gets larger and particularly as it expands its electoral activity, its ability to develop government or private foundation resources will decrease. ACORN's staff, therefore, has increasingly begun to institutionalize internal fund-raising, and the organization predicts 90 percent self-sufficiency by 1986.

While supporting 85 percent or more of the budget through internal means is impressive, fund-raising is, at this point, still chiefly the responsibility of the staff. Not only does this fact sometimes contribute to staff-leadership conflict, since all ACORN finances are centralized in New Orleans, but it has also increased the tasks of already overburdened organizers and taken time away from other aspects of organizational development. ACORN cannot maintain its level of actions and, at the same time, increase its self-sufficiency without increasing the membership's involvement and commitment to internal financial development.

ACORN's Potential: The Organizational Ledger

This book's examination of ACORN's history, methods, and development leads to the following conclusions:

Model: The ACORN model has allowed ACORN to replicate units of organization in forty geographic areas. The initial organizing drive results in the formation of a structure through which a local group can act, but also sets up staff/leadership role divisions that continue to prove problematic. While the model has been used successfully, the ratio of members to organizers (approximately 450 to 1) has led many new organizers to resign, being unable to keep up the pace.

Staff: Although the staff within the ACORN affiliated Service Employees Union is about 60 percent black, the staff of ACORN continues to be young, white, well-educated, and poorly paid. On one hand, after fifteen years of organizing, ACORN has developed considerable staff depth and expertise. On the other hand, the lack of formal ongoing training, the inability to maintain staff cadre, and the lack of success in hiring people at the state or national level who

INTERNAL ORGANIZATION AND SOCIAL STRUCTURE

have not come up through the staff ranks have made the maintenance of staff continuity difficult. In addition, the latent organizational structure that points to staff oligarchy, male dominance, and a heavy dependence on Rathke as the organization's chief strategist—even as both staff and leaders articulate a commitment to ACORN as a participatory democracy—inhibits both the straightforward development of staff people as leaders within the organization and the ability of the indigenous leadership to challenge organizational direction. This situation, however, may also be changing, since twelve-year veteran Steve Kest in September 1984 assumed the role of executive director of ACORN, in which he handles external contacts, while the internal job of chief organizer, long held by Rathke, is now divided among three other people.

Leaders: The leadership pool reflects the general constituency. However, with the exception of Association Board members, indigenous leaders do not take part in the initial debates concerning organizational direction. They therefore tend to have less investment in the organization. Although the leadership training and delegation of financial responsibility to local leadership has mitigated against this trend, local leadership remains the organization's largest underutilized resource.

Electoral strength: ACORN claimed 150,000 registered after the 1984 campaign. A June 1985 mailing to supporters pointed to the possibility of local campaigns to elect an ACORN supporter as the first Black mayor of Bridgeport as well as electoral drives in St. Louis, Pittsburgh, Little Rock, and New York City. With the Democratic Party in shambles nationally, it is unclear how significant local electoral victories may be in building ACORN's party presence. However, each of the proposed drives is linked to a local group demand that will make candidate accountability, or lack of it, clear to local members.

Issues: Although ACORN has posited the need since early 1979 to develop a civil rights thrust in the Latino community, no campaign plan has materialized. However, beginning in 1982 the organization did move several local campaigns on budget cutbacks. In addition, the organization has started new coalition initiatives in the peace and labor communities. These efforts, coupled with the reinitiation of low-income campaigns (squatting actions and agreements with developers in three cities to hire local low-income residents), and a noticeable recognition of women's issues (the Spring 1985 issue of the *United States of ACORN* (*USA*) headlined, "ACORN declares War on Rape"), may well have moved the organization into a position to work with a broad variety of groups and constituencies.

Reputation: ACORN has the reputation of being unwilling to work with other local community groups. While relations with unions (in particular) and with churches are good, winning the support of the local CO competition will not be easy. Outside the community organizing networks, ACORN's consistent militance has earned it a reputation for tough, uncompromising, and creative actions, which the organization is beginning to transform into more national media coverage. ACORN's national lobbying efforts have also been enhanced by moving all the research/publications staff to Washington, D.C.

Ideology: In the last few years a number of internal memos have identified ACORN as "left" and have advocated strategy in terms of class conflict. While the staff of the organization still resists labels, most of the staff people were comfortable with defining the organization as "anticorporate" and in favor of economic democracy.[55] However, while finally placing itself on the left, ACORN has staunchly resisted the question "left of what?"

Internal solidarity: While the organization still tends to be weak in terms of developing an internal alternative culture, the evolving radio stations in two states have forced questions of culture and ideology to become part of staff and leadership discussions. With regard to finances, ACORN stands head and shoulders above any other community organization, with 85 percent internal funding, through dues (45 percent) and a combination of grassroots events and canvassing.

External response: Movements on the left have received the most attention from the state, followed by those on the right, with little atention being paid to movements or organizations in the center. Thus ACORN's ideological neutrality, down-home Americanism, and dogged assertions that all it wants is its fair share—coupled with its folksy acronym—have until recently rendered it relatively safe. However, the use of VISTA volunteers in some of its more abrasive actions, the undisguised political nature of its 1980 and 1984 campaigns, and the recent decision to step out as a movement/builder are making ACORN more susceptible to government harassment (since 1978 the Association has been audited three times, and organizer arrests have gone from one in the first nine years to over forty in the last two years), as well as penetration from the organized left.

Constituency: ACORN has a large working-class, 70 percent minority constituency of roughly 60,000 members in twenty-seven states. While the new campaigns (jobs and squatting) have appealed to younger constituents, the age of most members is above thirty-five. The current organizational base is established in forty urban and rural areas. ACORN's "penetration" strategy has resulted in the initiation of a sister union affiliated with the AFL-CIO, two radio stations with pending applications for 30 more, and applications for three low-power TV stations.

In summary, the organization has done an effective job of mobilizing human, financial, and external political resources to represent the interests of low-income people. In terms of ideological development—which ACORN partisans argue is unnecessary—while ACORN has not developed a structured ideology, that lack of definition has probably been appropriate for organizational development to this point. Further expansion and development, however, may require a more specific ideological position.

ACORN's premise has been that the building of collective oppositional experience is more important than formal ideological articulation. This has been a fruitful approach to developing both organizers and leaders, but it does not take people far enough along to sustain them over time. The organization's four-year-old leadership school may increase participants' skills so that agenda-setting and financial development can become more the responsibility of the indigenous leadership. Yet it is characteristic of ACORN to view this problem and attempt to solve it on the leadership level without making the same sort of in-service training formally available to ACORN staff. Without restructuring leadership responsibilities and increasing internal skills and political development for both leadership and staff, the organization may not be able to maintain present staff levels, or generate the new staff expertise necessary to expand the organization.

In the next and final chapter, I will examine ACORN's position in the forefront of Community Organizing in comparison to the other major CO forces and evaluate ACORN's and other groups' ability to play a role in the development of a progressive movement for social justice.

9

The Prospects for Community Organizing

> *To continue to do our own thing in the '80's and 90's may well do us in.*
>
> —Tim Sampson, member, ACORN and C/LEC, Nov. 1984

What are the prospects for the community organization movement that ACORN represents? Some on the left have called the movement parochial, implying it has little future. Even among those sympathetic to and involved with the movement, there is a wide range of opinion. Mike Miller, writing in the mid-1970s, found "beneath the despair of Watergate the emergence of a new brand of democratic populism"[1] Similarly, Harry Boyte's *Backyard Revolution* identified CO with an alternative popular democratic thread of insurgency in the United States.[2] Steven Holt, a former organizer for both ACORN and the Citizen Action network, holds a more pessimistic view:

> We might as well start with where we are today. We don't have much, not any of us. We've got a constituency of 125 million people, and if you lump us all together we've got maybe 100,000 names on membership cards, but there's nothing frank about that figure. Throw out the 20,000 Fair Share members who've never talked to

> anyone but a canvasser, and the 20,000 ACORN members who haven't paid dues or come to a meeting in over a year, and all the similar "members" in New Hampshire and Illinois and any other state where we have businesses operating.
>
> We've got probably 200 organizing offices around the country, but if we're going to be frank we can close the doors on a third of them, either because the doors are closed today for lack of staff and money or because we haven't trained the folks we've got there to do their work. Maybe they'll be able to do it next year, but if we're going to be frank we'll have to wait until next year to claim them.[3]

But Rathke, writing of ACORN, claims:

> There are some things that just plain make us what we are, and why we are fundamentally different than others. It is not our history itself that shows this road, as much as the fact that our road has always been marked by the same sense of direction no matter how many twists and turns we have had to take to get there. That vision has been shared deeply at all times by a core of the staff and by significant numbers of the leadership. It has always been bigger than any of us, and it has always carried us along the way.
>
> ACORN is a community organization. We are multi-issued. We are multi-racial. We are a majority constituency. Although this was virtually non-existent 10 years ago, it is almost too common today. We were born in the time of Saul Alinsky and George Wiley. To say that others have followed our lead and broken ground in other corners of the country is equally apparent, even if not always flattering. But, *we are not our fathers, nor can our faces be seen in the mirrors of our sons and daughters* [emphasis added].[4]

THE PROSPECTS FOR COMMUNITY ORGANIZING

Probably neither Rathke's optimism nor Holt's "realism" fully reflects the true state of community organization. While competition among the networks will continue to spark arguments over the numbers of active members and states, win/loss records on local actions, and credit for initiating particular campaigns, this level of assessment would miss the significance of the emerging movement. Community organizations currently struggle in two arenas: they pose demands for immediate economic improvements, in terms of the distribution of the social wage, and they demand democratic rights and liberties.

Community organizations are the major instrumentalities through which fiscal struggles with the state are waged. They link the provision of collective goods and services to geographically defined class interest; by so doing, they create new avenues for understanding power and inequality.[5] The process of organizing, over the last ten years, has demystified the production and allocation of collective goods, and created replicable local organizations that encourage and validate a contradictory system of oppositional behavior.[6]

While these accomplishments in consciousness-building, coupled with concrete local victories, are indeed important, one must ask: has the movement reached its limits? Did community organization peak in the early 1980s? Will the movement continue to expand, mobilizing an increasing percentage of local residents into more and more powerful organizations? Finally, will organizational expansion ever be focused to encompass the structural problems of United States society or of other societies? In order to answer these questions, we must examine the range of community organizations currently operating, and how the major CO networks have attempted to redirect their strategic efforts in light of both the relative success of the movement and the current political climate.

The State of Community Organization

Boyte,[7] Miller,[8] and Perlman[9] tend to tout both the effectiveness and the similarities of community organizations around the country. Similarly, Burlington[10] grouped ACORN with the Citizen Action

Program in Chicago, the Powder River Resource Council in Wyoming, Fair Share in Massachusetts, the Buckeye Woodland Community Congress in Ohio, and the Citizens' Action League in California. Cockburn and Ridgeway[11] added to the list Tom Hayden's Santa Monica–based Campaign for Economic Democracy, the Ohio Public Interest Campaign (OPIC), and the Illinois Public Action Council (IPAC) as part of the newly formed Progressive Alliance.

As of mid-1982, the Citizens' Action Program, the Buckeye Woodland Community Congress, and the Progressive Alliance were defunct, OPIC was in serious financial trouble, and the initial organizers of Fair Share, as well as the Citizens' Action League, had affiliated with ACORN. The differences among organizations, however, are not simply added up in terms of affiliations or even the ability of the organization to stay afloat; they are more fundamental. Piven and Cloward argued that many organizations have opted to work with a more stable working-class constituency, leaving the poor essentially unorganized.[12] Citing Massachusetts Fair Share as a case in point, they note a marked tendency for community organization's class makeup to drift upwards, as well as a reduction of militant tactics, a move toward bureaucratization, and greater emphasis on state regulatory agencies than corporations as targets. Amplifying their point, Piven and Cloward insist that the constituencies organized by many citizen action groups include members who have access to aldermen and city councils—the notable exception being ACORN.

Part of the shift, in their view, is located in a change in the attitude of organizers. "As long as 'the people' were actively trying to win their rights, the morale of community organizers remained high, and young activists flocked into their ranks. The organizers shared a faith in the power of citizens to 'control their own destiny' and in their own skills at helping the process along. They had, in other words, a faith in the democratic possibilities of American institutions—if prodded (ever so slightly). That faith was rapidly disappointed."[13] If one tendency in responding to this disappointment was the vertical drift to a more stable constituency, another equally problematic response was ACORN's horizontal expansion into cities where existing organizations viewed the geographic turf, if not the low-income constituency, as their organization prerogative. While social science analysts term "wasteful" the tendency of organizations with similar goals to compete with each other in undesirable ways,[14] activists refer to the tendency as "sectarian." Steve Holt underscored this point in an unpublished essay entitled "Searching for the Line: Thoughts on Colleagues and Competition in Organizing":

> Having organized now in a dozen cities in four states, I haven't been able to maintain much respect for state lines as anything more than artificial boundaries. NHPA's [New Hampshire People's Alliance] membership and staff can work like hell until the sun comes up in New Hampshire but if organizing isn't going well in the rest of the country, we won't accomplish much more than a stop sign or two up here. If this work is worth doing, then it's got to be worth the attempt to develop a vision which says we are all working for the same leadership, that all our campaigns are fragments of the same great campaign, and that the weaknesses and problems in each of our organizations need the attention and the help of all our organizations.
>
> What were we doing, what did we think we were doing, and what was all that talk about changing the country? How did we form a vision which allowed us to define every colleague as a competitor if the logo on the button was different? . . .
>
> *I have got to wonder where Wade* [Rathke] *does draw the line. Are there any principled reasons out there on which ACORN would decide not to compete with another organization?* I don't mean reasons based on funding, or friendship, or pie-carving deals, or non-intervention pacts. I mean reasons based on a shared vision of what we are trying to

accomplish, and on a mutual interest in providing support to each other as those efforts proceed. If that vision exists, then it would mean that we would all look at each other's soft spots as places where we may be able to help out, not as targets for the next strike.[15]

Holt's questions to ACORN raise a larger question for community organizations in general: what is the potential for the existing CO networks to coalesce and, if they did, what difference would it make?

Generally, each of the major community organizing networks has made more progress in working with other progressive organizations than with each other. For instance, Citizen Action, a multistate network of statewide groups built mostly on the coalition model and brought together by the Midwest Academy in 1979, successfully transformed the ability to build local coalitions of neighborhood groups and organized labor into the national Citizen/Labor Energy Coalition (C/LEC) which is supported by the UAW and public service unions. In addition, because the Academy has specialized in training women's groups, Citizen Action has made connections with many of the national progressive women's organizations as well as the SEIU-affiliated Local 925 (Nine-to-Five). Citizen Action has also invested staff time in developing the Central America Peace Campaign, shifting Karen Thomas, former director of the Academy, into a full-time training role with groups opposed to U.S. intervention in Latin America.

In contrast, the Long Island–based Industrial Areas Foundation (IAF) has moved into coalitional formations only on the local level. Even so, those local partners have markedly enhanced the organization's ability to generate resources and legitimacy through (usually Catholic) churches. Funded by large allocations from the Catholic Campaign for Human Development, the IAF has developed a "go deep" as opposed to "go wide" strategy. Arguing that in order for people to be truly empowered, significant social institutions must be mobilized on the behalf of the oppressed, and utilizing a model developed by Ernesto Cortez (a Chicano organizer and former

THE PROSPECTS FOR COMMUNITY ORGANIZING

minister of the United Church of Christ), the IAF has mounted a strategy whose initial step is developing the political acumen of key actors in significant church institutions. This approach has led the IAF to build successful local organizations in Texas, Los Angeles, and Baltimore, and to develop ecumenical church-based organizing committees in a number of other communities. Variations on this project that attempt to include labor have been initiated by the San Francisco–based Organize Training Center in San Francisco, Fresno, and Portland, Oregon.

National People's Action has taken yet another tack on the question of coalition. Like the Midwest Academy's training sessions, which developed the social relations necessary to consolidate groups into C/LEC and Citizen Action, NPA developed out of the work conducted by Shel Trapp as the chief trainer for the National Training and Information Center (NTIC). NPA's approach was to deliver benefits and consolidate relations among constituent groups through a yearly national action targeting a Washington, D.C.–based federal agency. Notable targets were HUD and the Federal Home Loan Bank Board. Building on its success with housing issues, in 1982 NPA initiated a "Reclaim America" campaign that attempted to focus a series of local and national actions on both state regulatory and corporate targets, culminating in a march on Wall Street. Unfortunately, this major coalition attempt fell flat when fewer than 2,000 people attended the Wall Street rally, and financial difficulties have plagued the organization in its subsequent attempts to consolidate its base.

All of the four largest community organization networks have attempted to build working relationships with labor and church organizations while maintaining, for the most part, competitive relationships with each other. Moreover, community organizations have entered the fray of interest-group politics at a time when the insiders from labor and the liberal establishment have closed ranks. The fight to establish the pecking order of community organizations takes place in the relatively unfamiliar arena of electoral politics, where organizational and constituent interest is very often traded for political muscle.

THE PROSPECTS FOR COMMUNITY ORGANIZING

Three major factors will determine whether community organizations can effectively influence national politics. First is the ability of the CO networks to mobilize and allocate resources—both funds and personnel, since maintaining a working-class base, developing the analytical prowess of grassroots leadership, and accommodating the needs of both experienced cadre staff and new recruits is as important as the ability to raise money. In addition, the question of resource allocation is related to the groups' ability to collaborate with each other and to lend their expertise to non-class-based movements: organizations addressing peace, racial, and women's issues.

Second is the ability of community organizations to establish a national presence, including a developing competence in the arena of (particularly local) electoral politics. Equally important, however, will be CO's ability to take public credit for electoral success. Media relations, therefore, will have a powerful impact on the development of the movement.

The third factor is the level of opposition to CO efforts. While all of these factors are interrelated, *external opposition in an era of political conservatism may well be the controlling variable in determining the future of community organization.*

A National Support Infrastructure

In order to parlay local wins into political muscle, each of the networks has attempted to "profile" its strength and enhance its clout by developing relations or establishing an office in Washington, D.C. This trend was led by the establishment of Ralph Nader's Center for the Study of Responsive Law, which successfully addressed issues of automobile safety, radiation control, and food standards, and was supplemented by a growing network of technical assistance organizations in the capital, including the Center for Community Change, the Food Research and Action Center, the Conference on Alternative State and Local Government, and the Low-Income Housing Coalition. All of these supplied community organizations with legislative analysis. The trend was further legitimated through the work of the Movement for Economic Justice, which provided intramovement contact and communication through organized strategy meetings on key issues and through its newsletter, *Just Economics*, which attempted to reflect the work of all of the local and national networks.

The Youth Project, a national foundation based in Washington, D.C., provided many groups with seed money and acted as an advocate for the burgeoning movement in the funding world, leveraging hundreds of thousands of dollars every year for the movement. Moreover, progressive advocates for community organization found that the physical closeness of the governmental bureaucracy opened up additional opportunities. For instance, many groups within the community organizing movement had rejected funding from the Office of Economic Opportunity/Community Services Administration offices as "co-optive," preferring to generate financial resources internally through dues and grassroots activities and externally through the liberal foundation network. But when two of "their own," Sam Brown and Marjorie Tabankin, became directors of the ACTION agency and the VISTA program during the Carter administration, over three million dollars was funneled directly to ACORN, National People's Action, Citizen Action,[16] and the Industrial Areas Foundation in both training contracts and VISTA volunteers.

By 1980, three of the four national groups (the exception being the IAF) had established some "presence" in Washington, and by 1982 many were cultivating contacts on Capitol Hill and making plans for the 1982 mid-term elections. Citizen Action, in general, followed through on ground broken by ACORN's 1980 campaign, and both the Midwest Academy and the North Carolina–based Grassroots Leadership Project currently offer courses in electoral work to local community leaders. The shift in emphasis has left some local leaders disaffected, however. Fair Share's leaders were not altogether happy with the electoral thrust, and after years of direct action many community leaders, including some in ACORN, were unsure about the efficacy of the electoral arena.

Goal Transformation

When ACORN first entered electoral politics, it took a relatively new direction for community organizations. As of the presidential election in 1984, however, hundreds of community and labor groups were gearing up to "take back the government" through electoral politics. While this puts community organizations squarely in the center of the movement toward the repoliticization of the United States electorate and therefore in tune with dominant societal trends, we must also ask: how does this tendency affect the membership and change the goals of the organizations?

When the 1982 Fair Share convention, where there was a lively discussion on the pros and cons of getting involved in electoral work, voted to support the shift, observer Theresa Funicello of the New York–based Downtown Welfare Advocacy Center saw "a lot of discontent from low-income people over the vote."[17] In part, that discontent reflects the discomfort of many members in moving toward a more national political arena. Piven and Cloward note that in the welfare rights movement, the less central the concern to the constituency, the lower the participation rate of members; in the 1972 Children's March for Survival, for example, "it was doubtful that welfare recipients comprised one per cent of the crowd."[18] Generalizing the point, Day Creamer of Women Employed writes, "Time and time again organizations have sacrificed local programs as attention has shifted to the national arena. . . . After a number of years in local organizing, organizers and the leaders get tired of the local nitty gritty since building the organization at the local levels is painstaking and at times tedious."[19]

One tendency, then, of local groups is to attempt to move into the national arena, sometimes at the expense of their local bases. Shel Trapp, as director of the National Training and Information Network, noted another explanation for the trend. In a 1979 interview in *Just Economics*, Trapp argued that the local issues on which his Chicago-based group had won concessions had to be addressed in Washington. His experiences were replicated in other organizing networks.[20]

THE PROSPECTS FOR COMMUNITY ORGANIZING

The Level of Opposition

As community organizations began to consolidate, to develop a national presence, and to move their power base into the electoral arena, another important external variable changed: the level of opposition. As the *New York Times* and *Wall Street Journal* began to feature the successes of ACORN, the Citizen/Labor Energy Coalition, and other organizations, opposition from CO's targets—local politicians, the heads of federal regulatory agencies, and corporations—began to emerge in an organized way. Lipsky points out that organized protest generates organized response: (1) the dispensing of symbolic satisfaction rather than tangible payoffs, including public hearings and promises to "study the situation," or giving a benefit to one member in a group of three hundred; (2) targets appearing to be constrained in their ability to grant protest goals; (3) the discrediting of protest leaders and organizations; and (4) postponing action.[21]

In a 1976 article entitled "The Radicals Are Coming: Are You Ready?" William Braznell, Jr., public relations manager of the Del Monte Corporation, cited Alinsky's *Rules for Radicals* and noted, "These people are good. They include some of the best minds our universities produce—researchers, lawyers, writers. They do their homework and their ability to manipulate the news media is simply uncanny. The way they handle the press puts us all to shame." Braznell advised targets not to take groups on in their own territory but to use third-party experts to outtalk them, to screen all internal documents, and to take the offensive with careful redefinition of the issue.

> If "obscene profits" are the issue, let's not try to justify our God given *right* to obscene profits! Let's tell the American people why we need profits, what they do for the people, how profits relate to jobs, better living conditions, and so on. And then let's tell them why we need *more* profits—to do a better job and to build an even better standard of living for all Americans.[22]

THE PROSPECTS FOR COMMUNITY ORGANIZING

There have been other kinds of target response to confrontational tactics, as well. Ernest Morial, mayor of New Orleans, proposed in 1979 to have all ACORN activities investigated by the National League of Cities. Both corporate and city government officials have written to the Catholic Campaign for Human Development (a primary source of external funding for ACORN and others) to protest the awarding of Catholic monies to radical organizations. And under the Reagan administration, the tactic of publicly jamming progressive funding sources has been stepped up. By mid-1984 the National Conservative Political Caucus had labeled the Catholic Campaign for Human Development a left-wing foundation and repeatedly attacked its grants to local organizing efforts, particularly the successful Texas projects of the IAF.

Some conservative forces have gone beyond press attacks to lawsuits. In 1984 two progressive foundations granted small allotments for local organizing to a Chicano land rights organization in the Southwest. Political opponents, claiming that the money was used for electioneering, initiated legal action against both the local organization *and* the foundations. This sort of action has systematically discouraged even "radical" funding sources from supporting local grassroots entitlement projects.

Even without political disincentives, smaller and smaller shares of foundation monies are being allocated to grassroots organizing efforts. In 1983–84 the lion's share of progressive funding was channeled to voter registration; foundation liberals hoped that low-income, minority, and women voters would stem the conservative tide at the ballot box. Buying into this tactical thrust, many community organizations also set up voter registration programs.

Such efforts have clear advantages and disadvantages. On the plus side, many organizations have in this way been able to develop relationships with local Democrats, to meet their organizational goals for registration, and to introduce many new individuals to the electoral arena, often on the basis of issues that directly affect them. This was especially true of the registration efforts that took place on cheese lines and in the welfare offices.

At this point, however, the minuses of this effort far outweigh the pluses. Since the voters registered are seldom recruited into the community organization, the action becomes a benefit for the Democrats at little or no cost to the party. A great deal of organizational time and energy is expended on registration efforts with very little tied to ongoing organizational activities. The effort also opens up a new flank to attack from conservative forces: currently, two multistate programs are being sued for "partisan" registration efforts. Moreover, there is absolutely no accountability of candidates to any program or policy. And finally, very often the registration efforts are not coordinated with those of existing minority organizations that have been working on voter registration for the last ten years, increasing tension between minority organizations and the CO movement.

The idea to register voters as a strategy for major change was advanced, interestingly enough, by scholar-activists Piven and Cloward, who published an article entitled "Toward a Class-Based Realignment of American Politics: A Movement Strategy," in *Social Policy* magazine in the winter of 1983. The article not only gave voter registration political and intellectual legitimation but also loosened up major financial resources for voter registration in the liberal funding world—to the detriment of almost everything else.

In part, Piven and Cloward's argument reflected a basic political fact: shrinking state budgets and widespread sentiment against welfare and social spending conditioned the basic strategic choices open to many community organizations; their major thrust and focus in 1984 necessarily became the national election. Given this shift, many local organizations—particularly single-issue housing, welfare, and civil rights groups either unable to unwilling to change focus—have folded. Reagan's victory has given others pause and an opportunity to reevaluate. Electoral activity is still a relatively new thrust for many community organizations, and the attraction of having finally entered the main arena may for the moment have overshadowed other considerations, but increased electoral experience will sharpen their ability to make tactical decisions. ACORN's experience demonstrates that if electoral work—though tactically problematic, by itself—can be combined with disruptive tactics, it is potentially useful in enhancing the power of the organization, particularly at the local level.

Internal Organizational Development

Electoral activity has caused at least one of the major networks to reassess its organizing model. Citizen Action's definitive plan appears to follow the "progressive coalition" model, but as Miles Rapoport writes:

> I think it is also necessary for our organizations to have our own independent base. That is, we cannot rely on organizing primarily through other institutions (whether that be unions or churches). I think the only way that I've seen that you can really have a coalition that means something is when you bring some independent power, when your organization brings some troops, some people, some leadership, as well as ideas and a plan. I think that organizations that primarily build themselves through existing institutions are going to have serious weaknesses.[23]

The concerns that Rapoport raises are related to the ability of community organizations to continue to serve the interests and develop the leadership potential of a working-class base. Harry Boyte has described one Massachusetts Fair Share campaign as follows:

> Prompted by undue optimism and economic pressure to move beyond neighborhood issues to more dramatic and impressive offensives—the greater the name recognition and media attention, the larger the donations by which such an organization survives—Fair Share undertook a statewide campaign in 1976 to reform utility rate

THE PROSPECTS FOR COMMUNITY ORGANIZING

structures. It failed. The Associated Industries of Massachusetts successfully branded the group as subversive, communist, and a threat to the livelihood of every working person in the state. The association warned that large numbers of corporations would leave the state if they had to pay electric rates comparable to those paid by homeowners—and Fair Share's counter-arguments were simply overwhelmed. Furthermore, the dynamics of the campaign exacerbated tendencies toward staff domination, a chronic problem in citizens' groups, for a staff often has the knowledge and time to shape strategy more efficiently and quickly than members can.[24]

Four factors undermined the campaign: media pressure; level of opposition; weak analysis; and staff/leadership relations—all common and interrelated reasons why many community organizations have lost local fights. Two, however—media pressure and the level of opposition—are situational, external to the organization, and thereby difficult to control. The other two—analytical prowess and staff/leadership relations—are at once incremental, interactive, and internal, which should make them easier to control.

The analytical prowess of an organization depends first on its goals and general ideology, and second, on the organization's ability to elaborate these goals in concert with the collective experience of its membership. A third level relies on the analytical and strategic positions taken by powerful actors in the organization. For many years, the development of analysis in community organizations was totally dependent on some combination of the organizer's analysis and his/her ability to debrief local collective actions and generalize from local experience. However, given experiences like the Fair Share campaign described above, many organizers became convinced that this approach, while necessary in local campaigns, was not sufficient for expanding the analytical scope of either local leaders or organizers.

That realization, plus the electoral shift and the policy analysis that accompanied the establishment of Washington, D.C., operations, led many community organizations to develop formal structures for the political education of members. These needs were articulated by Miles Rapoport in a 1977 speech at the Midwest Academy retreat:

> It's been my experience that so many people, after they get into the organization (after eight months or so) say, "I really like what we're doing but I really don't know how the whole thing fits together." Well, since I *do* know how the whole thing fits together, then I should be communicating it to them, and if we're not, I think we're making a serious mistake. But what's happening in these new issues we're taking on . . . the statewide issues, the national issues . . . is *not* that you have to convince people there's an issue out there, that what they need is to get off their asses and work on it. What you need to do is fight against contrasting and vicious interpretations of what the problems and solutions are. If people don't get more explicit political education, they will not be able to make sound decisions.[25]

In the last four years, three of the four major CO networks have initiated leadership training efforts. The agendas of these training sessions address micro relations of power, how to work with media, resource development, negotiation, and campaign planning—all important *skill* areas. However, with the exception of recent discussions in ACORN and NPA as to the relationship between budget cuts and military spending, and the Citizen Action's training initiatives around Latin American intervention, none of the internal training efforts has explicitly addressed macro sociopolitical relations. Consciously or unconsciously, the organizers continue to operate out of an analytical framework which, because it is latent rather than manifest and therefore not subject to criticism or discussion, remains a source of tension in most community organizations.

This gap in political education is present not only between organizers and leaders but also between "senior staff" and new organizers. For many long-term staff people, the initial impulse to work as organizers was rooted in the political upheaval of the late 1960s

THE PROSPECTS FOR COMMUNITY ORGANIZING

and early 1970s. Their motivations, experiences, and values, therefore, are markedly different from those of new staff recruits who have not had the experience of either cultural upheaval or successful organizing.

Rapoport, emphasizing the need to build better staff with less turnover, longer stability, better political education, and better training, advocates salaries larger than the average $6,000 annually (1979) for organizational work.[26] Rathke writes that ACORN has a recruiting model insufficient for the organization's needs. While the staff is strong in the nuts and bolts of organizing, the proportion of white to minority organizers represents a major failure of the organization, and there are other gaps, particularly in the areas of external contacts, campaigns, and political understanding. Clearly the issues related to building and maintaining a stable staff are different for each organization.

In addition, the needs of the various groups within the staffs are different. For instance, the requirements of experienced organizers, many of whom are nearing their late thirties and early forties, have changed both politically and personally. Societal pressure to settle down and personal interest in having a relatively normal family life have made these organizers less willing or able to work a seventy-hour week for poverty-level pay. For them, increased salaries, regular hours, and organizational stability are important considerations. Minority organizers with no financial backup find it even more difficult to work for poverty wages. However, given the hundreds of minority organizations that are staffed by low-paid activists or volunteers, money is clearly *not* the bottom line. The bottom line is the relationship of the organization to issues about which people feel most strongly. In minority communities issues of welfare rights, housing and service cutbacks, coupled with an increasing interest in international issues (especially in the wake of the Jackson presidential campaign), define the areas of concern of many minority activists. Organizations that do not address these concerns will have a difficult time recruiting minority staff. In order to develop relationships with minority organizers, the major CO networks may well need to coalesce and work with local single-issue organizations on *their* issues.

Will community organizations survive this combination of a hostile political environment and the need to make major internal changes to accommodate the needs of both staff and leadership? Clearly, many won't. The internal pressures will likely be ignored, while the external attacks on community organizations by conservative forces will cause many organizations to fold. National People's Action, several statewide Citizen Action affiliates, and a number of ACORN statewide operations have been perched on the brink of financial disaster for the last two years. The lack of financial resources has forced much more collaboration within the CO movement over the last three years, but as I've said, the collaboration is more often between a CO network and other progressive actors than among the CO networks. Interorganizational competition, for the most part, continues.

Of the major networks, Citizen Action has the best infrastructural relations: media, money, and ties to other progressive forces. The IAF has the most solid financial base, being grounded in local churches and a number of very well-developed local organizations. NPA is by far the most eclectic network, encompassing a wide variety of local grassroots groups, but it is in the deepest financial hole. ACORN has developed the most effective mechanism for financial self-sufficiency and is the most standardized and disciplined national organization.

Given the general state of community organization, the current electoral thrust, and the conservative political environment, what is the potential relationship between community organizations and an emerging movement for social justice?

Community Organization's Movement Potential

Former ACORN staff members Borgos and Adamson have written that while community organizing has been the most forceful expression of social protest since the eclipse of the civil rights movement, its failure to have a collective impact on the configuration of

THE PROSPECTS FOR COMMUNITY ORGANIZING

power in the United States is due to falling prey to racism, cooptation, parochialism, and to the increased sophistication of targets. (And, I might add, lack of resources.) The most important factor, in their view, is failure of CO to generate a mass response or social movement.[27] How possible is it to build such a response? Clearly the political climate under Reagan has changed far more than any analyst predicted prior to his taking office. His domestic social policies and hawkish international policies have created the potential for mass mobilization around social justice issues: civil and immigrants' rights, comparable worth, reproductive rights, peace, disarmament, and anti-intervention—all issues that community organizations have, for the most part, avoided.

The old notion of community organization was that it would demand material concessions from the state and to play the combination role of watchdog and loyal opposition. Unfortunately, this formulation no longer works, for a number of reasons. First, the majority of CO members always have been and continue to be women—women whose consciousness has been raised both through the CO movement and despite it. Minorities also make up a significant percentage of CO membership, and for them the lack of jobs and cutbacks in services have not been remedied by local organizations. Strategically, then, the networks must assess their ability to develop tactics that will gain and hold adherents and reach objectives in a conservative political climate.[28]

Community organizations are at a pivotal point in their history. They can either work and strategize to consolidate a budding movement of forces organized around social justice issues, or they can struggle to transform the not-so-radical wing of the Democratic Party. Although these choices are not necessarily mutually exclusive, they do reflect two fundamentally different tactical approaches. The former would emphasize a movement forcing the state to react to planned disruptive activities. The latter would concentrate on the development of political IOUs in concert with the direct election of progressive candidates from a local organizational base.

It may well be that the division of labor to address both strategies already exists within the CO movement. Of the four networks discussed, ACORN and Citizen Action stand at the crossroads of the two directions. Citizen Action's major strategic thrust is the penetration of the electoral arena, while ACORN ambitiously hopes to keep a foot in two doors by both initiating electoral activity and influencing the development of a major movement mobilization.

In my view, neither of these efforts can be successful without the other. Citizen Action does indeed have the expertise to mount the electoral thrust but does not have the working-class or minority base to keep its action accountable. ACORN, on the other hand, has the base but has not yet developed either sufficient access to key political actors or the leverage to call in political favors from elected officials. Neither of these groups as presently constituted can have a significant impact on U.S. politics without some degree of negotiated cooperation. Doing our own thing will not work in the 1980s and '90s.

Factors necessary for the success of a coalition effort that would mobilize a mass movement response include, first, the increased politicization of the major CO networks. Without a more manifest and developed ideological position, especially racial and gender-based issues as well as foreign policy, community organizations—for all their developed infrastructure—will not be able to collaborate with new social movement organizations. Second, community organizations must begin to see themselves as sources of strategic experiences and be willing to work with other (peace, racial, gender-based) groups on issues defined by those groups in order to develop ongoing relationships. Third, since the electoral work is to continue, community organizations need to connect Democratic Party accountability to a specific set of programmatic demands and be prepared to withdraw support if the demands are not met. Fourth, in order to play a role in national movement-building, the CO networks must begin to develop their primary resources: staff and leadership. Until the problems of internal staff stability and the development of both the skills and the analytical prowess of the membership of these organizations are systematically addressed, the existing CO networks will not be in a position to maintain their own organizations, much less act as a force in movement-building. Fifth,

THE PROSPECTS FOR COMMUNITY ORGANIZING

electoral strategies must become one of a *number* of approaches that CO networks use, in a tactical repertoire that includes new *disruptive* actions to compliment the electoral thrust.

Will the community organizing networks make the changes necessary? According to Tim Sampson, who serves as a board member of the Human SERVE Voter Registration Fund and relates both to ACORN (as a member of the ACORN-affiliated Citizen's Action League) and to Citizen Action (as a C/LEC member of the board), "We haven't got a choice. More than anything else, the Reagan administration has demonstrated to us that registration without social action and political education is pointless. To continue to do our own thing *may well do us in!*"[29]

Probably the CO networks will not be "done in." The *real* question, however, is not whether they will survive, but whether they will develop the internal structures and external strategies necessary to grow beyond a group of organizations waiting for a movement into a progressive movement for social justice.

Notes

Author's note: The major research for this study was conducted between January 1979 and December 1983. Contextual data were gathered chiefly from interviews and library sources, as well as ACORN files. Cited newspaper articles listing "ACORN Archives" as the primary source were reproductions made available to me from the ACORN Archival Collections in Little Rock, New Orleans, and Washington, D.C.; these did not always show reporters' names, page numbers, or dates.

Preface

1. Cited in Rex Laird, "You Can Fight City Hall and These Iowans Do," *Des Moines Tribune*, n.d., ACORN Archives.
2. John Herberss, "Citizens' Activism Gaining in Nation," *New York Times*, 16 May 1982.
3. The work of Frances Fox Piven and Richard A. Cloward has informed my examination of the role of the state (*Regulating the Poor: The Functions of Public Welfare* [New York: Pantheon, 1971]; *The New Class War* [New York: Pantheon, 1982]) as well as strategic and organizational development (*Poor People's Movements: How They Succeed and Why They Fail* [New York: Pantheon, 1977]; "Who Should Be Organized? 'Citizen Action vs. Jobs and Justice,'" *Working Papers*, May/June 1979).

NOTES

4. Warren C. Haggstrom, "The Organizer," mimeographed, June 1966; "The Practice of Socio-Analysis," mimeographed, 1971, author's files.

5. Manuel Castells, *Economic Crisis and American Society*, (Princeton, N.J.: Princeton University Press, 1980); *The Urban Question: A Marxist Approach*, (Cambridge, Mass.: MIT Press, 1977); "The Wild City," *Kapitalistate* 4–5 (Summer 1976); James O'Connor, *The Fiscal Crisis of the State*, (New York: St. Martin's Press, 1973); "The Fiscal Crisis of the State Revisited," *Kapitalistate* 9 (1981); "The Democratic Movement in the United States," *Kapitalistate* 7 (1978); Norman I. Fainstein and Susan S. Fainstein, eds., *Urban Policy under Capitalism*, (Beverly Hills, Calif.: Sage Publications 1982).

6. John D. McCarthy and Mayer N. Zald, eds., *The Dynamics of Social Movements*, (Cambridge, Mass.: Winthrop Publishers, 1979); "Resource Mobilization and Social Movements: A Partial Theory," *American Journal of Sociology* 82 (May 1977): 1212–39.

Chapter 1

1. Jurgen Habermas, *Legitimation Crisis* (Boston: Beacon Press, 1975), 52–53.

2. Frances Fox Piven and Richard A. Cloward, *The New Class War* (New York: Pantheon, 1982), 125.

3. President's Commission on Law Enforcement and the Administration of Justice, *The Challenge of Crime in a Free Society* (New York: Avon Books, 1968).

4. H. Kaplan, "Urban Renewal Politics: Slum Clearance in Newark," in Norman I. Fainstein and Susan S. Fainstein, eds., *Urban Policy under Capitalism* (Beverly Hills, Calif.: Sage Publications, 1982), 172.

5. Fainstein and Fainstein, *Urban Policy under Capitalism*, 161–78.

6. Ibid.

NOTES

7. Cited in Manuel Castells, "The Wild City," *Kapitalistate* 4–5 (Summer 1976): 22.

8. Fainstein and Fainstein, *Urban Policy under Capitalism*, 166.

9. Ibid., 167.

10. For a detailed analysis of the role of the Rand Corporation and the Brookings Institute in moving minorities out of urban centers, see Henry DeBernardo, "Analysis of HUD's Regional Housing Mobility Program" (unpublished, 1979), available through Community Legal Services of Philadelphia. For background reading on the notion of "spatial deconcentration," see I. S. Lowry, "Seven Models of Urban Development: A Structural Comparison" (Rand Publication #P-3673); A. H. Pasial, "The Analysis of Residential Segregation," #P-4234; "The Rationale for a Policy on Population Distribution," #P-4374-1.

11. James O'Connor, "The Democratic Movement in the United States," *Kapitalistate* 7 (1978): 15.

Chapter 2

1. Cited in Wade Rathke, "Drawing the Line," *Just Economics* 5, no. 8 (November 1977), and 6, no. 1 (January 1978). ACORN Archives.

2. Janice Perlman, "Grassrooting the System," *Social Policy* 10, no. 2 (September/October 1976).

3. Kenneth Clark, "The Civil Rights Movement: Momentum and Organization," *Daedalus* 95 (Winter 1965): 241.

4. Ibid., 243.

5. Ibid., 245.

6. Although Wiley had been part of an NAACP voter registration drive during his army stint in Virginia in 1957, he did not assume a leadership role until he joined CORE in 1962.

7. Hardy Frye, *Black Parties and Political Power* (Boston: G. K. Hall, 1980), 29.

NOTES

8. Cited in Paul Booth, "What the 1960's Mean in the 1970's" (Midwest Academy, July 1974), 4.

9. Bayard Rustin, "From Protest to Politics: The Future of the Civil Rights Movement," *Commentary* 39, no. 2 (February 1964): 25–31.

10. Howard Zinn, *SNCC: The New Abolitionists* (Boston: Beacon Press, 1964), p. 13.

11. Cited in Kirkpatrick Sale, *SDS* (New York: Vintage, 1973), 101.

12. Ibid.

13. Ibid., 135.

14. Robert Kramer and Norman Fructer, "An Approach to Community Organizing," *Studies on the Left* 6, no. 2 (1966): 36.

15. Ibid., 38.

16. Sara Evans, *Personal Politics* (New York: Vintage, 1980).

17. Milton Kotler, *Neighborhood Government* (New York: Bobbs-Merrill, 1969), 31.

18. Saul Alinsky, *The Professional Radical* (New York: Harper & Row, 1970).

19. In particular, Marilyn Gittell's *Limits to Citizen Participation* (Beverly Hills, Calif.: Sage Publications, 1980) delineates the problems and limitations of community organizations.

20. See for instance Ralph M. Kramer and Harry Specht, "Mobilizing the Poor for Social Action," in Kramer and Specht, eds., *Readings in Community Organization Practice* (Englewood Cliffs, Prentice-Hall, N.J.:1969), 223–32.

21. For a discussion of the utility of building social institutions that increase social cohesion prior to direct action confrontation, see S. M. Miller's "Toward a Progressive Use of Durkheim," *Social Policy* 10, no. 2 (September/October 1979): 5–7.

22. Tabankin has become a pivotal figure in the 1970s and 1980s as a progressive funder. As cofounder of the Youth Project, a national foundation that has funded many community organizations, and later as director of the controversial VISTA program under the Carter administration, Tabankin was to direct millions of dollars to community organizations.

23. The organization was first called "Campaign Against Pollution."
24. Conversation with author, March 1982.
25. The original idea for this campaign, which was called "greenlining" to counter the banks' redlining of poor neighborhoods, was developed by Jim Keck, lead organizer for the Southwest Parish and Neighborhood Federation, a CAP affiliate.
26. Ernesto Cortes, an IAF-trained organizer from Communities Organized for Public Services (COPS) in San Antonio, has modified the Alinsky model one step further. He has used his initial entree into the Catholic Church to transform the church itself as an institution, as well as using its legitimacy for organizing efforts.
27. Booth, "What the 1960's Mean," 5.
28. Richard A. Cloward and Frances Fox Piven, "A Strategy to End Poverty," *The Nation* (May 2, 1966). This article was used by social work professionals all over the country in mobilizing thousands of students, organizers, and welfare recipients to jam the welfare rolls.
29. Cited in Frances Fox Piven and Richard A. Cloward, *Poor People's Movements: How They Succeed and Why They Fail* (New York: Pantheon, 1977), 278.
30. George Wiley, "Building a New Majority: The Movement for Economic Justice," *Social Policy* (September/October 1973).
31. Michael Lipsky, "Protest as a Political Resource," *American Political Science Review* 62 (December 1968).
32. Ronald Aronson, "The Movement and Its Critics," *Studies on the Left* (January/February 1966): 7–8.
33. Cited in Wade Rathke, Seth Borgos, and Gary Delgado, "ACORN: Taking Advantage of the Fiscal Crisis," *Social Policy* 10, no. 2 (September/October 1979).
34. Harry C. Boyte, *The Backyard Revolution* (Philadelphia: Temple University Press, 1980), 27.
35. Booth, "What the 1960's Mean."
36. Wini Breines, *Community Organization in the New Left: 1962–1968* (New York: Praeger, 1982), 133.
37. Ibid., 50.

NOTES

38. David Moberg, "Chicago's Organizers Learn the Lessons of CAP," *Working Papers* (Summer 1977): 17.
39. Jo Freeman, "The Tyranny of Structurelessness," *MS* (July 1973).
40. Aronson, "The Movement and Its Critics."
41. Booth, "What the 1960's Mean."
42. Moberg, "Chicago's Organizers."
43. Mike Miller, "Notes on Institutional Change," *Social Policy* (November/February 1972): 40.
44. Danny Schecter, "Reveille for Reformers II," *Studies on the Left* (January/February 1966): 25.
45. Steve Max, "Words Butter No Parsnips" (mimeographed, 1964). Author's files.
46. Cited in Sale, *SDS*, 159.
47. Aronson, "The Movement and Its Critics," 13.
48. Moberg, "Chicago's Organizers," 18.
49. Saul Alinsky, "Community Analysis and Organization," *American Journal of Sociology* 41 (1946): 797.
50. Harry C. Boyte makes this argument in a series of articles published in *Socialist Revolution*, most notably "The Populist Challenge," 32 (1977), and (with Frank Ackerman) "Revolution and Democracy," 16 (July/August 1973).
51. Steve Max, "Class Consciousness and Community Organization," Midwest Academy mailing to the Committee of Correspondence (Fall 1977), 3–4, cited in Boyte, *Backyard Revolution*.
52. Boyte, *Backyard Revolution*, 52.
53. William H. Friedland et al., *Revolutionary Theory* (Totowa, N.J.: Allanheld, Osmun, 1982), 162.

Chapter 3

1. Andrew Kopkind, "ACORN Calling: Door to Door Organizing in Arkansas," *Working Papers* (Summer 1975).
2. Conversation with author, May 1979.

3. Steven Kest and Wade Rathke, "ACORN: An Overview," *Community Organizing Handbook #2* (New Orleans, La.: Institute for Social Justice, 1979), 4.

4. Wade Rathke, "ACORN Organizing in Arkansas," *Southern Exposure* 2, no. 1 (n.d.):71. ACORN Archives.

5. Ibid.

6. Ibid.

7. Conversation with author, March 1973.

8. Kest and Rathke, "ACORN: An Overview."

9. Cited in an interview in *Christian Science Monitor*, 11 November 1978. ACORN Archives.

10. Conversation with author, June 1978.

11. Cited in Paul R. Wieck, "Citizens at Work," *Republic*, 28 September 1974.

12. The press release was written by the author in conjunction with Reverend Hobby. Author's files.

13. *Houston Post*, n.d.. ACORN Archives.

14. From author's prepared statement and *Arkansas Gazette*, 14 October 1970.

15. *Arkansas Gazette*, 15 January 1971. ACORN Archives.

16. *Arkansas Gazette*, 6 June 1976. ACORN Archives.

17. The purpose of the campaign was actually to address discrimination at local employment agencies.

18. The North Little Rock school superintendent was the target of an ACORN-initiated federal lawsuit.

19. *Arkansas Gazette* 11 February 1972. ACORN Archives.

20. This citation is from an article by Martin Kirby, a reporter for *Arkansas Democrat*, published in *Southern Voices* 1, no. 2 (May/June 1974).

Chapter 4

1. "ACORN Community Organizing Model" (mimeographed, n.d.). The original draft was compiled in 1972, and subsequent drafts have only minor changes.

NOTES

2. Author's field notes, March 1979, New Orleans.
3. ACORN Model, 2.
4. Ibid., 3.
5. Ibid.
6. Shel Trapp, "A Challenge for Change," in "Special Essays on Community Organization Leadership" (mimeographed, 1976), 1. Author's files.
7. ACORN Community Organizing Manual, 1977, 4, cited in John J. Miller, "ACORN's Model of Community Organizing: Successful Theory and Practice," paper presented at the annual meeting of the Society for the Study of Social Problems, 1978.
8. A crisscross directory lists people's names by their street address. A "safe petition" is one circulated solely to develop a list. It does not require the signer to do anything but give a name, address, and phone number, and the statement is usually so motherhood-and-apple-pie-ish and innocuous (for example, "I support the efforts of XYZ group to improve the quality of education in our schools") that most people in a given neighborhood will sign.
9. Organizers for ACORN spend roughly 18–20 hours per week doorknocking.
10. "ACORN Model," 9.
11. Ibid.
12. Meg Campbell, "Elements of a Successful Campaign," *Community Organizing Handbook #3* (New Orleans, La.: Institute for Social Justice, 1979).
13. Interview with Cesar Chavez, ACORN training materials (mimeographed), originally published in *Farm Labor* 1, no. 5 (April 1964): 23.
14. "ACORN Model," 11.
15. Ibid.
16. Steve Kest and Wade Rathke, "ACORN: An Overview," *Community Organizing Handbook #2* (New Orleans, La.: Institute for Social Justice, 1979), 7.
17. John Beam, "Actions from Start to Finish," *Community Organ-*

izing Handbook #3 (New Orleans: Institute for Social Justice, 1979), 7.

18. This article appeared as a lead editorial in the *Arkansas Democrat*, 10 February 1978.

19. See *Community Organizing Handbook #3*, 9–10.

20. John Beam, "Actions from Start to Finish," 8.

21. This position was taken by organizers in newspaper interviews in New Orleans, Des Moines, Houston, Detroit, Little Rock, Memphis, and St. Louis.

22. Cited in *Houston Post* interview, 7 May 1979, p. 3A. ACORN Archives.

23. Cited in *Houston Chronicle*, 23 January 1977. ACORN Archives.

24. Richard Rothstein, "What Is an Organizer?" (Midwest Academy, mimeographed, 1973), 2–3.

25. Nicholas Von Hoffman, "The Good Organizer," speech given in the early 1960s (mimeographed). Author's files.

26. Mike Miller, "What Is an Organizer?" (mimeographed, n.d.). The original appeared in *The Movement*, 1965. Files of the Organize Training Center, San Francisco.

27. Richard Harmon, "Organizing Is Teaching" (mimeographed, Industrial Areas Foundation, 1974).

28. Rothstein, "What Is an Organizer?"

29. Larry Grossman, "Ideological Stances on Change in the United States" (School of Social Welfare, University of California, Spring 1968).

30. Kest and Rathke, "ACORN: An Overview," 6.

31. Warren C. Haggstrom, "The Organizer," mimeographed, June 1966.

32. William Appleman Williams, "Radicals and Regionalism," *Democracy* 1, no. 4 (October 1981): 90.

33. William P. Hognaki, "What Is a Neighborhood?" *Social Policy* 10, no. 2 (September/October 1979), 50.

34. Williams, "Radicals and Regionalism," 88.

35. Conversation with author, February 1979.

36. See Barry Greever, "Tactical Investigations for People's

Struggles" (mimeographed, available from The Youth Project, Washington, D.C.) and "The Militant Observer" (Geneva, Switzerland: Institute for Cultural Action, IDAC, 1974).

37. Suzanne Keller, *The Urban Neighborhood: A Sociological Perspective* (New York: Random House, 1968), 4.

38. For a discussion of this point, see R. L. Warren, "A Community Model," in Ralph M. Kramer and Harry Specht, eds., *Readings in Community Organizational Practice,* (Englewood Cliffs, N.J.: Prentice-Hall, 1969).

40. Michael Silver, "Organizer's Housemeeting Technology" (unpublished, 1978), 3–4. Author's files.

41. Haggstrom, "The Organizer."

42. Ibid., 5.

43. Ibid., 14.

44. Mike Silver's essay on "Actions" was published in *The Organizer* (Spring 1980). The citation here is from an unpublished version in the author's personal files.

Chapter 5

1. Steven Kest and Wade Rathke, "ACORN: An Overview," in *Community Organizing Handbook #2* (New Orleans, La: Institute for Social Justice, 1979), 10.

2. Wade Rathke, "ACORN Organizing in Arkansas," *Southern Exposure* 2, no. 1 (n.d.):71. ACORN Archives.

3. Ibid.

4. Ibid.

5. Ibid.

6. Kest and Rathke, "ACORN: An Overview," 10.

7. Rathke, "ACORN Organizing in Arkansas."

8. Martin Kirby, a former reporter for the *Arkansas Democrat*, shared his files with the author. This article, for which there is no date, appeared in the *Democrat* in mid-1974.

9. Rathke, "ACORN Organizing in Arkansas."

10. John Beam, "Electoral Politics," in *Community Organizing Handbook #2*, 30.
11. Ibid.
12. Ibid. The debate on the vote, however, was the subject of discussion and editorials in four local newspapers.
13. Cited in Andrew Kopkind, "ACORN Calling: Door to Door Organizing in Arkansas," *Working Papers* (Summer 1975): 19.
14. Steve Kest, "Energy," in *Community Organizing Handbook #2*, 20.
15. Ibid., 21.
16. Conversation with author, February 1980.
17. Kest and Rathke, "ACORN: An Overview." 3.
18. This statement is the sidebar on all literature of the Institute for Social Justice.
19. Cited in Kopkind, "ACORN Calling," 19.
20. Conversation with author, March 1979.
21. Cited in *Arkansas Gazette*, 6 June 1976. ACORN Archives.
22. Ibid.
23. Kest and Rathke, "ACORN: An Overview," 13.
24. ACORN Staff Memo, 26 December 1976. Author's files.
25. Cited in Rex Laird, "You Can Fight City Hall and These Iowans Do," *Des Moines Tribune*, n.d. ACORN Archives.
26. Conversation with author, February 1979.
27. Wade Rathke, "ACORN Update: More of a Movement, More of a People's Machine," *Community Organizing Handbook #2*, 15.
28. Interview with John Beam appearing in *Memphis Press Scimitar*, 1 December 1976. ACORN Archives.
29. Interview with Wade Rathke appearing in *New York Times*, 6 October 1976. ACORN Archives.
30. Rathke, "ACORN Update," 15.
31. Ibid., 17.
32. Ibid.
33. References to the "Futures Committee" were located in two undated pre-1978 memos and in Rathke's "ACORN Update," 18.
34. *New York Times*, 6 October 1976.

35. Cited in an April 1979 ACORN staff memo, written by the author.
36. *Florida Star* (Jacksonville), 4 June 1977. ACORN Archives.
37. Conversation with author, March 1979.
38. Richard A. Cloward and Frances Fox Piven, "Who Should Be Organized? 'Citizen Action vs. Jobs and Justice,'" *Working Papers* (May/June 1979).
39. Conversation with author, November 1980.
40. The outside-agitator label did not really hurt ACORN until after 1975, when it became clear that the organization's agenda was not limited to Arkansas.
41. Interview with the administrator of the North Little Rock Housing Authority, *Arkansas Democrat*, 13 February 1979. ACORN Archives.
42. Conversation with author, June 1979.
43. Conversation with author, June 1979.
44. Citing a report issued by Congressman Robert Michel, an Illinois Republican, reporter Elizabeth Shores began an exposé series on ACORN in May 1979; it appeared for five straight days in the *Arkansas Democrat*.
45. Cited in *Arkansas Democrat*, 22 April 1979. ACORN Archives.
46. Author's conversation with six potential minority recruits in July 1979.
47. *Houston Post*, 7 May 1979. ACORN Archives.
48. *Denver Post*, 12 August 1979. ACORN Archives.
49. *Houston Post*, 7 May 1979. ACORN Archives.
50. Earlier, *Mother Jones* 1 no. 1 (February/March, 1976), had actually given ACORN rave reviews in an article by Bo Burlingham, "They've All Gone to Look for America."
51. This is one of the few occasions where left/liberal periodicals have taken sides in an organizing/expansion dispute.
52. Wade Rathke, ACORN staff/board memo, 18 December 1979.
53. Ibid.
54. Conversation with author, April 1979.
55. Conversation with author, February 1980.

Chapter 6

1. *Arkansas Gazette*, 15 January 1971. ACORN Archives
2. Steve Kest and Wade Rathke, "ACORN: An Overview," *Community Organizing Handbook #2* (New Orleans, La.: Institute for Social Justice, 1979), 10.
3. This strategy was advocated by Frances Fox Piven and Richard A. Cloward in an article entitled "A Strategy to End Poverty" that appeared in the *Nation* in May 1966. It was further elaborated by Piven and Cloward in *Regulating the Poor: The Functions of Public Welfare* (New York: Pantheon, 1971).
4. Kest and Rathke, "ACORN: An Overview," 4–5.
5. Rathke, in-house memo, 3 January 1976.
6. Conversation with author, October, 1980.
7. Conversation with author, December 1980.
8. Conversation with author, February 1979.
9. ACORN has used excerpts from Robert L. Morlan, *Political Prairie Fire: The Non-Partisan League 1915–1922* (Minneapolis: University of Minnesota Press, 1955), as a part of the organization's training materials since 1971.
10. Conversation with author, February 1979.
11. ACORN staff/board memo, Summer 1978.
12. Rathke memo to Citizens' Committee entitled "Notes Toward an Organizing Plan for a New Party" (n.d.).
13. Association Staff conversation with author, March 1979.
14. Note from staff organizer to author, April 1979.
15. Conversation with author, April 1982.
16. The platform included planks in nine issue areas; among the more interesting were proposals that doctors whose education had been government subsidized be required to work for three years in an area with a shortage of medical personnel; that bank charters be granted for periods of five years only, subject to citizen review; that intangible property be taxed; and that all corporations with over $10 million in assets include worker representatives and low- and moderate-income members of the community on their corporate

NOTES

boards. Another plank advocating the expansion of the urban homesteading programs that confiscate abandoned properties and turn them over to low-income people, is the basis for ACORN's current ten-city squatting campaign.

17. Cited in Alexander Cockburn and James Ridgeway, "Is There Hope for the 80's?" *Village Voice*, 26 March 1979.

18. Danny Cantor, ACORN staff/board memo, February 1979.

19. Notes from ACORN Association staff meeting, October 1979. Author's files.

20. Alexander Cockburn and James Ridgeway, "It's Now or Never in Iowa: Door to Door with ACORN," *Village Voice*, 21 January 1980.

21. Dewey Armstrong, ACORN staff/board memo, "Report on Rules Committee," 19 July 1980.

22. *Detroit News*, 31 July 1979. ACORN Archives.

23. ACORN Board materials, item 14A, 6 October 1979.

24. A staff memo in July 1980 listed the following endorsements of the ACORN Commission: Colorado, 170 precinct caucuses in Denver and Colorado Springs; Florida, state delegation to the Demcratic National Convention; Iowa, 77 precinct caucuses; Louisiana, Baton Rouge Parish Convention; Montana, Democratic Central Committee; Nevada, State Democratic Party Convention; North Carolina, 80 precinct caucuses; North Dakota, Democratic Central Committee; Oklahoma, 66 precinct caucuses and State Democratic Party Convention; South Carolina, Richland County caucus; South Dakota, Minnehaha County Democratic Central Committee; Texas, 150 precinct caucuses and 7 senatorial district caucuses; Tennessee, State Democratic Executive Committee and State Delegation to the Democratic National Convention.

25. Rathke, ACORN staff/board memo, 18 July 1980. The average ACORN staff salary in 1980 was $500 per month.

26. Conversation with author, September 1980.

27. Conversation with author, September 1980.

28. Conversation with author, August 1980.

29. Dewey Armstrong, ACORN staff memo, 3 March 1981.

30. Conversation with author, October 1980.
31. Conversation with author, July 1981.
32. Although the ACORN Executive Board subsequently did vote to support the ERA, a number of women's groups remained lukewarm to ACORN.
33. Conversation with author, April 1982.
34. Minutes of ACORN Executive Board meeting, April 1982.
35. Conversation with author, April 1982.

Chapter 7

1. Wade Rathke, "Drawing the Line," *Just Economics* 5, no. 8 (November 1977), and 6, no. 1 (January 1978). ACORN Archives.
2. Ibid.
3. Ibid.
4. Wade Rathke, memo to Heather Booth, 18 November 1979.
5. Larry Ginsburg and Wade Rathke, ACORN staff memo (undated, 1981).
6. Rathke, "Drawing the Line."
7. Author's conversation with organizers from Citizen Action network, June 1980.
8. Wade Rathke, ACORN staff memo, March 1980.
9. Steve Bachmann, ACORN staff memo, December 1980.
10. Wade Rathke, "ACORN's Role in These Times," internal memo, 3 May 1982.
11. Conversation with author, May 1983.
12. Conversation with author, November 1984.
13. ACORN press release, August 1984.
14. Conversation with author, October 1984.
15. Asserted in an internal memo by Mike Shea, Spring 1982.
16. Conversation with author, October 1984.
17. Becker's statement appears in an organizational profile of ACORN put together by Jack L. Brummel for the New World Foundation, 3 August 1984.

NOTES

Chapter 8

1. Conversation with author, June 1979.
2. Meg Campbell, "The ACORN Maintenance Model" (mimeographed, no date). ACORN Archives.
3. Mike Miller, "Leaders and Their Self-Interest," Handout #5, Organize Training Center, San Francisco.
4. Mark Lindberg, "How Community Organizers Develop Community Leadership: Seven Principles" (New England Training Center, mimeographed, no date).
5. Steve Max, "Four Steps to Developing Leaders" (Midwest Academy, July 1973), 1.
6. Neil Gilbert, *Clients or Constituents* (San Francisco: Jossey-Bass, 1970), 70.
7. *New York Times*, 14 October 1976. ACORN Archives.
8. Conversation with author, July 1979.
9. Conversation with author, June 1979.
10. *The Telegram* (Bridgeport, Conn.), 4 September 1979. ACORN Archives.
11. Cited in Andrew Kopkind, "ACORN Calling: Door to Door Organizing in Arkansas," *Working Papers* (Summer 1975), 19.
12. Gilbert, *Clients or Constituents*, 161.
13. Timothy J. Sampson, "Role of Professionals in Movement Organizations" (mimeographed, author's files, December 1980).
14. Joan Lancourt, *Confront or Concede: The Alinsky Citizen Action Organization* (Lexington, Mass.: Lexington Books, 1978), 134.
15. Ibid., 122.
16. Conversation with author, July 1979.
17. Conversation with author, May 1979.
18. Kopkind, "ACORN Calling."
19. Conversation with author, August 1979.
20. *Austin American Statesman*, 25 July 1979. ACORN Archives.
21. *Denver Post*, 12 August 1979. ACORN Archives.
22. Conversation with author, August 1980.
23. Conversation with author, July 1979.

24. Alexander Cockburn and James Ridgeway, "Is There Hope for the 80's?" *Village Voice* (March 26, 1979).
25. Author's conversation with ACORN leadership, October 1979.
26. Conversation with author, August 1980.
27. In *Austin American Statesman* (July 25, 1979). ACORN Archives.
28. Both Komorovsky's *Blue Collar Marriage* (1964) and Lillian Rubin's *World of Pain: Life in the Working Class* (1976) are cited in Ronald Lawson and Stephen Barton, "Sex Roles in Social Movements," *Signs* 6, no. 2 (Winter 1980).
29. Conversation with author, August 1979.
30. Conversation with author, April 1979.
31. Essentially, the percentage of women in key positions on the staff of the organization has not increased.
32. Madeleine Adamson, "Women Organizers Spell Out Concerns," *Just Economics* (n.d.), 10. ACORN Archives.
33. *Arkansas Democrat*, 19 March 1978. ACORN Archives.
34. Cited in Kopkind, "ACORN Calling."
35. Lancourt, *Confront or Concede*, 104.
36. Adamson, Madeleine, "Organizing Needs Affirmative Action," *Just Economics* (Spring 1979): 14.
37. Martin Kirby, *Southern Voices* 1, no. 2 (May–June 1974).
38. Adamson, "Organizing Needs Affirmative Action," 12.
39. Barry Mclaughlin, *Studies in Social Movements* (New York: Free Press, 1969), 14.
40. Amitai Etzioni, *A Comparative Analysis of Complex Organizations* (New York: Free Press, 1961), 250, cited in Lancourt, *Confront or Concede*, 210.
41. Lancourt, *Confront or Concede*, 120.
42. Mancur Olson, *The Logic of Collective Action* (Cambridge, Mass.: Harvard University Press, 1965).
43. Cited in Jack L. Brummel, "An Organizational Profile of ACORN," New World Foundation (New York: 1984).
44. Ibid.
45. Wade Rathke, "Drawing the Line," *Just Economics* 5, no. 8 (November 1977), and 6, no. 1 (January 1978).

NOTES

46. Franz Schurman, *Ideology and Organization In Communist China* (Berkeley: University of California Press, 1968), 22, 38, 39.
47. Janice Perlman, "Grassrooting the System," *Social Policy* 10, no. 2 (September/October 1976): 20.
48. Campbell, "Principles and Foundations," in "The ACORN Maintenance Model," 3.
49. Harry Boyte's and Lawrence Goodwyn's writing, including Boyte's *Backyard Revolution* (Philadelphia: Temple University Press, 1980) and Goodwyn's *Populist Moment* (New York: Oxford University Press, 1978), tends to equate democratic processes and anticorporate sentiments with revolutionary potential. This position dominates in community organizing circles.
50. For a critique of Frances Fox Piven and Richard A. Cloward, *The New Class War* (New York: Pantheon, 1982), see Gary Delgado and Howard Winant, "The End of Reaganism?" in *Socialist Review* 66 (November/December 1982).
51. Cited in Brummel, "An Organizational Profile."
52. Cited in Bo Burlingham, "They've All Gone to Look for America," *Mother Jones* 1, no. 1 (February/March 1976).
53. Cited in Brummel, "An Organizational Profile."
54. "How Washington Funds the Left," *Conservative Digest* 8, no. 4 (April 1982). This entire issue was devoted to listing left-liberal groups that received government money. ACORN was mentioned four times.
55. Conversation with author, November 1982.

Chapter 9

1. Cited in Harry Boyte, *The Backyard Revolution* (Philadelphia: Temple University Press, 1980), 92.
2. Ibid., xiv.
3. Steve Holt, "Searching for the Line: Thoughts on Colleagues and Competition in Organizing" (unpublished, January 1980). Author's files.

4. Wade Rathke, "Drawing the Line," *Just Economics* 6, no. 1 (January 1978); 6, no. 2 (March 1978). ACORN Archives.

5. This argument has been made by Ira Katznelson et al., "Race and Schooling: Reflections on the Social Bases of Urban Movements," in Norman I. Fainstein and Susan S. Fainstein, eds., *Urban Policy under Capitalism* (Beverly Hills, Calif.: Sage Publications, 1982).

6. This argument has been made by Manuel Castells in *The Urban Question: A Marxist Approach* (Cambridge, Mass.: MIT Press, 1977).

7. Harry Boyte, *Backyard Revolution*.

8. See Mike Miller, "Community Organization, Vision and the Electoral Tactic," *Socialist Review* 63–64 (May/August 1982): 185–97.

9. See Janice Perlman, "Grassroots Empowerment and Government Response," *Social Policy* 10, no. 2 (September/October 1979):16–21.

10. Bo Burlingham, "They've All Gone to Look for America," *Mother Jones* 1, no. 1 (February/March 1976).

11. Alexander Cockburn and James Ridgeway, "Is There Hope for the 80's?" *Village Voice*, 26 March 1979.

12. Frances Fox Piven and Richard A. Cloward, "Who Should Be Organized? 'Citizen Action vs. Jobs and Justice,'" *Working Papers* (May/June 1979): 38–39.

13. Ibid., 35.

14. See F. E. Emery and E. L. Trist, "The Causal Texture of Organizational Environment," *Human Relations* 18, no. 1 (February 1965).

15. Holt, "Searching for the Line."

16. Citizen Action was not formed until 1980. Prior to that it was a loose-knit federation of statewide community organizations with two things in common: (1) most of the top staff leadership had emerged from SDS, and (2) many of the groups had coalesced through the Chicago-based Midwest Academy, which was directed by Heather Booth. Married to *Port Huron Statement* coauthor Paul Booth, Heather came to community organization with contacts from both the SDS and her own work in the women's movement.

NOTES

17. Conversation with author, March 1982.
18. Frances Fox Piven and Richard A. Cloward, *Poor People's Movements: How They Succeed and Why They Fail* (New York: Pantheon, 1977), 314.
19. Cited in Boyte, *Backyard Revolution.*
20. Cited in *Just Economics* (n.d., 1979). ACORN Archives.
21. Michael Lipsky, "Protest as a Political Resource," *American Political Science Review* 62 (December 1968).
22. William Braznell, Jr., "The Radicals Are Coming: Are You Ready?" *Journal of Public Relations* (December 1976).
23. Miles Rapoport, "The Fifth Year and Beyond: Community Organizing Strategies for the 80's," transcript of speech delivered at Midwest Academy retreat, Summer, 1979.
24. Harry Boyte "Citizens in Revolt," *The Progressive* (January 1978) 46:16–19.
25. Rapoport, "The Fifth Year and Beyond."
26. This is a point of difference among the organizing networks. Of the four, only IAF pays lead organizers $20,000 plus per year.
27. Madeleine Adamson and Seth Borgos, *This Mighty Dream* (Boston: Routledge & Kegan Paul, 1984) 125.
28. Barry Mclaughlin, ed. *Studies in Social Movements* (New York:Free Press, 1969), 20.
29. Conversation with author, November 1984.

Bibliography

Ackerman, Frank. "The Melting Snoball: Limits of the 'New Populism' in Practice." *Socialist Revolution* 7, 5 (September/October 1977): 113–24.
Adamson, Madeleine. "Born Again Democracy." *The Progressive* 44 (May 1980): 40–41.
———. "Organizing Needs Affirmation Action." *Just Economics* (Spring 1979): 14.
———. "Women Organizers Spell Out Concerns." *Just Economics* 6, no. 6 (October 1978): 10–13.
Adamson, Madeleine, and Borgos, Seth. *This Mighty Dream*. Boston: Routledge & Kegan Paul, 1984.
Alinsky, Saul. "Community Analysis and Organization." *American Journal of Sociology* 41 (1946): 797–808.
———. *The Professional Radical*. New York: Harper & Row, 1970.
———. "The War on Poverty: Political Pornography." *Journal of Social Issues* 21 (January 1965):41–47.
Allen, Ernie. "Dying from the Inside." Dick Cluster, ed. *They Should Have Served That Cup of Coffee*. Boston: South End Press, 1979.
Aronson, Ronald. "The Movement and Its Critics." *Studies on the Left*, January/February 6, no. 1 (1966): 3–19.
Beam, John. "Actions from Start to Finish." *Community Organizing Handbook No. 3*, New Orleans: Institute for Social Justice, 1979.
———. "Electoral Politics." *Community Organizing Handbook No. 2*. New Orleans: Institute for Social Justice, 1979.

Berger, Peter L., and Luckman, Thomas. *The Social Construction of Reality*. Garden City, N.Y.: Doubleday and Co., 1967.

Booth, Paul. "What the 1960's Mean in the 1970's." Mimeographed. Chicago: Midwest Academy, July 1974.

Boyte, Harry C. *The Backyard Revolution*. Philadelphia: Temple University Press, 1980.

———. "Citizens in Revolt." *The Progressive* 46 (January 1978): 16–19.

———. "The Populist Challenge." *Socialist Revolution* 7, no. 32 (1977): 39–81.

———, with Ackerman, Frank. "Revolution and Democracy." *Socialist Revolution* 3, no. 16 (July/August 1973): 7–74.

Braznell, William. "The Radicals Are Coming: Are You Ready?" *Journal of Public Relations*, December 1976.

Breines, Wini. *Community Organization in the New Left: 1962–1968*. New York: Praeger, 1982.

Brill, Harry. *Why Organizations Fail*. Berkeley: University of California Press, 1971.

Brummel, Jack L. "An Organizational Profile of ACORN." New York: New World Foundation, 1984.

Burlingham, Bo. "Community Unions." *Working Papers for a New Society* 4 (Winter 1977); 20–22.

———. "They've All Gone to Look for America." *Mother Jones* 1, no. 1 (February/March 1976).

Campbell, Meg. "Elements of a Successful Campaign." *Community Organizing Handbook No. 3*. New Orleans: Institute for Social Justice, 1979.

Castells, Manuel. *Economic Crisis and American Society*. Princeton, N.J.: Princeton University Press, 1980.

———. *The Urban Question: A Marxist Approach*. Cambridge, Mass.: MIT Press, 1977.

———. "The Wild City." *Kapitalistate* 4–5 (Summer 1976): 2–30.

Chavez, Cesar. "The Organizer's Tale." *Ramparts* 5, no. 2 (July 1966).

Clark, Kenneth. "The Civil Rights Movement: Momentum and Organization." *Daedalus* 95 (Winter 1965).

Cockburn, Alexander, and Ridgeway, James. "Is There Hope for the 80's?" *Village Voice*, 26 March 1979.
———. "It's Now or Never in Iowa: Door to Door with ACORN." *Village Voice*, 21 January 1980.
Curtis, R. L., and Zurcher, L. A. "Stable Resources of Protest Movements: The Interorganizational Field." *Social Forces* 52 (September 1973): 53–61.
Delgado, Gary, and Winant, Howard. "The End of Reaganism?" *Socialist Review* 2, no. 6 (November/December 1982): 125–32.
Domhoff, G. William. "Why Socialists Should Be Democrats: A Tactic for Class Struggle in Corporate America." *Socialist Revolution* 71, no. 1 (January/February 1977): 25–36.
Emery, F. E., and Trist, E. L. "The Causal Texture of Organizational Environment." *Human Relations* 18, no. 1 (February 1965).
Etzioni, Amitai. *A Comparative Analysis of Complex Organizations.* New York: Free Press, 1961.
Evans, Sara. *Personal Politics.* New York: Vintage, 1980.
Fainstein, Norman I., and Fainstein, Susan S., eds. *Urban Policy under Capitalism.* Beverly Hills, Calif.: Sage Publications, 1982.
Freeman, Jo. "The Tyranny of Structurelessness." *MS*, July 1973.
Friedland, William H. et al. *Revolutionary Theory.* Totowa, N.J.: Allanheld, Osmun, 1982.
Frye, Hardy T. *Black Parties and Political Power.* Boston: G. K. Hall, 1980.
Gilbert, Neil. *Clients or Constituents: Community Action in the War on Poverty.* San Francisco: Jossey-Bass, 1970.
Gittell, Marilyn. *Limits to Citizen Participation.* Beverly Hills, Calif.: Sage Publications, 1980.
Goodwyn, Lawrence. *The Populist Moment.* New York: Oxford University Press, 1978.
Gortz, Andre. *Strategy for Labor.* Boston: Beacon Press, 1964.
Gramsci, Antonio. *Prison Notebooks.* New York: International Publishers, 1971.
Green, Gerson. *Who's Organizing the Neighborhood?* Washington, D.C.: Community Anti-Crime Program. U.S. Department of Justice, September 1978.

Greever, Barry. "Tactical Investigations for People's Struggles." Mimeographed. Washington, D.C., 1978.

Grossman, Larry. "Ideological Stances on Change in the United States." Dittoed. School of Social Welfare, University of California, Spring 1968.

Habermas, Jurgen. *Legitimation Crisis*. Boston: Beacon Press, 1975.

Haggstrom, Warren L. "Can the Poor Transform the World." Irwin Deutscher and Elizabeth J. Thompson, eds. *Among the People*. New York: Basic Books, 1968. 67–110.

———. "The Organizer." Mimeographed. June 1966. Author's files.

———. "The Practice of Socio-Analysis." Mimeographed. 1971. Author's files.

Hamilton, Charles V. *Black Power: The Politics of Liberation in America*. New York: Vintage, 1967.

Harmon, Richard. *Making an Offer We Can't Refuse*. Pamphlet, Industrial Areas Foundation, Chicago, 1973.

———. "Organizing Is Teaching." Mimeographed. Chicago: Industrial Areas Foundation, 1974.

Hognaki, William P. "What Is a Neighborhood?" *Social Policy* 10, no. 2 (September/October 1979).

Holt, Steve. "Searching for the Line: Thoughts on Colleagues and Competition in Organizing." Unpublished, January 1980. Author's files.

James, Hulbert. "From Politics to Protest: A Black Agenda for the '80s." *Just Economics* 8, no. 1 (January/February 1980): 4–8.

Kahn, Si. *How People Get Power: Organizing Oppressed Communities for Action*. New York: McGraw-Hill, 1970.

Keller, Suzanne. *The Urban Neighborhood: A Sociological Perspective*. New York: Random House, 1968.

Kest, Steve. "Energy." *Community Organizing Handbook No. 2*. New Orleans: Institute for Social Justice, 1979.

Kest, Steve, and Rathke, Wade. "ACORN: An Overview." *Community Organizing Handbook No. 2*. New Orleans: Institute for Social Justice, 1979.

Kopkind, Andrew. "ACORN Calling: Door to Door Organizing in Arkansas." *Working Papers for a New Society*, Summer 1975, 13–20.

———. "Fair Share's Ballot Box Blues." *Working Papers for a New Society*, Winter 1977, 26–32.

Kotler, Greta Smith. "Case Study Summary and Analytical Report of the National Commission on Neighborhoods." Washington, D.C.: GPO, 1979.

Kotler, Milton. *Neighborhood Government*. New York: Bobbs-Merrill, 1969.

Kramer, Ralph M., and Specht, Harry, eds. *Readings in Community Organization Practice*. Englewood Cliffs, N.J.: Prentice-Hall, 1969.

Kramer, Robert, and Fructer, Norman. "An Approach to Community Organizing." *Studies on the Left* 6, no. 2 (1966): 36.

Lancourt, Joyce. *Confront or Concede: The Alinsky Citizen Action Organization*. Lexington, Mass.: Lexington Books, 1979.

Lawson, Ronald, and Barton, Steven. "Sex Roles in Social Movements." *Signs* 6, no. 2 (Winter 1980).

Lenin, V. I. *Selected Works*. New York: International Publishers, 1967.

Lindsey, Mark. "How Community Organizers Develop Community Leadership." Mimeographed, New England Training Center, n.d. Author's files.

Lipset, Seymour Martin. *Political Man: The Social Basis of Politics*. Garden City, N.Y.: Doubleday, 1960.

Lipsky, Michael. "Protest as a Political Resource." *American Political Science Review* 62 (December 1968).

Mao Tse-tung. "On Methods of Leadership." *Selected Works*, Vol. 4. New York: International Publishers, 1954.

———. *On Practice*. Peking: Foreign Languages Press, 1966.

Marx, Karl. *Capital*. 3 vols. New York: International Publishers, 1967.

———. *The German Ideology*. New York: International Publishers, 1947.

Max, Steve. "Class Consciousness and Community Organization." Chicago: Midwest Academy, Fall 1977. Author's files.

BIBLIOGRAPHY

———. "Four Steps to Developing Leaders." Mimeographed, Chicago: Midwest Academy, July 1973.

———. "Words Butter No Parsnips." Mimeographed, 1964. Author's files.

McCarthy, John D., and Zald, Mayer N. "Resource Mobilization and Social Movements: A Partial Theory." *American Journal of Sociology* 82 (May 1977); 1212–39.

Mermelstein, David, ed. *The Economic Crisis Reader.* New York: Vintage, 1979.

Merton, Robert. "The Latent Functions of the Machine." Edward Banfield, ed. *Urban Government.* New York: Free Press, 1969.

Michels, Robert. *Political Parties and Sociological Study of Oligarchical Tendencies of Modern Society.* New York: Free Press, 1969.

Miller, John J. "ACORN's Model of Community Organizing: Successful Theory and Practice." Paper presented at 1978 Annual Meeting of Society for the Study of Social Problems.

Miller, Mike. "Community Organizations, Vision and the Electoral Tactic." *Socialist Review* 63–64 (May/August, 1982): 182–97.

———. "Leaders and Their Self-Interest." photocopied, Handout No. 5, Organize Training Center, San Francisco, n.d.

———. "Notes on Institutional Change." *Social Policy*, November/December 1972.

———. "What Is an Organizer?" Mimeographed. San Francisco: Organize Training Center, n.d.

Miller, S. M. "Toward a Progressive Use of Durkheim." *Social Policy*, September/October 1979: 5–7.

Moberg, David. "Chicago's Organizers Learn the Lessons of CAP." *Working Papers for a New Society,* Summer 1977: 17.

Mollenkoff, John Hill. "Neighborhood Political Development and the Politics of Urban Growth: Boston and San Francisco 1958–1978." Unpublished, 1978. Author's files.

Morlan, Robert L. *Political Prairie Fire: The Non-Partisan League 1915–1922.* Minneapolis: University of Minnesota Press, 1955.

Moynihan, Daniel Patrick. *Maximum Feasible Misunderstanding: Community Action in the War on Poverty.* New York: Free Press, 1969.

O'Connor, James. "The Democratic Movement in the United States." *Kapitalistate* 7 (1978): 15.

———. *The Fiscal Crisis of the State.* New York: St. Martin's Press, 1973.

———. "The Fiscal Crisis of the State Revisited." *Kapistalistate* 9 (1981): 41–62.

Olson, Mancur. *The Logic of Collective Action.* Cambridge: Harvard University Press, 1965.

O.M. Collective. *The Organizer's Manual.* New York: Bantam, 1971.

Perlman, Janice. "Grassrooting the System." *Social Policy*, September/October 1976.

———. "Grassroots Empowerment and Government Response." *Social Policy*, September/October 1979.

Piven, Frances Fox, and Cloward, Richard A. *The New Class War.* New York: Pantheon, 1982.

———. *Poor People's Movements: How They Succeed and Why They Fail.* New Orleans: Pantheon, 1977.

———. *Regulating the Poor: The Functions of Public Welfare.* New York: Vintage, 1971.

———. "A Strategy to End Poverty." *The Nation*, May 1966.

———. "Who Should Be Organized? 'Citizen Action vs. Jobs and Justice.'" *Working Papers for a New Society*, May/June 1979.

Plotke, David. "Notes on the Democratic Party: A Response to Domhoff." *Socialist Revolution* 31 (January/February 1977). 37–58.

Rapoport, Miles. "The Fifth Year and Beyond: Community Organizing Strategies for the 80's." Transcript of speech. Chicago: Midwest Academy, Summer 1979. Author's files.

Rathke, Wade. "ACORN Organizing in Arkansas." *Southern Exposure* 2, no. 1 (n.d.): 71. ACORN Archives.

———. "ACORN Update: More of a Movement, More of a People's Machine." *Community Organizing Handbook No. 2.* New Orleans: Institute for Social Justice, 1979.

———. "Drawing the Line." *Just Economics* 5, no. 8 (November 1977) and 6, no. 1 (January 1978).

Rathke, Wade, Borgos, S., and Delgado, G.. "ACORN: Taking

Advantage of the Fiscal Crisis." *Social Policy*, September/October 1979.

Reissman, Frank. "The Alinsky Model of Social Action: Tactics Without Strategy." *Transaction*, September 1965.

———. "The Myth of Saul Alinsky." *Dissent* 14, no. 4, 469–478.

Rustin, Bayard. "From Protest to Politics: The Future of the Civil Rights Movement." *Commentary* 39, no. 2 (n.d.): 25–31.

Sale, Kirkpatrick. *SDS*. New York: Vintage, 1973.

Sampson, Timothy J. "Role of Professionals in Movement Organizations." Dittoed, 1980. Author's files.

Schecter, Danny. "Reveille for Reformers, II." *Studies on the Left*, January/February 1966.

Schurman, Franz. *Ideology and Organization in Communist China*. Berkeley: University of California Press, 1968.

Shearer, Derek. "CAP: New Breeze in the Windy City." *Ramparts*, October 1973.

Silver, Michael. "Organizer's Housemeeting Technology." Unpublished, 1978. Author's files.

Stinchcombe, Arthur L. "Social Structure and Organization," in James March, ed. *Handbook of Organizations*. Chicago: Rank, 1965.

Trapp, Shel. "A Challenge for Change," in "Special Essays on Community Organization Leadership." Mimeographed, 1976. Author's files.

Tucker, Robert C., ed. *The Marx-Engels Reader*. New York: W. W. Norton & Company, 1972.

Weber, Max. *From Max Weber*. (Hans Girth and C. Wright Mills, trans.) New York: Oxford University Press, 1946.

Wieck, Paul R. "Citizens at Work." *New Republic*, 28 September 1974. ACORN Archives.

Wiley, George. "Building a New Majority: The Movement for Economic Justice." *Social Policy*, September/October 1973.

Williams, William Appleman. "Radicals and Regionalism." *Democracy* 1, no. 4 (October 1981).

Wilson, J. *Introduction to Social Movements*. New York: Basic Books, 1973.

Wilson, James Q. "Planning and Politics: Citizen Participation in Urban Renewal." *Journal of the American Institute of Planners* 29 (November 1963): 242–49.

Yoes, Jr., E. D. "COPS Comes to San Antonio." *The Progressive* 41, no. 5 (May 1977), 33–36.

Zald, Mayer N., ed. *Organizing for Community Welfare*. Chicago: Quadrangle Books, 1967.

Zald, Mayer, and Ash, R. "Social Movement Organizations: Growth, Decay and Change." *Social Forces* 44 (March 1966).

Zinn, Howard. *SNCC: The New Abolitionists*. Boston: Beacon Press, 1964.

Index

Abourezk, James, 101
ACORN Anthem, 196
ACORN Commission, 143, 144, 145–51
ACORN Conventions: 1978, Memphis, 129, 130; 1979, St. Louis, 136, 140; 1980, New York, 148–50
ACORN Marches On (song), 197
ACORN Model, 61, 63–66, 82, 89, 90, 108, 123, 202
ACORN Organizing Handbook, 45
ACORN Organizing Song, 197
ACORN People's Platform, 133–37, 139, 183
ACORN People's Platform Committee, 140
ACORN structure. *See* Structure, organizational
ACTION, 110
Adamson, Madeleine, 113, 130, 154, 167, 181, 224
Affiliations, 114, 130. *See also* Carolina Action; Citizens' Action League; Georgia Action
AFL-CIO, 154, 171–72, 205
African People's Socialist Party, 35
Aid to Families with Dependent Children (AFDC), 40
Alinsky, Saul, 21, 23, 37, 80, 118, 208
Alinsky model, 21–22, 24, 40

Alinsky organizations, 4, 11, 30, 32, 33, 40, 46, 66
Alliance for Justice, 168, 170, 197
Allies: ACORN's new initiatives with, 159–73; in 20/80 campaign, 156; within the organizing campaign, 65
Ansara, Michael, 120, 121
Anti-nuclear movement, 166
Anti-war organizations and movement, 3, 4, 11, 18, 165
Arkansas, 43, 44
Arkansas Community Organizations for Reform Now, 3, 45, 53
Arkansas Council for Human Relations, 50, 53
Arkansas Institute for Social Justice (AISJ). *See* Institute for Social Justice
Arkansas leaders of ACORN, 109–10
Arkansas Welfare Rights, 53, 58–60
Armstrong, Dewey, 101, 112, 144, 145, 150
Aronson, Ron, 29, 33, 35

Bachmann, Steve, 131, 163
Beam, John, 73, 96, 107, 121, 127, 167
Becker, Bill, 172
Bissenden, Sue, 167
Black Muslims, 18
Black Panther Party, 15

263

INDEX

Black Power Conference, 18
Black Power Movement, 34–35
Blair, Pam, 45
Boggs, Carl, 35
Bok, Derek, 94
Bolshevik League, 35
Booth, Heather, 22, 23, 25, 120, 161
Booth, Paul, 23, 31, 33, 120, 161
Borgos, Seth, 94, 95, 131, 144, 152, 167, 188, 225
Boston, ACORN's expansion into, 117–21
Boston Model, 24, 41, 63, 64, 71
Bowen, Barbara, 41, 113, 120, 121
Bowler, Andy, 43
Boyte, Harry, 37, 38, 189, 207, 209, 220
Braznell, William, 217
Breines, Wini, 131
Brock, Bill, 147
Brookerd, William (Bill), 116, 178
Brookings Institute, 8
Brown, Ron, 155
Brown, Sam, 215
Buckeye Woodland Community Congress, 210
Bumpers, Dale, 56–57, 59, 92, 94

Campaign: definition by organizer, 86–87; multistate, 108–9, 152
Campaign for Human Development, 212, 218
Campbell, Meg, 68, 96, 101, 105, 176, 185, 189, 198
Candidate endorsement, 131–32, 154–56
Cantor, Danny, 141–42, 167
Carmichael, Stokeley, 35
Carolina Action, 113, 114, 130, 138, 167, 168
Carter, Jimmy, 128, 142, 144–46, 156
Carter, Rosalyn, 145

Center for Community Change, 214
Center for the Study of Responsive Law, 214
Chambers, Ed, 32, 190
Chavez, Cesar, 22, 46, 69, 83
Chelsea Organizing Project, 113
Cities, the fight for, 4–11
Citizen Action, 28, 117, 119, 120, 161, 198, 207, 212, 215, 220, 222, 224, 226
Citizen/Labor Energy Coalition (CLEC), 207, 212, 217
Citizens' Action League (CAL), 114, 130, 153, 167, 168, 210, 227
Citizens' Action Program (CAP), 23, 25, 33, 36, 181, 209–10
Citizens for Adequate Welfare, 19
Citizens for the Abolition of Poverty, 52, 61, 172, 227
Citizens' Party, 132
Civil rights movement, organizations of, 3, 4, 11, 14–18, 29, 34, 36
Cloward, Richard, and Piven, Frances Fox. See Piven, Frances Fox
Coalitions, ACORN's attitude towards, 160–68
Collective social action, 21, 71, 85, 87, 88
Community, definition of, 83
Community Action Training Center (CATC), 23–24, 33, 80
Community Development Block Grants (CDBG), 146
Conference on Alternative State and Local Government, 212
Congress of Racial Equality (CORE), 14–16, 23, 24
Connecticut Citizens' Action Group (CCAG), 117
Conservative Digest, 201
Constituency, 20, 30, 39, 47–48, 60, 111–12, 132, 162, 212
Contact work, 67

INDEX

Convention, Democratic, 125, 128, 131, 134, 141, 148, 150, 156
Convention, Republican, 128, 131, 141, 146, 147, 148, 156; in 1984, 169–70
Cortez, Ernesto, 212
Cox, Paul, 178
Creamer, Bob, 23, 120
Creamer, Day, 216

Davis, Rennie, 19–20
DeLeeuw, Bert, 13, 41, 112, 120
Democratic Convention. *See* Convention, Democratic
Democratic Party, 122, 123, 125, 127–29, 146–51, 156–57, 165, 226
Democratic Socialist Organizing Committee (DSOC), 140
Demonstrations, ACORN, 72. *See also* Collective social action; Protest
Displacement, in cities, 7
Downtown development, urban, 7
Downtown Welfare Advocacy Center (DWAC), 148, 216
Dues, membership, 48, 67, 69, 71, 105, 200

Economic Research and Action Project (ERAP), 19, 20
Education, political, 222–23
Electoral politics: ACORN's strength in, 203; first campaign, 60; tactical shift toward, 29
Equal Rights Amendement, 134, 139, 188
Etzioni, Amitai, 193
Evaluation: of ACORN's political campaign, 156–57; of action, 73, 88–89
Evans, Faith, 186
Evans, Sara, 20

Fanon, Franz, 35
Farmers' Union (South Dakota), 136
Fazio, Tony, 101

Fellowship of Reconciliation, 15
Finances, of ACORN, 102, 104, 200–202
Fiscal crisis takebacks, 4
Fiske, Mary Ann, 106
Flat grant, 25, 42, 46, 58
Food Research and Action Center, 214
Ford, Pearl, 117
Fraser, Douglas, 154
Freeman, Jo, 32
Friedland, Roger, 7
Friedland, William, 38
Friedman, Barbara, 178, 179, 189
Fundraising, 167–68, 202
Funicello, Theresa, 216
Furniture campaign, 41, 50
Furniture for Families, 53

Gaudett, Tom, 30
Generic drug pricing, 99
Gentrification, 8, 9
Georgia Action, 113, 130, 135, 167
Gilbert, Neil, 177, 180
Ginsberg, Larry, 103, 161
Goodwyn, Lawrence, 199
Grassroots Leadership Project, 215
Gray, Jesse, 19
Grievance day, 41
Guaranteed income plank in ACORN platform, 136
Gully, Dub, 114

Haggstrom, Warren, 33, 34, 40, 80, 86, 87
Hamilton, Charles, 35
Hampton, Barbara, 59
Hangii, Elena, 130, 195
Harmon, Richard, 77
Harvard University connection, 93–95
Hayden, Tom, 19, 35, 163
Henry, Marcia, 41
Hessey, Jay, 114, 123, 149, 150
Highlander Folk School, 30

265

INDEX

Hill-Burton Act, 57
Hobby, Peter, 32, 33
Holt, Steve, 96, 101, 185, 207, 209, 211–12
Housemeetings, 22, 86
U.S. Department of Housing and Urban Development (HUD), 6, 213
Human SERVE Voter Registration Fund, 227

Ideological compatability, 84, 85, 114
Ideology, role of, 34; in ACORN generally, 179, 186, 198, 204; in ACORN platform, 139, 152–54; in community organizing, 37
Illinois Public Action Council (IPAC), 210
Independent unions, ACORN's formation of, 104–5
Industrial Areas Foundation (IAF), 11, 13, 21, 23, 26, 30, 32, 33, 37, 40, 71, 84, 117, 182, 192, 212–13, 215, 224
Infrastructure, intellectual, 31
Institute for Social Justice, 68, 101–2
Intangible wealth assessment, 100
Internal dissatisfaction, 109
Issues: in cities, 5; that ACORN addresses, 187–88, 203; within the 1960s movements, 28–38
Issues of racial minorities. *See* Racial issues
Issues of women. *See* Women's issues

Jackson, Jesse, 157, 168, 171, 182
Jobs and Justice campaign staff, 112, 113, 120, 130
John Birch Society, 136
Johnson, Willard, 177, 178, 189
Just Economics, 113, 130, 215–16

Keith, A. M. Sandy, 39
Kennedy, Ted, 142–46, 153–56
Kest, Jon, 143
Kest, Steve, 45, 94–95, 124
King, Dr. Martin Luther, 14, 15, 18
Kirby, Martin, 58, 190
Kirkland, Lane, 154
Kitchen, Bill, 94
Kopkind, Andrew, 44
Koppelman, Charles, 121
Kotler, Milton, 21
Kydd, Andrea, 115, 186

Lancourt, Joan, 181, 190, 193, 194
Landry, Kathy, 41
Lassen, Ann, 184
Lassen, Mary, 96, 127
Leader/organizer dichotomy, 176, 181–82
Leadership, 70, 74–75, 109–10, 119, 138, 176–79, 182–83, 195
League for Industrial Democracy, 19
Lifeline electric rates, 99–100, 103, 109, 200
Lindberg, Mark, 176
Linton, Rhoda, 24, 41
Lipsky, Michael, 29
Little Rock, 42, 43, 44
Localist tendency in community organizing, 37, 38
Low-Income Housing Coalition, 214
Lowndes County Freedom Organization, 15
Lynd, Staughton, 23

Maintenance versus expansion, 128, 130–31
Majority constituency, 47, 48
Male dominance, 187–89
Manipulation, by organizers, 178–79
Massachusetts Fair Share, 113, 117–20, 161, 210, 216, 220–21

INDEX

Massachusetts Welfare Rights Organization (MWRO), 45, 46
Max, Steve, 35, 37, 177
Maximum feasible participation, 3
McDonald, Steve, 58, 138, 139
McGovern, George, 55
McGovern Rules, 149, 153
Meredith, Judy, 144
Mid-America Institute, 80
Middle South Utilities (MSU), 93, 94
Midwest Academy, 25, 77, 120, 177, 212, 215, 222
Miller, Mike, 33, 77, 114, 176, 207, 209
Minimum stadard of need, 41, 52
Minority population shifts in central cities, 6, 7
Mississippi Freedom Democratic Party, 15
Model, definition of, 89–90. *See also* ACORN Model; Alinsky Model; Boston Model; Welfare rights organizing model
Moore, Phil, 185
Movement for Economic Justice, 13, 112, 113, 114, 120, 215
Movement versus organization, 52
Multi-issue approach, 66
Multistate campaigns, 108–9
Multistate expansion, 101, 103–9

Nader, Ralph, 214
National Association for the Advancement of Colored People (NAACP), 14, 16
National People's Action (NPA), 26, 28, 66, 213, 215, 222, 224
National School Lunch Act, 54
National Tenants' Organization (NTO), 42
National Training and Information Center (NTIC), 28, 66, 213
National Welfare Rights Organization (NWRO), 13, 15, 23, 25, 30, 39–43, 49–51, 58–61, 66, 124, 137
Neighborhood meeting, 70–71
Newark Community Union Project (NCUP), 19
New England Training Center, 176
New Left Notes, 31
New University Thought, 31
New World Foundation, 195
Nonpartisan League, 106, 127, 186
Northern Student Movement, 19
Nuclear power plank in ACORN platform, 136–38

Occupational Health and Safety Act (OSHA), 141
O'Connor, James, 9, 31
October League, 35
Office of Economic Opportunity (Arkansas State), 44, 52
Ohio Public Interest Campaign (OPIC), 210
Olson, Mancur, 194
Opposition: to community organizations, 214, 217–20; neutralizing, 65, 106
Organize Training Center, 213
Organizer/leader dichotomy. *See* Leader/organizer dichotomy
Organizer's role, 76–89, 182–83; in ACORN platform process, 134–35; as social reconstructionist, 76–89. *See also* Leader/organizer dichotomy
Organizing committee, 67–70, 85
Organizing drive, 64–71
Organizing Support Center, 110
Orselli, Val, 185

Pastreich, Bill, 24, 41, 45, 172
Patriots, Bois d'Arc, 117
Perlman, Janice, 198, 209
Piven, Frances Fox, and Cloward, Richard, 5, 23, 24, 32, 199, 210, 216, 219

267

INDEX

Planned shrinkage, 7
Platform, ACORN People's. *See* ACORN People's Platform
Platform, ACORN's first, 56, 123
Platform, Democratic Party, 125
Pollett, Zach, 96, 127, 175
Powder River Resource Council, 210
President's Commission on Law Enforcement and the Administration of Justice, 6
Progressive Alliance, 210
Protect Our Land Association (POLA), 92
Protest, tactical uses and limitations of, 29. *See also* Tactics
Protestant churches, and Alinsky organizations, 23

Quorum Court takeover, 96–99, 103, 124, 127, 131

Racial issues, 15, 162, 189–93
Radical, definition of, 81
Radio stations, ACORN's creation of, 104
Rainbow Coalition, 168–69
Ramparts, 31
Rand Corporation, 8
Rapoport, Miles, 220, 222–23
Rathke, Lee, 43, 51
Rathke, Wade, 41–51, 55, 95, 103–8, 118, 120–21, 125–26, 155–56, 160–63, 172, 179; early background, 185–88, 198
Reagan, Ronald, 147, 164–65, 169–70, 173, 219
Reaganomics, 163
Recruitment, 69, 93, 166, 184–85, 192–93, 223
Redlining, 9
Republican Convention. *See* Convention, Republican
Republican Party, 129, 141, 147–48, 156

Republican strategy, in 1980 campaign, 146–48
Reputation, of ACORN, 204
Research, 65; centrally gathered for campaigns, 108
Resource mobilization, 199, 214
Response, external, of ACORN, 204
Revitalization, urban, 7, 143
Robin Hood in Reverse policy, 4
Rockefeller, Winthrop, 44, 52–53, 55–56, 172
Ross, Fred, 22, 23, 40, 80
Rothstein, Richard, 75–77
Rustin, Bayard, 18

Safe petition, 67
Salaries, ACORN, 116, 183, 223; of affiliates, 167; minority, 192
Sale, Kirkpatrick, 19
Sampson, Tim, 114, 180, 207, 227
Save Health and Property (SHAP), 92
Save the City campaign, 60
Schecter, Danny, 33–34
Schurmann, Franz, 198
Scope and size of organization, 37–38
Self-interest, 22, 69, 93
Semi-autonomous social institutions, 30–31
Senate Select Committee on Human Needs, 55
Service Employees International Union (SEIU), 172, 212
Share Our Wealth Clubs, 186
Shea, Gerry, 41, 172
Shea, Mike, 149, 169, 171
Sheehan, Terry, 149, 185
Silver, Mike, 85, 88
Smart, Annie, 43
Smith, Mary Ellen, 152
Social composition, of ACORN, 175–87, 193
Solidarity, internal, of ACORN, 193–94, 204

Southern Caravan, of NWRO, 42
Southern Christian Leadership Conference (SCLC), 14–16, 32, 42
Southern Tenant Farmers' Union (STFU), 44, 106, 111, 186
Spatial deconcentration of cities, 8, 9
Splain, Mark, 41, 113, 120–21, 143
Sponsoring committee, 66
Staff, ACORN, 74–75; composition, 183, 202; decision-making, 192; turnover, 130
Staples, Lee, 113, 121
State government: as an arena for conflict, 5; as a target for CO, 124
Student Nonviolent Coordinating Committee (SNCC), 14–17, 19, 32, 114
Students for a Democratic Society (SDS), 13, 18, 19, 32, 35, 36; Conference on Economic Issues and Community Movement (1964), 35
Structure, organizational, 33–34, 73–77, 101, 176, 182, 193

Tabankin, Margery, 22, 115–16, 215
Tactics, 29, 152, 199
Talbot, Madeleine, 74, 96, 178
Teamsters ACORN Engineers Movement (TEAM), 171–72
Texas Women's Political Caucus, 154, 188
Thomas, Bruce, 3, 24
Tillmon, Johnnie, 44
Tipps, Paul, 145–46, 149
Trapp, Shel, 66, 213, 216
20/80 Plan, 103–4, 125–32

Unemployed Workers' Organizing Committee (UWOC), 57
United Autoworkers' Union (UAW), 154, 156, 212
United Farm Workers (UFW), 69, 83

United Labor Unions (ULU), 112–13, 171–72, 183
Urban League, 14
Urban renewal and revitalization, 7

Vietnam Veterans' Organizing Committee (VVOC), 57, 58
Vietnam War, 15, 34
VISTA (Volunteers in Service to America), 60, 110–11, 115–16; ACORN's contract with, 110, 166
Von Hoffman, Nicholas, 77
Voter registration, 67, 169–70, 218–19

Welfare, issue of, 42
Welfare rights organizations, 4, 11, 13. *See also* National Welfare Rights Organization
Welfare rights organizing model, 24, 40
White Bluff Power Plant campaign, 92–95, 112
Wiley, George, 15, 24–25, 32, 39, 43, 58, 120, 208
Williams, William Appleman, 80, 81, 89
Wimberly, George, 103
Women's Action Alliance, 132
Women Employed (WE), 216
Women's issues within ACORN, 188–89, 193
Women's liberation movement, 20, 33
Workers' Alliance to Guarantee Employment (WAGE), 112
Workers' rights plank in ACORN Platform, 136–38

Young, Coleman, 143, 146
Youth Project, 215

Zinn, Howard, 19